REAL ESTATE FINANCE

William R. Beaton

Florida International University

Prentice-Hall, Inc., Englewood Cliffs, N.J.

Library of Congress Cataloging in Publication Data

Beaton, William R
   Real estate finance.

   (Prentice-Hall series in real estate)
   Includes bibliographies.
   1. Real estate business—Finance. I. Title.
HD1375.B334   332.7'2   74-18432
ISBN 0-13-762708-4

Prentice-Hall Series in Real Estate
© 1975 by Prentice-Hall, Inc., Englewood Cliffs, N.J.

Printed in the United States of America

10 9 8 7 6 5 4 3 2

PRENTICE-HALL INTERNATIONAL, INC., *London*
PRENTICE-HALL OF AUSTRALIA, PTY. LTD., *Sydney*
PRENTICE-HALL OF CANADA, LTD., *Toronto*
PRENTICE-HALL OF INDIA PRIVATE LTD., *New Delhi*
PRENTICE-HALL OF JAPAN, INC., *Tokyo*

To
Lillian
and
Robert

Contents

Preface

The purpose of this book is to provide an introduction to the basic and elementary principles and practices of real estate finance. The book is written as a textbook for persons planning to enter a career in the real estate finance field, particularly the branch of mortgage lending. The book will also serve as a useful refresher and reference source for persons already in the business. It is also suitable for courses in real estate finance and mortgage lending presented by junior and senior universities, and trade and professional organizations.

The book is written in non-technical language and the emphasis is on residential finance, though certain aspects of financing income-producing property are covered. Chapter 1 introduces the reader to the broad field of real estate finance. Chapter 2 covers the mortgage market, within which the lender must operate. The legal aspects of the mortgage are discussed in Chapter 3 since every lender must be familiar with the nature of the basic instrument in his field of business. Chapters 4, 5, and 6 are concerned with the operations of the lender in the areas of permanent financing, construction financing, and residential mortgages. The lease is an important instrument of real estate finance and is discussed in Chapter 7. Lenders must have an understanding of valuation principles and techniques and Chapters 8 and 9 cover valuation. Chapter 10 examines real estate investment trusts, which are a major source of funds for real estate finance. Mortgage brokerage regulations and ethics are discussed in Chapter 11. Unusual financing techniques are discussed in Chapter 12 on "Creative Financing." Syndication, Tax Shelter, and the Limited Partnership are covered in Chapter 13.

Many persons contributed to this book in the form of materials or constructive comments on the manuscript. Acknowledgement and appreciation is extended to the following: M. J. Simon, mortgage broker, Jacksonville; Ronald Ames, Ames Mortgage Associates, Inc., Miami; Bernard A. Epter, Miami; Frank W. Reed, Orlando; Raymond F. Powers, Jr., mortgage broker, Tampa; C. E. Burnette, Tallahassee; and Ronald W. Thomas, James H. Allen, Jr., and Joseph M. Ehrlich of the Office of the Comptroller of Florida. Also, making contributions of ideas and materials are David Smith and Ruth Callahan of Advance Mortgage Corporation, Miami; William B. Smith, and Dennis Wilson of Financial Federal Savings and Loan Association, Miami Beach; John Atler, Chief Appraiser, Federal Housing Administration, Miami; and my university colleague, Assistant Professor of Real Estate, Terry Robertson.

Appreciation is also extended to the two reviewers of the manuscript: Professor Karl G. Pearson, University of Michigan, and Professor W. H. Hippaka of California State University at San Diego.

Editorial and typing assistance was provided by Mrs. Susan Schur, Mrs. Irene Young, Mrs. Maria Leon, Mrs. Toby Levin, and Mrs. Carolyn Medina. Miss Cheryl Smith of Prentice-Hall, Inc., was the production editor.

Any errors and shortcomings in the book are, of course, the sole responsibility of the author.

This book is dedicated to my family—my wife, Lillian, and my eight year old son, Robert. It is through their motivation and inspiration that the long hours at the typewriter make it all worthwhile!

William R. Beaton

Florida International University

ONE

Real Estate Finance Business

The money for financing real estate comes from numerous sources and is disbursed by these sources through a variety of technical, and sometimes complex, arrangements. Government at all levels is involved directly or indirectly, through regulation and taxation, in every transaction. Many professional and business enterprises participate in the financing process. There are specialized terms and trade expressions as well as distinctive methods of property and risk analysis.

The purpose of this chapter is to give an introduction to the broad scope of the business of financing real estate. Many of the subjects will be covered in greater detail in other parts of the book. The discussion which follows is divided into three parts: (1) sources of funds; (2) financing instruments, with emphasis on the mortgage; and (3) participation of various non-lender professional and business enterprises in the real estate finance business. The mortgage funds market within which the business operates, and the influence of government on the business and the market will be discussed in a later chapter.

SOURCES OF FUNDS

The money in a real estate investment is usually made up of (1) borrowed or debt funds; and (2) equity funds, that is, funds supplied by an owner with which he acquires an ownership interest in the property. The primary sources of borrowed funds or debt capital are institutional and individual lenders. Equity capital comes primarily from (1) the owner's personal resources; (2) the build up of equity in the property through amortization of the debt; (3) appreciation in the value of the property; and (4) direct investment of funds into a project by an institutional investor in exchange for an equity participation. A real estate investment requires a large sum of money and equity capital is usually relatively limited and expensive. Heavy reliance is placed on the use of borrowed funds from institutional lenders, namely, savings and loan associations, life insurance companies, commercial banks, mutual savings banks, mortgage bankers, mortgage brokers, real estate investment trusts, and pension funds. The principal characteristics of these institutions are discussed below.

Savings and Loan Associations

Savings and loan, or building and loan, associations are found in nearly every community. Most of the loans made by these institutions are to buyers of single-family, owner-occupied residences but they are also active in lending funds for residential and commercial construction, land acquisition and development, apartment and condominium projects, office buildings, shopping centers, mobile home parks, and industrial properties.

Associations are essentially local in their primary market lending, though they do invest funds on a national scope through buying whole loans or participations in loans made by other associations throughout the country and through the government-sponsored secondary mortgage market. Loans on single-family houses are made primarily on a conventional, amortized mortgage basis, at loan to value ratios of 75-95 percent; a market rate of interest at the time of the loan; a 20-25 years maturity; and with the use of private mortgage insurance (PMI) on the 90-95 percent loans.

A savings and loan association is a financial intermediary. That is, it obtains funds from savers and then invests these funds in mortgages. The association sometimes faces a situation where yields on other kinds of investments, such as government securities, are higher than the association is able to pay on its savings accounts. Savers withdraw their money and invest it directly in the higher yield investments. Such a process is termed disintermediation and can reduce the flow of funds into the home mortgage market.

Life Insurance Companies

Life insurance companies are located in every state and make real estate loans on a national basis. The companies obtain their funds from policyholder premiums which accumulate in reserves and give the companies a continuous large pool of long-term capital for investment.

Insurance companies prefer to make large loans, and in recent years they have preferred loans on apartment projects and commercial and industrial developments. Loans are for the most part long-term, permanent financing, rather than construction financing. Some life insurance companies have, through subsidiaries, participated directly in the ownership and development of large scale projects, such as planned communities. Companies also buy packages or blocks of residential mortgages. A conventional loan on a single-family house may be available from a life insurance company depending upon the community, money market conditions, and the lending policy of the company at a given time.

Life insurance companies make loans either directly through their home or branch offices or through a loan correspondent. The correspondent is a community-based independent business firm, usually a mortgage banker, and represents the insurance company for a fee for the origination and servicing of loans in that area. Mortgage brokers package loan proposals for presentation to life insurance companies but brokers do not retain the servicing of the loan.

Commercial Banks

Commercial banks are usually a good source of funds for real estate financing though the availability of such financing will vary with the geographic location and financial assets of the bank, competitive conditions from other lenders, the attitude of management, and regulatory limitations. Banks have historically been required by law to maintain a high degree of liquidity and have been closely regulated as to their investments. Their primary lending activity has been making short-term business loans.

Commercial banks, particularly in metropolitan areas, make **land** acquisition, development, and construction loans for developers of residential, commercial and industrial projects. Permanent financing is usually available for the ultimate consumer or user of the project, though the funds may come from another lender, such as a life insurance company. Banks may also provide construction funds to a developer on a straight line of credit.

Commercial banks also lend money on a short-term basis to other lenders, particularly mortgage bankers. The latter may need temporary or interim funds for handling a loan between the time of origination and sale to a permanent investor. The mortgage banker pledges mortgages held in its inventory as security for the loan. Such operations are known as mortgage warehousing.

Permanent, long-term mortgage loans on single-family houses may also be available from commercial banks. The volume of such loans varies, however, with the bank's size, loan policy, and location. In some rural areas commercial banks may be the only institutional source for long-term home loans. Sometimes commercial banks make home loans only on a "preferred customer" basis, meaning that preference is given to regular customers of the bank. Conventional loans may have a shorter maturity, lower loan-to-value ratio, and a lower interest rate than loans of other lenders.

Mutual Savings Banks

Mutual savings banks are located primarily in the Northeast, particularly in Massachusetts, New York, and Connecticut. They are major lenders on all types of real estate in this region. Their influence is felt on a national basis through their purchases in the secondary mortgage market of blocks of mortgages already originated by other lenders or through mortgage brokers.

Mortgage Bankers

The mortgage banker, or mortgage company, is concerned exclusively with the financing of real estate. The primary function of these institutions is to originate or initiate loans; sell them to investors, such as life insurance companies, savings and loan associations or mutual savings banks; and then service the loans for the investors. Mortgage bankers usually have a contractual agreement by which the investor agrees in advance to commit itself to a certain number and type of loans. The continuing relationship is known as the correspondent system. In recent years, however, investors have been reluctant to issue advance commitments.

Both the mortgage banker and the correspondent system have changed considerably in recent years. Mortgage bankers have become more active in originating and servicing loans on income-producing properties, construction lending, equity-mortgage combinations, creative financing techniques, and structuring and packaging of whole financial deals. They have also created real estate investment trusts (REIT's), issued GNMA pass-through securities, and broadened their investor relationships.

Mortgage bankers have expanded the structure and financial capacity of their organizations by acquisition of or merger with other institutions, such as commercial banks. Some mortgage companies have obtained additional capital direct from the market through the issuance of various types of securities. Mortgage bankers no longer depend heavily on long-term commitments from investors; purchase for immediate delivery is now the more common practice. Mortgage bankers need to inventory mortgages to meet the changed preferences of investors. Further, investor affiliations become more diffuse as the mortgage bankers increase in size and financial strength. The close correspondent relationship between mortgage banker and investor has given way to a more independent relationship whereby investors operate according to their immediate needs and obtain business from a variety of sources offering the best yields. Mortgage bankers are larger in size, have greater capitalization, and operate on a national basis in seeking origination and investment outlets. Greater risks will be taken and there will be active efforts to seek new markets. The correspondent system continues to play a vital role in the flow of mortgage funds, though the role is performed in a different manner from its early years.[1]

Mortgage banking has changed considerably in recent years and change continues to take place. One mortgage banking executive gives the following changes thrust upon the industry: [2]

1. The transition of FNMA into a quasi-public, profit-motivated institution and its entry into the conventional mortgage field. FNMA has, in fact, become the primary investor for many lenders. (FNMA is the Federal National Mortgage Association.)
2. The declining importance of the Federal Housing Administra-

[1] "Quarterly Economic Report," prepared by Miles L. Colean in *The Mortgage Banker*, August, 1972, pp. 24A–24C.
[2] Jess Hay, "Mortgage Bankers Must Adapt to Changing State of the Art," *The Mortgage Banker*, July, 1973, pp. 38–39, 46–47, 78.

tion in terms of its share of the total mortgage market and the resulting challenge to the mortgage banking industry to reduce its dependence on FHA.

3. The advent and gradual acceptance of private mortgage insurance, presenting at least the possibility of increasing liquidity in conventional mortgage investments, and offering to the mortgage banker a significantly new opportunity to participate in this important sector of the mortgage market.

4. The aggressive entry into mortgage banking by commercial banks and other major financial institutions, signaling a new competitive dimension within the industry.

5. The almost total disappearance of the warm, paternalistic relationship between investors and their correspondents, and the increasing sophistication and yield orientation of the typical savings institution.

6. The liberalization of lending by the Federal Home Loan Bank and the creation of the Federal Home Loan Mortgage Corporation. These events hastened the decline of FHA and have challenged the position of the mortgage banking industry in the total mortgage market.

7. The secondary marketing of GNMA and the Federal Home Loan Mortgage Corporation, a factor which has resulted in a much greater and more frequent sensitivity in the mortgage markets to general money market conditions; and a factor which frequently floods the markets with huge quantities of mortgage investments at bargain prices.

8. The almost complete change from 1/2 percent to 3/8 percent servicing fees, and the recent pressure from some in the industry to further reduce the rate. Some investors charge 1/4 percent.

The changes have challenged the mortgage banking industry to modify its character so that is reflects the character of the real estate industry and its competitive environment. Among the modifications are the following: (1) offering, to the extent possible, comprehensive financial services to developers on a national basis; (2) becoming equipped with greater capital resources, greater volume of production and servicing, more alternative investor outlets, greater and easier access to capital and credit markets, and geographic diversification—all of which would contribute to production and servicing volume and enable the mortgage banker to better serve a critical function in the distribution of mortgages through the secondary markets. The mortgage banker is assuming the role of money manager. Financial resources are needed to create mortgage inventory for immediate delivery and assume the risks of not having an advance allocation of money from investors. Mortgage bankers have expanded their own capital resources, or organized new sources of investors such as pension funds and limited partnerships.[3]

Mortgage Brokers

The real estate mortgage broker brings the borrower and lender together. There is the broker for individual loans and the broker in money centers. The broker is similar to the mortgage banker but yet has some distinct characteristics which separate the two. The broker is strictly a middleman whose main function is to originate loans for institutional lenders. Loan applications are solicited and loan packages are prepared for submission to a lender. The mortgage broker does not invest his own funds in a mortgage nor does he retain the servicing on mortgages placed with investors.

The mortgage broker is a marketing specialist who serves both the mortgage banker and the institutional investor. The broker serves the mortgage banker in two ways: (1) timing, and (2) expansion and diversification. The broker devotes full time to calling on current and potential mortgage investors and is able to place a package of loans at the time the mortgage banker is ready to sell. Timing also benefits the investor because the broker has ready offerings available to meet unplanned-for investment periods. The expansion and diversification benefit is derived from the fact that brokers call on large numbers of current and potential lenders in varied geographical areas. Many investors who are active participants with mortgage bankers acquired their first assigned and serviced mortgages through a mortgage broker.[4]

The institutional investor is served in four ways: (1) selection; (2) timing; (3) experience; and (4) resale of mortgages. The broker has an obligation to select among mortgage offerings and mortgage bankers and to recommend the best proposal to investors. The broker will have inspected offerings and areas before selling them to investors. As for timing, the broker seeks to have various types of mortgage packages for preferred delivery periods whenever the investor decides to buy. The broker also has a wide range of experience in mortgage lending. He negotiates many placements in a given year and knows both the mortgage banking function and the investor function. Further, brokers may have qualifications for specialty type loans and be better qualified than others to place them. Another service is the reselling of blocks of mortgages for

---

[3] Ibid.
[4] Adrian I. Bradford, "The Mortgage Broker," The Mortgage Banker, September, 1971, pp. 74–75.

investors who want to dispose of a portion of their portfolio. Brokers, through their daily contact with the market, are able to effect such sales with efficiency and at a minimum cost.[5]

It should be pointed out that while the mortgage broker is primarily a marketing man or marketing tool in the lending field, he is more than simply an individual who delivers mortgage loan requests to the mortgage banker. The mortgage broker, like the mortgage banker, is fully involved in the loan-originating process in every respect. The mortgage broker, like the mortgage banker, goes out and solicits mortgages, puts packages together, and delivers them to lenders. A primary difference between the mortgage banker and the mortgage broker is that the mortgage banker can, at his option, make loans in his own name and can, if he has an established contractual arrangement to this effect, then service the loans for a lender.

Real Estate Investment Trusts

Real estate investment trusts (REIT's) are of two types: (1) equity, and (2) mortgage. The mortgage trust obtains its funds from the public sale of shares and commercial paper and then invests the pool of money in loans on real estate. The income of REIT'S is not taxed, as would be true if the entity was a corporation, provided the trust meets certain requirements set forth by the Internal Revenue Service. Among these requirements is the need to have a minimum of 100 shareholders with at least 90 percent of the trust income distributed to the shareholders.

Pension Funds

Corporate, trade union, and public employee pension and retirement funds have substantial assets seeking investment outlets. Preference has been shown for corporate securities, and the funds have not been a major source of real estate loans, largely because of management's unfamiliarity with mortgage investments. Pension funds in recent years, however, have invested more of their assets in mortgages, particularly through the use of mortgage bankers and mortgage brokers.

TYPES OF FINANCING INSTRUMENTS

Lenders in the real estate finance business require some form of written document setting forth the terms of the loan and serving as a legal instrument to take action on in the event the borrower defaults

[5] *Ibid.*

on the obligation. Instruments frequently used are: (1) promissory note; (2) mortgage; (3) land contract; (4) deed of trust, and, (5) lease.

Promissory Note

The person who signs a promissory note incurs a personal liabilty to repay the debt. The note is the obligation. The assets of the person may be sold to pay off the debt in the event of default on the note. The note does not pledge any specific asset as security for the loan but is a general lien against all of the property of the debtor. The note is usually used with a mortgage to secure the typical real estate loan. Some states use a bond instead of a promissory note.

Mortgage

The mortgage pledges a specific property as security for a loan and secures the note. If the borrower defaults the lender may foreclose on the mortgage and sell the specific property to satisfy the mortgage. When a mortgage is accompanied by a promissory note the lender may: (1) sue on the note; (2) foreclose on the mortgage; or (3) foreclose on the mortgage and sue on the note for any deficiency in the foreclosure sale. Mortgages are usually recorded at the courthouse and constitute a lien against the property.

There are several types of mortgages used in the real estate finance business. Their classification is based upon their provisions and the situations to be covered. One mortgage may be a combination of several types.

PERMANENT vs. CONSTRUCTION MORTGAGES. Long-term mortgages, usually given to the ultimate user or investor in a property, with the funds disbursed in a lump sum and repaid by the borrower in a series of payments over a period of time, are known as permanent mortgages, permanent financing, or end loans. Construction mortgages are short-term funds used for the construction of a project. The funds are disbursed in a series of installments as construction progresses. The construction loan is repaid in a lump sum when the construction is completed, usually with funds from a permanent or end mortgage. Construction may, however, be included in the permanent mortgage.

CONVENTIONAL—FHA—VA. The three residential mortgages most commonly utilized in the real estate finance business are the conventional, the Federal Housing Administration insured mortgage, and the Veteran's Administration guaranteed mortgage. The conventional is any mortgage which is not an FHA or VA mortgage, that is, has no government backing in the form of insurance or guarantee. The terms of the mortgage are set by individual lenders and the interest rate is the market rate at the time of the transaction. Most mortgages are of the conventional type.

The FHA mortgage is insured by an agency of the federal government. The lender uses his own funds to make the loan and the FHA insures the lender against loss in event of default. The borrower pays a fee for this insurance feature for the lender. FHA mortgages carry a fixed or pegged rate of interest set by the federal government and the terms of the mortgage are standardized by law.

The VA mortgage is guaranteed, in part, by the Veterans Administration, to the lender in event of default. The lender makes the loan with his own funds; there is no fee to the borrower for this guarantee for the lender. The VA mortgage initially is limited to qualified veterans, though non-veterans may assume an existing loan, and maximum terms and interest rate are fixed by law.

PURCHASE-MONEY. The purchase-money mortgage is any mortgage given by the buyer to the seller as part of the purchase price of a property. The seller takes back from the buyer a mortgage and is thereby helping to finance the purchase. The buyer makes payments to the seller. This is in contrast to a regular mortgage, where the borrower obtains financing from a source other than the seller, such as an institutional lender.

BLANKET. The blanket is a single mortgage which covers or blankets several properties. It is frequently used in financing subdivisions (a developer acquires a tract of land and subdivides it into lots). The blanket mortgage is on the entire tract. As the lots are developed and sold they are released by the lender from the mortgage lien in exchange for an agreed upon price.

PACKAGE. The package mortgage covers both real estate and items of personal property, fixtures, or chattels in the same mortgage. The mortgage may include, for example, such items as garbage disposals, dishwashers, refrigerators, and air-conditioning units.

OPEN-END. The open-end mortgage permits the borrower to obtain additional funds at a later date under the same original mortgage. This privilege eliminates the need for a new mortgage if a borrower wants money for, say, home improvements. The additional funds may be limited to the maximum amount of the original mortgage, the interest rate on the new money will be the market rate at the time of their disbursement, and there may be some closing costs on the new funds.

PARTICIPATION. The participation mortgage is a single mortgage on a property in which several persons share or participate. Investors lend money on the property and receive certificates of beneficial interest showing the extent of their participation in the mortgage. The participants receive their respective share of each payment on the mortgage. The participation mortgage generates a pool of capital from several investors.

DEED OF TRUST. The deed of trust, or trust deed mortgage, provides that an independent third party (trustee) holds title to the property as security for a loan. The borrower transfers title to the trustee and in the event of default the trustee may foreclose on the mortgage and sell the property without going through the usual court foreclosure process. The deed of trust serves the same purpose as a regular mortgage, namely, to pledge specific property as security for a debt, but gives the lender the advantage of a quicker and less expensive sale than court foreclosure.

FIRST AND SECOND MORTGAGES. Mortgages may be classified as to their priority of claim or lien against a property. The mortgage recorded first becomes the first mortgage, unless stipulated otherwise. A first or senior mortgage has first claim on the income and foreclosure sale proceeds. A second or junior mortgage has subordinate claim, that is, the senior mortgage must be paid off or satisfied before the holder of the junior lien is entitled to receive any payment. There may not be sufficient funds to pay off the second mortgage holder. Several junior mortgages may be on a single property—second mortgage, third mortgage, and so on.

EQUITABLE. An equitable mortgage may be construed from any financing arrangement in which the intent of the transaction is to secure a loan even though the document used is not a mortgage form. A deed, for example, may be given to secure a loan. There is no intent to transfer title though the instrument form—a deed—is normally used for that purpose. The transaction will be deemed an equitable mortgage.

Priority of claims is usually established by either: (1) date of the mortgage; (2) date of recording; or (3) agreement of the parties. The holder of a first mortgage on land, for example, might agree to subordinate his lien to the lender on a construction mortgage, such as a savings and loan association, who by law cannot lend on a second mortgage. Or, a junior mortgage holder may agree to keep the junior mortgage in a junior status, even if the first mortgage is fully paid.

Payment Plans

Mortgages may also be classified as to payment arrangements, that is, the method by which the borrower repays the loan. The basic plans are term and amortized, with several variations of these two.

TERM. Under the term mortgage the principal sum of the loan remains the same through the period of the mortgage, that is, it is not periodically reduced by a payment. For example, a person borrows $1,000 for five years at 8 percent interest. At the end of five years the borrower still owes $1,000. During the five-year period the borrower has paid only periodic interest on the loan but has not reduced the principal sum of the debt.

AMORTIZED. The amortized mortgage provides for the regular periodic reduction of the principal sum of the debt. Payments include both interest and principal and often include an amount to build up an escrow fund for property taxes and hazard insurance premiums (PITI—principal, interest, taxes, and insurance). Most home mortgages from institutional lenders are of the amortized type, with payments on a monthly basis.

BALLOON. The balloon mortgage is a variation of the amortized mortgage. Periodic payments are usually the same amount except for the last one which is larger or a "balloon."

SPLIT AMORTIZATION. The amortization schedule on a mortgage may be arranged so that payments in the early years of the loan are amortized at a slower rate than in the later years. Different schedules of amortization may be developed to serve various needs of the borrower and lender.

Mortgage Loan Terms

The terms of a mortgage loan vary somewhat with lenders. There are, however, certain basic items which all lenders take into consideration and which may serve as comparisons between lending policies, particularly for residential mortgages.

LOAN-TO-VALUE RATIO. The amount of a loan is usually a percentage of the appraised value of the property. This relationship is known as the loan-to-value ratio or percentage. The maximum percentage is often set by law for institutional lenders, such as commercial banks and savings and loan associations.

MAXIMUM AMOUNT. Lenders usually have a maximum loan amount for a given property or situation. The amount may be determined by management policy of the lender or set by law.

INTEREST RATE. The interest rate on a mortgage may reflect several factors: (1) the cost of money to the lender; (2) the yields on competitive investments, such as government and corporate securities; (3) interest rates charged by competitors; (4) the type of property; (5) the borrower; (6) the attitude of the lender's management and its portfolio policy; and (7) the amount of the loan. Interest rates may be (1) fixed; (2) variable, that is, rise or fall according to changes in a specific index; (3) a range, such as 7-9 percent, with the upper rate in effect only in event of default by the borrower; and (4) a stated percentage above prime. The latter is used in loans on commercial property.

The Truth-in-Lending Law requires that a lender on residential mortgages disclose the interest rate on the mortgage in two ways: (1) contract rate; and (2) annual percentage rate (APR). The contract rate is the stated rate for the loan, such as 7½ percent. The APR is the true or effective rate which takes into account certain items of loan costs, such as discounts or points.

AMORTIZATION. Mortgage loans, both residential and commercial, are today paid off, both as to principal and interest, on a regular periodic basis. Home loans are usually amortized on a monthly basis; commercial loans may be amortized monthly, quarterly, semi-annually, or anually. The method and length of amortization is usually an item of negotiation between the lender and borrower.

DURATION OF MATURITY. Closely related to the amortization feature is the term of the mortgage, that is, its duration or maturity date. Most institutional lenders are limited by law as to the number of years for which a real estate mortgage of a given type may be issued. Some lenders limit the duration of the mortgage, say to 25 years, as a matter of management policy.

ESCROW. Lenders may require that borrowers, particularly on home mortgages, set aside each month a sum of money to build up a reserve to pay property taxes and hazard insurance premiums when they become due. The usual practice is to include a pro rata share of the estimated annual amounts for these items in the borrower's regular periodic payment. The lender holds these sums in escrow or trust for the borrower and pays the bills when due. The lender may or may not pay interest on escrow accounts. The payments into an escrow account are estimates and may need to be adjusted over a period of time. The lender may increase the payments or may decrease them and, after an analysis of the escrow account, refund any surplus to the borrower.

Another type of escrow account, used in commercial lending, is set up to insure the completion of unfinished space. The lender requires that the builder of a project who has leased space to a tenant set aside funds sufficient to finish the space. Interior space is usually not finished until it is leased and the escrow arrangement guarantees its completion.

The term escrow is also used in a third sense in connection with a deed of trust described earlier in this chapter. It refers to the independent third party who holds the deed in trust as security for a loan.

ANNUAL CONSTANT. The annual constant is used primarily in commercial lending. It is the amount of principal and interest needed to pay off a loan. The original face amount of the loan is divided into the number of years of the loan to compute the equal or constant payments for the duration of the loan. The debt service (principal and interest) is stated as a percentage of the original loan.

PREPAYMENT. A mortgage is a contract for the repayment of a loan over a specific period of time. The lender expects to have his money invested or working over that time. The lender may permit the borrower to pay off the loan faster, that is, to "prepay" the loan either in whole or in part before payment is due.

The prepayment privilege is given at the option of the lender and is not automatically found in all mortgages. Several arrangements are utilized in which the lender may: (1) permit full payment at any time and without penalty; (2) permit full or partial payment at any time, but with a penalty; and (3) permit limited prepayments, either with or without penalties. Penalties may consist of additional interest or a flat fee. The period of time on a commercial loan when prepayment is prohibited or restricted is known as the "lock in" period.

Borrowers, of course, prefer to have the option of full prepayment at any time without penalty. The prepayment privilege may be an item of negotiation between lender and borrower. Further, whether a lender will permit a prepayment at any given time depends on a number of factors: (1) the lender's need for money; (2) the interest rate on the existing mortgage as compared with current rates; and (3) the borrower's reason for the prepayment.

Land Contract

The land contract, or contract for deed, is usually used to finance real estate where the purchaser makes a low downpayment or perhaps none at all. The seller is not willing to immediately transfer title by deed and retains title under the land contract until the debt is paid off, either substantially or in full, at which time a deed will be given to the purchaser. A mortgage may replace the land contract after the purchase price of the property is paid off to a specified amount.

A major difference between a land contract and a mortgage is the party who holds title to the subject property. As emphasized above, the seller retains title under a land contract for a specified period of time. Under a mortgage the borrower or buyer receives or retains title to the property against which money is lent and the lender has a lien or charge against the property.

Since the lender under a land contract retains title, it is not necessary to go through the usual court foreclosure proceedings in event of default by the borrower. The lender simply cancels the contract, and keeps the payments already made by the borrower. Time and expense are saved in comparison with the mortgage foreclosure process.

The land contract may be used in the sale of any type of property but it is most commonly used in the sale of vacant lots, on the installment plan, with low or minimal downpayments, such as $40.00 down and $40.00 per month. The land contract may also be used for the purchase of improved property where normal mortgage financing is not available because either the property or the borrower or both are not acceptable to the lender.

Lease

The long-term lease may serve as security for a mortgage loan and leasehold mortgages are frequently used in financing commercial real estate projects. A developer, for example, leases ground from its owner for, say, 75 years under a ground lease. The developer then obtains a mortgage using his interest in the lease, known as the leasehold interest, as security for the loan. The lender looks to the tenant's or developer's leasehold rights—possession and use—in the event of default. The land still is owned by the ground lessor and may not be sold by the lender to satisfy the leasehold mortgage, unless the owner has subordinated his ownership rights to the lender.

RELATED FIELDS

The real estate finance business utilizes the services of various professional and business enterprises. Legal talent is called upon to prepare title abstracts, render title opinions, and prepare instruments for the closing of loans. Real estate finance techniques, such as syndication, sale-leaseback and joint venture, often require the services of both lawyers and income tax experts. Licensed engineers or surveyors prepare plats of survey.

The title insurance business is a direct outgrowth of the real estate finance business. Companies in this field provide policies to lenders and borrowers insuring against loss due to defects in title to property. Many lenders require title insurance on all loans.

Property insurance or hazard insurance is usually required by lenders on any property subject to a loan. Credit life insurance may be offered to borrowers. Mortgage insurance, which is a form of reducing term life insurance, is provided to pay off the balance of the mortgage if the borrower dies. The insurance industry also provides a wide range of coverage, necessary to obtain financing, for development and construction activities.

Every phase of the real estate business is utilized to some extent in the real estate finance business. Appraisers estimate the value of property for loan purposes. Land economists prepare feasibility studies. Environmental impact studies may be required before a loan is approved. Brokers know real estate markets and lenders seek their advice and counsel on many matters. Brokers also are a source of loans. Property managers advise on a project from its inception to the finished and occupied building. Cost estimators, quantity surveyors, and computer experts are needed to develop and analyze data for making financing decisions.

Architects, engineers, and land surveyors are needed to assist in the evaluation of projects on which loans are to be made. Plans and specifications of proposed projects must indicate a satisfactory physical security for the loan.

Local government is, of course, related to the real estate finance business through its numerous services and activities directly and indirectly affecting real estate. City and county property taxes, a major item affecting real estate finance, are assessed and collected by local government. Land planning and zoning is largely performed at the local level. Public records, including recorded mortgages, are maintained by the courthouse staff.

TYPES OF PROPERTIES

Almost any type of property or legal interest in real estate may be financed, either by an institutional lender or by an individual. The lending decision is basically one of having a sound property—physical, economic and legal—and management being willing and able (that is, funds are available and legally qualified to be disbursed) to take the risk of making the loan. Real estate loans are made on the following types of real estate:

Raw acreage and improved land
Single-family houses and subdivisions
Condominiums—residential, office, commercial, industrial
Apartments—garden, high-rise
Duplexes and fourplexes
Mobile home parks and communities
Shopping centers
Office buildings and office parks—high-rise, suburban
Warehouses
Industrial parks and individual industrial buildings
Farm properties—ranches, groves
Recreational land and facilities—campgrounds, golf courses, resorts,
    marinas
Hotels and motels
Nursing homes
Private college dormitories
Quick service food stores
Restaurants

BRIEF HISTORY OF LENDING PRACTICES

Real estate lending practices have gone through changes over the years. The most significant took place in the early 1930's. It is necessary to review the conditions existing in the economy, and in the real estate finance scene, at that time to understand the reason for the changes.

1. Short-term, such as 5 year, nonamortized mortgages were used for financing real estate. The term loans could often be called for full payment at any time at the option of the lender. Or, the loan would come due at a time when the borrower could not afford to pay it or obtain refinancing from other sources. The result was foreclosure since the lender, too, often needed funds at the same time. The lender had no amortization to provide a continual flow of funds.

2. Low loan-to-value ratios, such as 50-60 percent, were used along with the short-term loans. The low percentage loans often meant that purchasers needed second mortgage financing with high interest rates.

3. Appraisal practices were not well-developed nor were there any standards of qualifications for appraisers. Loans were often made on the basis of incorrect values, and some loans were in excess of the market value of the property. Or, an appraisal was made to justify the amount of the loan.

4. Construction standards were lacking and lenders had no way to judge quality. Loans were made on poorly built homes whose values did not hold up, and were later difficult to justify.
5. Lenders had no systematic method of evaluating the borrower. Reliance was placed largely upon the physical security of the real estate which, as indicated above, often was valued by weak practices.
6. There was no national market for real estate funds. Lenders depended upon local markets and there was no way to shift funds effectively and smoothly among geographic areas of the country to meet different demand and supply situations.

The result was instability in the real estate market and wide fluctuations in real estate values. Funds were not available for refinancing and lenders found their mortgages "frozen;" that is, the mortgages lacked liquidity. Foreclosure increased rapidly. Homeowners were often unable to pay taxes and insurance, or maintain their homes in proper repair.

The Depression period of the 1930's prompted significant changes in real estate lending practices. Steps taken by the Federal government included the establishment of the following agencies:

FEDERAL HOUSING ADMINISTRATION. The basic function of the FHA was to insure loans made on single-family housing. The insurance feature, in which the FHA paid the lender in event of default by the borrower, was designed to reduce some of the risk in mortgage lending and encourage lenders to make loans. The FHA was largely responsible for promoting other improvements in mortgage lending: (1) improved construction standards; (2) systematic appraisal practices utilizing sounder techniques; (3) lower interest rates; (4) amortized mortgages with long maturities; (5) higher loan-to-value ratios; (6) risk analysis of properties and borrowers; and (7) creation of a national mortgage market.

FEDERAL HOME LOAN BANK SYSTEM. The FHLB was created to provide a credit reserve, or institutional liquidity, for its members, savings and loan associations. The System is much like the Federal Reserve System for commercial banks. Member institutions borrow from the System to meet needs for liquidity. The System also exercises a regulatory function over its members.

FEDERAL SAVINGS AND LOAN INSURANCE CORPORATION. The FSLIC provides for the insurance of accounts in savings and loan associations. The safety of each account is insured up to a specified maximum amount. Associations must observe standards of operation and examinations of their operations are required.

HOME OWNERS LOAN CORPORATION. The HOLC made loans directly to homeowners facing foreclosure of their mortgages. In addition, the agency advanced cash to pay taxes, make repairs, and the like, with the advance added to the loan. Homeowners were helped in the refinancing of their mortgages and lenders received some liquidity when frozen mortgages were paid off by HOLC. The HOLC served its purpose and was liquidated in 1951.

FEDERAL NATIONAL MORTGAGE ASSOCIATION. The FNMA was created in 1938 with its primary function being to provide a secondary market for mortgages. Such a market provided a national market for FHA-insured mortgages by giving lenders a broader access to capital markets. It performed this function by buying mortgages from lenders in areas needing more funds and then seeking to sell these mortgages in areas where there was a surplus of funds for investment.

In 1944 the Federal government created the GI (government issue) loan for World War II veterans. The veteran was given a low interest rate, long-term home mortgage loan with little or no cash downpayment. The loan was guaranteed to the lender against default up to a specified percentage of the property value. The GI or VA (Veterans Administration) mortgage, like the FHA mortgage, provided for systematic and efficient construction and appraisal standards and techniques and required standardized lending forms and procedures.

RECENT DEVELOPMENTS

Real estate financing in recent years has been strongly influenced by developments and conditions in the economy, by needs of borrowers, and by active participation of government in the mortgage market. Inflation has generated a rising cost of land, labor, and building materials as well as increased fees for technical, professional, and financing services. Further, many real estate projects have become large-scale undertakings requiring vast sums of money. The result has been a need to create larger pools of capital and to develop financing techniques for the use of this capital.

REVIEW AND STUDY QUESTIONS

1. List the sources of (A) equity funds, and (B) borrowed funds, for investing in real estate.
2. Describe the characteristics and lending policies of the principal types of institutional lenders.

3. List the basic kinds of legal instruments frequently used in real estate financing and define the nature of each.

4. Describe each of the several types of mortgages used in the real estate finance business.

5. Describe the several posible payment arrangements by which a borrower may repay a mortgage loan.

6. What factors may be taken into consideration in comparing mortgage terms or lending policies of institutional lenders, particularly for residential mortgages?

7. Describe how the real estate finance business utilizes the services of several other professional and business enterprises.

8. Give a brief history of the changes which real estate lending practices have gone through over the years, including recent developments.

FURTHER READINGS AND REFERENCES

American Institute of Banking, *Home Mortgage Lending.* New York: American Institute of Banking, 1963.

American Savings and Loan Institute, *Lending Principles and Practices.* Chicago: American Savings and Loan Institute Press, 1971.

Beaton, William R, *Real Estate Investment.* Englewood Cliffs, N.J.: Prentice-Hall, Inc., 1971.

Bryant, Willis R., *Mortgage Lending.* New York: McGraw-Hill Book Company, 1962.

De Huszar, William I., *Mortgage Loan Administration.* New York: McGraw-Hill Book Company, 1972.

Hoagland, Henry E., and Leo D. Stone, *Real Estate Finance,* Fifth Ed. Homewood, Ill.: Richard D. Irwin, Inc., 1973.

1973 National Fact Book of Mutual Savings Banking. Published by the National Association of Mutual Savings Banks, New York.

Pease, Robert H., and Lewis O. Kerwood, *Mortgage Banking,* Second Ed. New York: McGraw-Hill Book Company, 1965.

TWO

Mortgage Market

The mortgage market is a segment of the overall capital funds market of the economy. The need for funds to finance real estate competes with the need for funds to finance business expansion, maintain inventories, provide government services, and deal in world commerce. The supply of funds is allocated by the market mechanism to the varying demands, including the need for mortgage funds. The availability and cost of real estate loans depends upon two interrelated factors: (1) the supply of and demand for loanable funds; and (2) the role of government in the economy. Persons concerned with analyzing the financial markets, including the mortgage market, must understand the principles and workings of these markets and plan to project interest rate movements and the impact of shifts in fiscal and monetary policy. Lenders must have an understanding of the basic structure and workings of money and capital markets since activities in the overall market directly influence the mortgage sector of the market. Lenders and borrowers on real estate must often adjust to financial market forces outside of the mortgage sector.

The discussion below is concerned, first, with the Federal Reserve System, and, second, with debt management by the U.S. Treasury. The operations of these two agencies have a significant impact on financial markets. Following this discussion, the two kinds of financial markets are described, namely, the capital markets and the money market. The concepts of inflation and deflation are next briefly covered. The bond market, gross national product, housing starts, and the credit crunch are discussed in relation to their impact on the mortgage market. The chapter concludes with a discussion of the mortgage market and disintermediation.

FEDERAL RESERVE SYSTEM

The principal function of the Federal Reserve System is to regulate the supply of money and credit in the economy; that is, it maintains and supervises the monetary system. It increases or decreases the money supply, which in turn influences interest rates. The flow of money and credit is controlled by managing its availability and cost to borrowers. Policies of the Federal Reserve have a direct and significant impact on real estate financing. The Federal Reserve works closely with the U. S. Treasury, which has the responsibility for management of the national debt.

The Federal Reserve exercises its control through three techniques of monetary regulation: (1) reserve requirements; (2) discount rate; and (3) open market operations.

Reserve

The Federal Reserve has the power to expand and contract the reserves of the commercial banking system. Banks must maintain a portion of their deposits in reserves, including cash on hand and deposits with the Federal Reserve Bank. The bank is not permitted to lend out all of its deposits. If a bank, for example, accepts a deposit of $100.00 and the reserve requirement is, say 15 percent, the bank must hold in reserve $15.00, leaving $85.00 available for loans. The reserve balance with the Federal Reserve Bank is equal to a specified percentage of demand and time deposits.

Congress establishes the minimum and maximum amounts of reserves that banks must maintain for each dollar of deposits. The Federal Reserve has the authority to change these reserves within the limits set by Congress. Changes in reserve requirements are not made frequently but are an important tool of Federal Reserve policy and can have a significant impact on the entire monetary system. A reduction in reserve requirements releases reserves and enables banks to make more loans and investments. If the released reserves give too much impetus to the economy, the Federal Reserve may sell securities to absorb the surplus funds and create a more balanced situation.

Discount Rate

The discount rate is the interest rate a commercial bank pays when it borrows from the Federal Reserve Bank. The bank uses the money to make additional loans or to adjust their reserve positions temporarily.

An increase in the discount rate increases the cost of money to the bank and it may not be attractive to discount notes. Further, an increase in the discount rate has a psychological impact on lenders, borrowers, investors, and market professionals. It influences expectations about the future of monetary policy and interest rates, and causes lenders to review their lending and investment policies. Increase in the discount rate increases the cost of money to the bank, which then reduces its borrowings from the Federal Reserve, which leads to a scarcity of funds and an increase in interest rates. The discount rate affects the short-term market through its influence on the level of interest rates for treasury bills and federal funds.

Open Market Operations

The Federal Reserve, through its open market committee, buys and sells government securities, such as notes, bills, and bonds, in the open market. The open-market operations will change the composition of the holdings of securities of the Federal Reserve so as to steer credit policy in a given direction.

The sale of securities by the Federal Reserve adds to the supply of securities with varying maturities, reduces prices because of the added supply, and raises interest rates because money becomes scarce. Commercial banks purchase the securities and thereby reduce the amount of dollars available for loans. Sale of securities also reduces reserves and banks must borrow or sell securities to maintain their reserves at the required level. The effect on the commercial bank of a reduction in its reserves is the reduction of its lending operations or sale of some of its investments. The objectives of the Federal Reserve in selling securities may be to reduce reserves, increase interest rates, tighten money, and reduce inflation.

When the Federal Reserve purchases securities, the objective may be to add to reserves and relax money conditions. Purchases withdraw securities from the market and the action tends to raise the price of the remaining supply. The Federal Reserve pays the dealer, who makes a deposit at the bank, and increases the reserves of the bank. The bank uses the expanded reserves for loans or investment in other assets.

DEBT MANAGEMENT

The U.S. Treasury provides the funds for the spending programs of the Federal government. These funds are obtained through Treasury borrowing in the open market. The borrowing is accomplished through the use of a variety of types of instruments. The level of interest rates is influenced through the size, terms, and timing of the borrowings. Debt management means that the Treasury arranges the volume of securities of different maturities so as to influence the level of interest rates.

The Treasury needs new money, or it needs money for refunding existing obligations as they mature or come due. The national debt continues to grow and must be continually refinanced. It is in the billions of dollars, and the Treasury needs to sell large sums of money market instruments to refund this debt, which is both short and long term. Treasury operations have an important influence on real estate financing and on the markets for securities.

Treasury borrowings take funds from the money and capital markets and have an impact on the availability of funds in the market. Further, the interest rates paid on the Treasury securities influence interest rate levels in the entire economy.

There is a market demand for securities of different maturities. In the long-term market if the supply exceeds demand, the Treasury will have to sell securities at higher rates to attract investors who usually prefer short-term obligations. A shift in supply will cause an increase in the interest rate level.

If the Treasury believes that short-term rates are not high enough to attract funds, it can increase its offerings of short-term securities. The excess supply raises short-term rates in relation to securities with longer maturities. If the Treasury believes that the volume of borrowing in the long-term market, which includes mortgages, is too heavy, it can issue additional long-term bonds to increase long-term market rates. Generally, as interest rates increase and government bonds become attractive, there is a reduction in the amount of funds for real estate financing. Funds for the real estate sector tend to increase in availability when government security rates are low and mortgage rates are higher.

Debt management policy is technical and complex and involves many factors in attempting to maintain a reasonably balanced debt structure. Policy is directed toward meeting domestic and international government objectives as well as economic policy. Decisions must consider international balance of payments, conditions in the short and long-term financial markets, costs of issuing new debt, and the effects on existing monetary instruments, such as fixed income securities.

FEDERAL DEBT AND SECURITIES MARKET

Federal debt is short, intermediate, and long-term. Direct and guaranteed Federal obligations which are negotiable and marketable are: (1) treasury bills, which have maturities of three months, six months, and one year; (2) certificates of indebtedness, with one year maturity; (3) treasury notes, with maturities of one to five years; and (4) treasury bonds, with maturities of over five years.

Marketable government securities change in price and yield with changes in interest rates in the short and long-term markets. Interest rate changes reflect supply and demand conditions. The latter conditions, however, are influenced by debt management of the Treasury and policy of the Federal Reserve System, particularly its open market operations in selling and buying securities of varying maturities.

Long-Term Markets

"Capital markets" are markets for long-term obligations. The Federal Reserve influences this market through its impact on the lending and investment policies of banks and other financial institutions. Changes in the discount rate and activity in open market operations have an immediate impact on short-term rates but also reflect on intermediate and long-term obligations, including mortgages. Indirect impact is through financial intermediaries.

The function of capital markets is to facilitate the buying and selling of long-term obligations. There are many separate but interrelated markets of varying degrees of organization. The market deals in mortgages, securities, and government and corporate bonds. Yields rise and fall in response to aggregate demand and supply though there is usually a spread between particular types of instruments. The spread between corporate bonds and mortgages, for example, is reduced during periods of tight money and high interest rates.

Short-Term Markets

The short-term funds market, which is for securities with maturities of one year or less, is known as the "money market". It is the market for financial assets which are close substitutes for money, or "near money". The market is a complex of institutions, instruments, and facilities which enable the transfer of short-term funds. The funds are used to finance the needs of the various segments of the economy, such as business, government, and individuals. Short-term funds in the open market are transferred and made available to others through intermediaries, such as commercial banks, government securities dealers, and Federal Reserve Banks.

Interest rates in the money market tend to have greater fluctuations than in the capital markets. During tight money and high interest rates, money market rates tend to rise above capital market rates. When loanable funds are plentiful and interest rates are low, money market rates tend to be lower than capital market rates. In the long run, rates in the money market tend to move together because of the close relationship between segments of the market. There is, however, variation in individual rates depending upon the flow of funds into given sectors of the market. Since the U.S. Government is the largest single borrower in the market, Treasury debt management and Federal Reserve open market operations have a significant impact on rate changes.

Instruments used in the short-term funds market are primarily (1) short-term government securities, such as Treasury bills and certificates; (2) federal funds, which are excess reserves which banks may lend to one another; (3) certificates of deposit—CD's; (4) bankers acceptances; (5) Federal agency securities, such as Fannie Mae and the Federal Home Loan Banks; and (6) commercial paper. Lenders, such as commercial banks and real estate investment trusts (REIT's), often borrow funds by selling commercial paper in the market. Such paper is essentially an IOU or promissory note backed by the general credit of the issuing institution.

Commercial paper is of two types: (1) directly placed, and (2) dealer placed. Institutions which have a national credit acceptance in the market can sell their paper directly. Most institutions sell their paper through dealers who receive a commission on the sales.

Federal Reserve policy has an immediate impact on short-term rates. An increase in the discount rate and in the prime rate can cause an increase in short-term interest rates. Rates on Treasury bills in particular influence rates on other short-term obligations. An increase in the rate on Federal funds borrowed between banks can put pressure on short-term rates.

MONETARY POLICY

Tight money is a condition in the money and capital markets wherein funds are scarce and expensive; that is, interest rates are high. The condition may be caused by a government monetary policy of restraint designed, for instance, to fight inflation.

A Federal Reserve policy of monetary restraint will limit the ability of commercial banks to make loans. The supply of bank credit becomes limited and borrowers must pay more for money. Total spending is reduced as projects are deferred, credit standards are raised by lenders, and attempts are made to eliminate marginal borrowers and credit. Sales of securities by the Federal Reserve removes money from the markets and reduces the lending ability of banks.

A policy of monetary ease means that the money supply is growing at a good rate, loans are available at relatively low rates, new projects are started, marginal buyers obtain loans, and there is an increase in general business and real estate activity. The Federal Reserve buys government securities and this tends to increase spending because banks can use the funds to increase lending activity.

BOND MARKET

The prices of long-term securities are influenced by changes in the general level of interest rates. Further, institutional investors may make shifts in the types of instruments in their portfolios. A restrictive credit policy, in which bank credit is scarce and expensive, can cause higher long-term yields. Institutions shift from short-term securities, such as Treasury bills, to the more attractive, higher yield, corporate and municipal bonds and mortgages. In an inflationary period the borrowers will repay these obligations with cheaper dollars. Shifts in types of instruments held by institutional investors decline during times when savings flows are declining because of the risk of price loss.

Investors, however, during periods of rising rates, may prefer to buy short-term obligations and reinvest again as rates go higher. Bonds may not be attractive and saleable at reasonable rates. During periods of declining rates, such as in a recession, investors prefer long-term obligations.

Banks usually prefer short-term obligations and savers prefer long-term instruments. The sale of Treasury bills will tend to increase total spending and the sale of bonds will tend to attract the savings market. The Treasury may attempt to sell bills in a recession and bonds during inflation. Short-term bills, however, have lower rates than bonds and the Treasury may decide to issue bills to reduce financing costs even though the action contributes to inflation.

GROSS NATIONAL PRODUCT

Gross national product is the sum of all goods and services produced and consumed in the country. An important factor in any consideration of the mortgage market is the general business outlook, the rate of business expansion, and the level of business activity. Elements of weakness and strength in the economy must be considered.

A slow growth of business activity may be caused by a number of factors. A decline in consumer confidence can reduce buying activity. Rising costs and a reduction of profits can reduce the rate of capital spending by industry. Reduction of Federal spending can slow business activity. A Federal monetary policy of restraint will reduce the ability of commercial banks to make loans.

A faster growth of business activity may be accounted for by several factors. A relaxation of monetary policy and fiscal restraints should increase spending by business and the consumer. It should be remembered, however, that changes in monetary and fiscal policy, either for restraint or ease, have a delayed impact on the economy and the full effect may not be felt for several months. Business activity should increase as business and Federal spending increase due to the availability of credit.

HOUSING STARTS

A high level of housing starts can result from a strong net inflow of savings into deposit and thrift institutions and from an expansionary monetary and fiscal policy. A positive government policy toward housing, backed by support from government housing agencies, can maintain a high level of activity. Liberalized lending policies for institutional lenders such as regulatory agencies permitting higher loan-to-value ratios, larger maximum loan amounts, and a larger percent of the lender's assets in certain types of loans, may also stimulate starts.

A decline in housing starts may be caused by a fiscal and monetary policy of restraint which results in tight money, high interest rates, and high prices. Excess demand may be reduced by increases in the discount rate, increase in bank reserve requirements, income tax increases, and wage and price controls. Moratoriums on government housing subsidy programs also reduce starts in these areas.

Housing construction in the United States is subject to almost constant fluctuations which have an impact on the economy. The extent of the fluctuations depends to a large extent on developments in the mortgage market. The relationship between the housing cycle and residential construction is aptly described as follows:

> Residential construction tends to be countercyclical. In all six of the previous postwar slowdowns, home building turned down well ahead of the peak in the business cycle and began picking up before recovery in the rest of the economy had begun.
>
> This countercyclical movement is largely the result of fluctuations in the availability of mortgage credit. Without credit, most people cannot buy a house or invest in income property. The amount of new housing that can be built, therefore, depends on the extent to which long-term mortgage funds are available.[1]
>
> The availability of mortgage credit is highly sensitive to movements in interest rates. In times of economic expansion, short-term interest rates usually rise relative to long-term rates—a movement in response to increases in credit demands and the restraining influence of monetary policy typical of such periods. Under such circumstances, mortgage funds tend to become scarce. Conversely, as the pace of economic activity slows and monetary restraint is relaxed, credit demands subside, short-term yields fall relative to long-term rates, and mortgage credit becomes more available.[2]

CREDIT CRUNCH

The impact of a "credit crunch" is usually heavy on the residential mortgage market. Money is scarce and expensive and housing starts are reduced considerably. Mortgage bankers can suffer warehousing interest losses as the prime rate rises above the FHA and VA rates. Losses also can occur if the mortgage banker has a substantial volume of outstanding mortgage commitments without firm purchase commitments from investors. Usually, if the flow of savings funds declines, forward commitments in mortgages decline because institutions wait for higher yields.

[1] "Residential Building—Extent of the Drop Will Depend Mainly on Mortgage Markets," *Business Review* of the Federal Reserve Bank of Dallas, November, 1973, p. 1.
[2] *Ibid.*

Lack of mortgage financing will reduce the sales of existing houses. Further, sales of new houses will also be reduced since potential purchasers are unable to sell their present houses. Builders are also unable to complete houses and a backlog of uncompleted housing develops. Financing is not available for houses scheduled for completion and in the final stages of completion.

MORTGAGE FUNDS

The funds for real estate financing must compete with the demand for funds from all users of credit in the economy. The demand comes from government and private securities, consumer loans, notes, commercial paper, and commercial loans to business enterprises. The supply of funds available to real estate depends upon the total supply of funds and credit in the economy and the surplus after competitive needs have been satisfied.

Net Savings

The basic source of funds for investment is the net savings of individuals, business firms, and governments. The savings may be loaned directly to borrowers or placed in financial intermediaries for lending. Savings depend on changes in income levels, expenses, and desire of the units to save. Individuals have fixed savings commitments through life insurance and pension programs. Further, many individuals have modest savings in securities, mutual funds, real estate, and institutional savings accounts of various forms. The bulk of individual savings is through financial intermediaries, and this preference is a major influence on the organization and operation of the residential mortgage market. The supply of savings attracted to these financial institutions fluctuates with demand from other sources and may result in curtailment of lending or a surplus of loanable funds and an increase in lending activity.

Business savings come from profits. Profits are reinvested in the business or paid to owners of the business, such as through stockholders' dividends. Undistributed profits are available for investment though these profits are subject to fluctuation.

Government savings are also subject to fluctuation due to shifts from deficit to surplus. Government enters the money markets and borrows funds during deficits. Surplus funds are used to reduce debts or are deposited in financial institutions. In both instances the result is to increase the supply of loanable funds in the market.

Mortgage Funds

The supply of funds available to financial institutions depends basically on net savings. There are, however, other sources of funds generated in the operations of the institutions which influence the total supply of loanable funds at a given time.

Savings and loan associations have four sources of loanable funds: (1) net savings gains; (2) periodic income from loan payments, prepayments, and payoffs of loans; (3) retained earnings after payment of interest and operating expenses; and (4) advances from Federal Home Loan Banks and other borrowed money, such as from local commercial banks. Sales of whole loans and of participating interests in blocks of loans are also sources of loanable funds.[3]

Life insurance companies obtain their supply of funds for investment from premiums on policies. Policyholders' reserves are accumulated and since these funds are long-term in nature and substantial in amount the companies are able to engage in permanent financing and make large loans on business and commercial properties. Life insurance companies also receive income from investments, such as mortgage repayments, government securities, and corporate securities.

Commercial banks receive their funds from depositors, trust accounts, borrowings, and return on investments in loans and securities. Funds available to banks vary with their share of the savings market and with government monetary policy.

Mortgage bankers obtain funds primarily from the issuance of securities, commercial banks, and commitments from institutional investors to purchase mortgages. Income is also available from servicing activities, sale of hazard insurance, mortgage fees, and equity participations in real estate projects.

DISINTERMEDIATION

Financial disintermediation is a term used to describe withdrawals of savings from thrift institutions by individuals who use the funds to invest directly in the money and capital markets. It is a shift

[3] American Savings and Loan Institute, *Lending Principles and Practices*. Chicago, Ill.: American Savings and Loan Institute Press, 1971.

of funds from financial intermediaries such as savings and loan associations to direct investments. The term has been broadened through usage to include withdrawal of funds from one type of financial institution and their redeposit into another institution paying a higher rate. Funds move from one intermediary to another as savers take advantage of differences in rates.

Disintermediation is not a new process. The term was coined specifically to describe the heavy withdrawal of funds from thrift institutions in 1966 and their direct reinvestment in securities. Disintermediation had occurred previously in 1959 and has again in 1973.

The process is a result of a rapid increase in open market interest rates, which creates a wide spread or differential between thrift or deposit institution rates and market rates. Rates paid to savers by thrift institutions, or deposit intermediaries, tend to lag behind increases in open market rates. Further, government imposes statutory ceilings on interest rates paid on savings accounts.

Thrift institutions must "borrow short and lend long". They compete in the market for short-term funds, including savings accounts which are subject to withdrawal on demand, at fluctuating rates. The short-term funds are invested primarily in long-term, fixed-rate mortgages. If thrift institutions increase their rate to meet open market competition, they must apply the increase to all deposits. Higher rates of return can be obtained, however, only on new investments. Substantial losses and a depletion of reserves would occur under such circumstances. Cost of money to the institution increases rapidly while its income increases slowly. The cost squeeze is particularly acute with savings and loan associations because of their long average asset maturity.

Disintermediation has an impact on the allocation and distribution of funds in financial intermediaries and on the flow of funds in the economy. Housing starts are reduced when funds flow out of thrift institutions with heavy investments in residential mortgages, such as savings and loan associations and mutual savings banks. If the funds flow into commercial banks there is a growth in funds for business loans. A shift of funds from any of these financial institutions into U.S. government securities may reduce funds available for the private business sector of the economy. Statutory ceilings on interest rates paid by thrift and deposit institutions may restrain a shifting of funds between them but may result in a decline of deposits in all of them as savers shift to direct investments without statutory rate limits.

Savings and loan associations are seeking to lengthen their deposits by use of certificates which have extended maturity dates and a loss of partial interest penalty for early withdrawal of the certificate funds. The certificates may not, however, deter disintermediation since holders may decide to withdraw and take the penalty if yields are higher on other investments, such as U.S. Treasury bills, commercial paper, and municipal bonds.

REVIEW AND STUDY QUESTIONS

1. Explain the three techniques of monetary regulation through which the Federal Reserve System exercises its control over the monetary system.
2. Briefly explain how the U.S. Treasury exercises "debt management".
3. What are "capital markets" and what are the primary instruments used in these markets?
4. What is a "short-term market" and what are the primary instruments used in this market?
5. Distinguish between "inflation" and "deflation," and "tight money" and "easy money."
6. What is the "gross national product" and how does it affect the mortgage market?
7. Explain how the availability of mortgage credit affects the level of housing starts and why residential construction tends to be countercyclical.
8. Explain the basic source of the supply of funds for residential mortgages and the effect on the mortgage market of (A) a "credit crunch," and (B) disintermediation.

FURTHER READINGS AND REFERENCES

Board of Governors of the Federal Reserve System, *The Federal Reserve System: Purposes and Functions.* Washington, D.C., 1961.

Goldsmith, R. W., *Financial Institutions.* New York: Random House, 1968.

Maisel, Sherman J., *Financing Real Estate.* New York: McGraw-Hill Book Company, 1965.

Pease, Robert H., and Lewis O. Kerwood, *Mortgage Banking.* New York: McGraw-Hill Book Company, 1965.

Polakoff, Murray E., et al., *Financial Institutions and Markets.* Boston: Houghton Mifflin Co., 1970.

Robinson, Roland I., *Money and Capital Markets.* New York: McGraw-Hill Book Company, 1964.

Smith, Paul F., *Economics of Financial Institutions and Markets.* Homewood, Ill.: Richard D. Irwin, Inc., 1971.

Woodworth, Walter G., *The Money Market and Monetary Management.* New York: Harper and Row, 1965.

THREE

Legal Aspects of the Mortgage

IMPORTANCE AND IMPACT OF THE MORTGAGE

The mortgage is the most frequently used instrument in real estate financing. It contains provisions covering the duties, rights, responsibilities, and liabilities of the parties to it. These provisions have an impact on the economics and even the societal aspects of a transaction, such as environmental requirements and antidiscrimination clauses. Borrowers, lenders, investors, developers, government, and society are affected by the legal environment of the mortgage instrument.

Importance of Legal Counsel

The real estate mortgage is a legal instrument and must be prepared and interpreted by an attorney at law. The discussion in this chapter is presented to make the lender and borrower aware of certain legal effects of a mortgage and the need to retain legal counsel in all transactions.

Institutional lenders have their own legal department or retain an independent law firm on a regular basis. Borrowers on a mortgage loan should retain an attorney to represent them in the transaction.

HISTORICAL DEVELOPMENT

Real estate has for centuries been used as security for loans. The mortgage is one of the oldest legal instruments used to secure the transaction. The mortgage instrument and the practice of mortgage lending has gone through changes over the years and reflects the changing concepts as to the protection of the rights of borrower and lender.

The early mortgage, beginning in the fourteenth century, was a deed of the property to the lender with a provision, known as the defeasance clause, for return of the property to the borrower upon full payment of the debt. The borrower lost the property to the lender absolutely, and all rights and interest of the borrower were cancelled, upon default in the obligation. There was no foreclosure sale and the lender took immediate possession. Actually, the lender was legally able to take possession of the property at the time the mortgage was made and remain in possession until the debt was paid. The lender, however, usually permitted the borrower to have possession.

The transfer of land title as security for a loan, possession by the lender, strict interpretation and enforcement of the mortgage by the courts, and the immediate forfeiture of the borrower's property upon default (regardless of the reason for the default or the value of the property or the balance of the debt) were gradually recognized by the courts as being unduly strict and inequitable. Mortgage law gradually changed to permit borrowers to redeem their property, that is, pay the debt after default. The new right, in full effect by 1625, was known as the borrower's "equity of redemption".

It was necessary, in fairness to the lender, to place a time limit on the equity of redemption of the borrower, or the lender, after taking over property upon default, would never know when the borrower would seek to redeem the property. The courts gave the lender a remedy known as "foreclosure". The purpose of foreclosure is to cut off or bar the equity of redemption of the borrower. The court would specify a period of time after default in which the borrower could pay the debt and, if it was not paid, the court would terminate the borrower's equity of redemption and all of his rights and interest in the property would cease. The action is known as "strict foreclosure" and is still used today to some extent.

A later development, and the common practice today, was foreclosure by sale, known as legal foreclosure or judicial sale. The property is sold by the court at public auction to satisfy the debt. Surplus funds from the sale above the balance of the debt are given to the borrower. The public sale cut off the equity of redemption. Some states have by statute given the borrower an additional period of time to redeem after the foreclosure sale. The right is known as the "statutory right of redemption".

Mortgage law has evolved to a general recognition today that the mortgage is a security instrument which creates a lien on property owned by the borrower. The borrower rather than the lender is the owner of the property. The lender has a security interest but title is not transferred to him until the borrower defaults and specified legal proceedings, such as foreclosure, are properly conducted.

DEFINITION AND PARTIES

The mortgage pledges a specific property as security for a debt. It creates a specific lien or charge which may be enforced by the sale of the property to satisfy the debt. The borrower is known as the mortgagor and the lender is the mortgagee. Some states use a deed of trust, or a security deed, rather than a mortgage.

Mortgageable Interests

The mortgage is typically used to finance a fee interest in real estate. It may be used, however, to finance almost any interest provided the lender is legally permitted and is willing as a matter of management policy to lend on a given interest. Examples of such interest are life estates and leases.

Form and Execution

No particular form need to be used for a mortgage. A mortgage may be written or typed for a given transaction. Institutional lenders have a printed form used in their respective institutions. Mortgage forms may be purchased at an office supply store. It is essential, however, that a mortgage form, in order to be enforceable, meet requirements prescribed by state statutes and that certain provisions be included for the protection of lender and borrower.

A mortgage must be properly executed if it is to be valid between the parties and if it is to be recorded. The borrower must sign the mortgage and deliver it to the lender for acceptance. Witnesses and acknowledgment are necessary for recording.

MORTGAGE AS PERSONAL PROPERTY

A mortgage is personal property, rather than real property, in the hands of the lender. The lender may sell and assign it to another party, which is frequently done in the mortgage market. The promissory note is also personal property to the lender.

Promissory Note and Parties

Most mortgage transactions involve a promissory note, or bond, along with the mortgage. The note is evidence of the debt and creates a personal liability on the part of the borrower to pay the debt. The note is a general lien against assets of the borrower. The borrower is known as the obligor and the lender as the obligee. The note may be a separate instrument or be included in the mortgage instrument, either in full or by reference.

LAW WHICH GOVERNS

Mortgages are governed by the laws of the state in which the property subject to the mortgage is located. National lenders must be aware of the laws in fifty states, the territories, and the Commonwealth of Puerto Rico.

TITLE THEORY VS. LIEN THEORY

In title theory states, the lender holds title to the property and has the right of possession until the debt is paid. If the debt is not paid the borrower automatically loses the property. In lien theory states, which are in the majority, the borrower retains title to the property and the lender has only a lien against it. The title theory has been modified in some states so that the borrower has the right of possession. If the lender takes possession he is held strictly accountable for the income, expense, and use of the property.

Defeasance

The defeasance clause gives the borrower, in title theory states, the right to redeem the property upon payment of the debt; the lender's rights in the property are defeated. If the borrower does not pay the debt, title to the property remains with the lender and the rights of the borrower cease.

EQUITY OF REDEMPTION AND STATUTORY REDEMPTION

The borrower under a mortgage has the right to redeem his property any time before a foreclosure sale by paying the amount of the debt and any costs incurred by the lender in the foreclosure action. The equitable right of redemption is for the protection of the borrower and may not be cut off except by foreclosure.

The statutory right of redemption, available in some states, gives the borrower a period of time to redeem his property after a foreclosure sale. Statutory redemption, granted by statute, is in addition to the equity of redemption and increases the period of time for redemption for up to two years, depending on the state.

Equity of redemption is before a foreclosure sale; statutory right of redemption, in states which have it, is after a foreclosure sale. The diagram below illustrates the distinction.

```
Date of                  Foreclosure              End of
Default ◄──────────► Sale ◄──────────► Statutory Period
       ╰─────────────────╯    ╰─────────────────╯
   Equity of Redemption      Statutory Right
                              of Redemption
```

ESSENTIAL ELEMENTS

No particular form is necessary for a mortgage, but certain elements are needed to have a valid instrument. The typical mortgage creating a lien upon real estate should contain the following elements: (1) competent parties to a written instrument; (2) a mortgaging clause; (3) statement of the obligation, its terms, and consideration; (4) legal description of the property; (5) an interest capable of being mortgaged; (6) covenants of the borrower; and (7) proper execution, and voluntary delivery and acceptance.

The parties to a mortgage, the mortgagor and mortgagee, must be legally capable of entering into the agreement. They should be properly identified in the mortgage, particularly as to their marital status. Names should be the same in both the promissory note and the mortgage. The mortgage must, according to the Statute of Frauds, be in writing to be enforceable since it involves an interest in real estate.

The mortgaging clause pledges the property as security for the debt. The exact wording of the clause will vary as to whether a state uses the lien theory or title theory.

The obligation, that is the debt, and its terms and consideration must be stated with reasonable certainty. Among the items to be identified are the principal sum of the debt, interest rate, terms of repayment, and evidence of the promissory note. The information about the debt in the note must be identical with that in the mortgage. The note may be made a part of the mortgage by reference to it in the mortgage. The note is not recorded while the mortgage should be and usually is recorded.

There must be a complete and accurate legal description of the property. Third parties have a right to rely upon the constructive notice of the public records as to the lender's interests and rights in a property. A third party purchaser or another lender may not be bound by an obligation if the property description is inadequate. It is also necessary to identify personal property in the mortgage so that the lender may include it in any foreclosure sale.

Any interest in real estate may be mortgaged if the lender is willing to accept the interest as security. The interest may be held at the date of the mortgage or acquired at a later date. Such "after-acquired" property is subject to claims against it at the time of acquisition.

Mortgages include covenants or promises setting forth the duties and responsibilities of the borrower as to the protection of the property. The covenants may be specified by statute or included as a matter of custom which has been recognized by the courts. Typical of such provisions are the following: defeasance clause, acceleration clause, waste or failure to properly maintain the property, payment of the debt, insurance on the property, marketable title, escrow deposits, removal or alteration of the property, and default.

A mortgage is executed by the borrower signing it. A corporation also affixes its corporate seal. Witnesses and a "SEAL" may be required by state statute. Acknowledgment is not necessary for a valid mortgage as between the parties to it unless required by state statute. A mortgage should be voluntarily delivered to the lender for his voluntary acceptance.

Statute of Frauds

The regular mortgage must be in writing to be enforceable and meet the requirements of the Statute of Frauds. An interest, or legal estate in real estate, is voluntarily and intentionally created or transferred.

Statute of Limitations

The Statute of Limitations prohibits a person from bringing court action on a debt after a specified period of time. The application of the statute to mortgages is varied since there is a distinction between: (1) the debt and the mortgage; (2) lien theory and title theory states; and (3) types of mortgages, such as deeds of trust, junior mortgages, equitable mortgages, and the mortgage with power of sale. The barring of action on the debt, for instance, may not necessarily bar action on the mortgage, though some courts take the opposite view.

INTEREST RATES

The interest rate on a mortgage has at least three legal aspects: (1) it must not be higher than permitted by state law or usury will be involved; (2) the borrower must be advised of the Annual Percentage Rate (APR); and (3) FHA and VA mortgages have a fixed or pegged maximum interest rate set by law. The interest rate may be fixed for the duration of the mortgage or it may be variable, that is, rise and fall according to changes in some index used by the lender. Or, it may float at a given number of points above prime. Prime is the interest rate charged by large commercial banks to its best customers. A national reference point for prime is usually the rate charged by certain banks in New York and Chicago.

Usury

Usury is a lender charging a rate of interest which is in excess of the maximum rate permitted by law. Difficulty may be encountered in determining whether the charge is for the use of money, that is, interest, or whether it is for services rendered in connection with the loan, such as a mortgage broker's commission. Usury statutes vary in detail among the states as do the penalties. Generally the borrower is not relieved of the obligation if the lender is guilty of usury. He must pay the debt and the legal rate of interest if he wants the mortgage discharged. The lender is barred from collecting interest in excess of the legal maximum. In some states the lender guilty of usury forfeits all of the loan and the obligation is declared void.

PREPAYMENT

The mortgage specifies the method and manner of its repayment, such as so many dollars per month for a given period of time. The lender is not required to accept advance payments unless there is a provision to this effect, known as the prepayment clause. The clause may permit prepayment in full or in part and the lender, at his option, may charge a penalty.

HAZARD INSURANCE

Lenders require that borrowers maintain proper insurance coverage as to type and amount on the mortgaged property. Policies contain a clause giving the lender first claim to the proceeds of any loss payment. The originals of the policies are kept by the lender and the borrower has copies. Premiums may be paid by the lender from the escrow account of the borrower. Borrowers may purchase the insurance coverage from a company of their choice though the company must be acceptable to the lender. Underwriting limits on exposure are sometimes required.

RECORDING

Recording is placing a copy of the mortgage on the public records. Notice is thereby given to the public of the rights of the parties in the mortgaged property. Recording is not to make a mortgage valid. It does, however, establish priority of claim to the proceeds of a foreclosure sale.

Mortgages are recorded in the court house in the county in which the land is located. If the land boundaries cross more than one county the mortgage is recorded in all counties in which the land is situated.

ASSIGNMENT

The mortgage is personal property, as compared to real estate, to the lender and, unless provided to the contrary, the lender has the right to transfer it without permission of the borrower. The borrower is obligated to the party receiving the assigned mortgage. The lender usually notifies the borrower of the assignment and directs that future payments be made to the new holder of the mortgage. Hazard insurance companies are notified of the assignment. The party assigning the mortgage is known as the assignor and the party receiving the assignment is the assignee.

The promissory note is assigned with the mortgagee. The assignment of note and mortgage is made by a formal written instrument and the assignee receives all of the rights of the original lender, including the rights to collect payments and to foreclose. The assignee records the assignment. In some jurisdictions a separate written instrument is not required.

The assignor provides the assignee with an estoppel certificate. This is a statement obtained from the owner of the property certifying: (1) that the mortgage is valid; (2) the amount of principal balance due; (3) the interest due; and (4) that there are no defenses or offsets to the obligation. The estoppel certificate protects the purchaser of the mortgage against the owner later making representations other than those in the certificate. A lender, for example, assigns a mortgage with a principal balance of $1,000 to an investor. The investor will require that the person who is liable on the mortgage, that is, the borrower, provide a statement verifying the amount. The borrower cannot later deny a fact which he has previously stated in writing as correct.

EXTENSION

A mortgage, such as a term mortgage, may be extended beyond its due date if the parties agree to the modification. The extension agreement is in writing, between the lender and borrower, and may be recorded. Since such an agreement changes the terms of the original mortgage it is important to obtain the approval of any other parties to the mortgage. For example, assume the seller of mortgaged property, who is the original mortgagor, transfers the property, with the new owner assuming the mortgage. The seller stands as a surety for the assumed mortgage and changes in the mortgage terms without his approval may, in some states, release him from liability on the mortgage.

SUBORDINATION

Subordination refers to an agreement between lien holders whereby one party agrees to place his lien in a junior or subordinate position to the other. A seller of land, for example, may already have accepted a mortgage on the land from a buyer. The buyer may need to have the seller subordinate the mortgage to a construction loan from an institutional lender since the latter needs a first mortgage as security. The seller should be willing to subordinate since the construction of proper improvements should enhance the value of the mortgaged property.

Subordination is also a feature of commercial leasehold financing. A developer leases ground under a ground lease. Financing of the improvements on the ground is by a leasehold mortgage, that is, the security for the loan is the developer's interest in the leasehold. In order for the developer to obtain maximum financing it is necessary for the land owner to subordinate his ownership interest in the land to the lender. Such subordination gives the lender the security of land as well as the leasehold.

SATISFACTION

The proper payment of a mortgage in full will discharge the obligation between the parties and cancel or satisfy the debt and lien. The borrower should obtain from the lender the original promissory note and mortgage and a written statement, called a satisfaction piece, certifying that the obligation is paid in full and satisfied. The satisfaction piece is recorded by the owner and this cancels the mortgage on the public record.

MERGER

Merger occurs when the owner of the property and the holder of the mortgage are the same party. The situation would occur if the owner-borrower took an assignment rather than a satisfaction piece for a mortgage paid in full. The mortgage would merge with the owner's fee interest and be discharged or cease to exist as a mortgage. The owner might prefer an assignment to a satisfaction, for example, in order to keep the mortgage alive and prevent junior mortgages from advancing to a first or senior position. The owner should state in the assignment that there is no intention to merge the fee with the mortgage. It is also possible to have the assignment made to a dummy or straw party, that is, a person other than the owner.

ASSUMPTION VS. SUBJECT TO

Real estate is often sold with the buyer "assuming" or taking "subject to" an existing mortgage on the property. Under either arrangement the buyer must make the payments on the mortgage and abide by its provisions or lose the property through foreclosure.

Under the assumption agreement, the buyer not only loses the property but may be held personally liable for any deficiency if the proceeds of the foreclosure sale are insufficient to pay the debt balance. If the buyer takes the property "subject to" the existing mortgage, there is no personal liability for a deficiency; the buyer loses only the property.

In both arrangements the original debtor remains liable to the lender on the promissory note and the lender may sue the original debtor or any assuming grantee or both to collect the debt. Sale of the property does not release the original debtor from liability to the lender unless the lender agrees to make such a release. The original debtor, under the assumption agreement, may sue the assuming grantee for any amount the debtor has to pay the lender.

For example, Doe buys a house for $60,000. There is an existing mortgage with a principal balance of $40,000 on the house. Smith is the owner-seller of the house and the party who originally signed the promissory note and mortgage which now have a principal balance of $40,000. If Doe "assumes" the $40,000 mortgage and the mortgage goes into default and foreclosure, Doe loses the house. If the foreclosure sale of the house brings only, say, $36,000, Doe is liable for the $4,000 deficiency. The lender can sue either Doe or Smith or both for the $4,000. If Smith has to pay it, he may then sue Doe for $4,000, since Doe had a contract (the assumption agreement) with Smith that he would assume liability for the debt. If Doe buys the house "subject to" the $40,000 and the same default, foreclosure, and deficiency situation occurs, Smith cannot recover the $4,000 from Doe since the latter did not agree to assume liability for any deficiency.

DEFAULT AND ACCELERATION

The acceleration clause gives the lender, at his option, the right to declare the entire amount of the debt due and payable at once upon default by the borrower. The due date of the mortgage is accelerated if the borrower fails to meet the terms of the mortgage. Default may be caused by the borrower: (1) failing to pay principal and interest when due; (2) failing to pay taxes and hazard insurance premiums; (3) selling the property without notifying the lender; (4) commiting "waste," that is, failing to keep the property in good repair; and (5) committing any other action which may impair the security of the loan.

Lenders permit a grace period before exercising the acceleration option. An attempt is made to assist a borrower delinquent in payments. Foreclosure is usually resorted to only when other efforts have failed. FHA and VA require a delay of 90 days before foreclosure.

If a mortgage does not contain an acceleration clause the lender must, unless the statutes or courts decree otherwise, wait until each payment is due and in default before taking legal action. Such a situation could involve the lender in a series of law suits.

A lender may provide in the mortgage that the interest rate will be increased or escalated during the period of delinquency or default. Such a penalty, for example, may provide for an interest rate of, say, 8 percent as long as the mortgage is current, but a rate increase to 9 percent during any period of default.

STRICT FORECLOSURE

Under strict foreclosure the court establishes a period of time in which a borrower must pay the debt. If the debt is not paid by the specified date, the borrower's equity of redemption is forever barred and absolute title is given to the lender. There is no legal foreclosure sale. The lender keeps any value of the property over the amount of the debt and thus may acquire a property in excess of the debt balance. The borrower may still be liable for any deficiency if the value of the property is not sufficient to satisfy the debt and costs in full. Strict foreclosure is seldom used and in most states has been abolished by statute.

VOLUNTARY DEED

The borrower may, instead of going through foreclosure, convey his property to the lender by deed. The lender accepts the voluntary conveyance and releases the borrower from liability on the note and mortgage. The method saves the time and expense of legal foreclosure.

There are limitations to this method of debt satisfaction. There is the possibility that the borrower may later claim duress or undue pressure from the lender and have the conveyance set aside. The fact that the borrower owes the lender money places the lender in a position of having to collect the debt by absolutely proper means with no hint of pressure. A voluntary conveyance of a valuable parcel of property for a nominal sum is easily open to question, despite the legitimate objective of the lender to help the borrower. Further, junior mortgages are not terminated by a voluntary deed. Also a lender may waive his right to obtain a deficiency judgment by accepting a voluntary conveyance.

POWER OF SALE

A mortgage may contain a provision which permits the lender, upon default by the borrower, to foreclose without going through court action. The procedure, known as power of sale or foreclosure by advertisement, is much the same as in legal foreclosure, namely, proper notice to all parties, advertising of the sale, a public auction sale, and distribution of the proceeds.

Statutory requirements and regulations must be strictly followed if the sale is to be valid. The method has several weaknesses: (1) the lender is handling the foreclosure rather than going through judicial proceedings and sometimes the title given in this type of sale is not readily acceptable for fear it is not marketable; (2) the lender may not be permitted to bid on the property at the sale; and (3) deficiency judgments may be limited or not available.

Power of sale has the advantage to the lender of savings in time and expense over the legal foreclosure method, which can be time-consuming and costly. This advantage must be weighed against the deficiencies of the method.

LEGAL FORECLOSURE

Default and foreclosure are discussed under one heading though default does not necessarily lead to foreclosure, except as a last resort. Foreclosure can be expensive and time consuming and lenders seek to work out a mutually satisfactory solution to a borrower's default.

Default is a breach by the borrower of a provision of the promissory note or mortgage. The usual items of default are: (1) failure to pay principal and interest when due or to maintain proper insurance premiums when due or to maintain proper insurance coverage; (3) failure to keep the mortgaged property in good repair (commit "waste") so as to impair the lender's security; and (4) failure of the borrower to provide an estoppel certificate when one is properly requested. Lenders provide a "grace period" after default before exercising the acceleration clause and initiating foreclosure action. The borrower may during this time cure the delinquency or default and bring the loan current.

Legal foreclosure or judicial sale is action by the lender, through judicial processes, to have the mortgaged property sold and the proceeds used to pay the debt. The foreclosure sale cuts off the equity of redemption of the borrower. A person buying a property at a foreclosure sale obtains title from the court and becomes the new owner of the property.

Mortgages specify the lender's remedies and rights to foreclosure. Foreclosure actions are, however, governed by state statutes and rules and must be conducted exactly according to these provisions. Details vary but generally legal foreclosure requires that: (1) there be a default; (2) all parties to the mortgage subordinate to the senior mortgage are joined in the foreclosure action so as to terminate their interests and rights; (3) all parties are properly notified of the action and the sale is properly advertised; (4) the sale is conducted as a public auction, usually at the court house by an officer, such as the sheriff, appointed by the court; and (5) the proceeds of the sale are distributed, first, to pay taxes and expenses of the sale, and, second, to pay the lender who brought the action. Any remaining funds go to junior lien holders and to the former owner of the property.

If a property does not bring an amount at the foreclosure sale sufficient to pay off the debt, the lender may be able to sue for a deficiency judgment on the promissory note, which created a personal liability of the borrower for the debt. Both the foreclosure action and the suit on the note may be combined in one action or may be separate. The lender through the deficiency judgment is able to look to other property of the borrower, rather than only the mortgaged property, for funds to pay the deficiency. Deficiency judgments have been abolished or limited by statute in many states, particularly where the lender is the purchaser of the property at the foreclosure sale.

RECEIVER

A lender may want to have a receiver appointed by the court to protect his interest between the date of default by the borrower and the foreclosure sale. There may be a considerable lapse of time during this period and an owner, knowing that foreclosure is coming, may not take proper care of the property. Rents on income property will continue to be collected but if a receiver is appointed the rents will be assigned to him for the lender. Or, the defaulting owner may "milk" the property, that is, collect as much rent as possible and do as little as possible to maintain the property, and it may be necessary for a receiver to take temporary possession of the property. The receiver represents the lender through the court, and is accountable to him and the court for income and expenditures on the property. The mortgage may provide for the appointment of the receiver; an agreement between the lender and borrower for the appointment may be made at the date of default; or the court may elect to appoint a receiver if a situation indicates need for such protection.

MORTGAGES AND LEASES

If a lease is on a property before the mortgage, the rights of the tenant may not be disturbed. A foreclosure action will not terminate the lease nor may the tenant be evicted before the expiration of the lease. If the lease is made after the mortgage has been placed on the property, the rights of the lender take precedence over those of the tenant. The lease is terminated by a foreclosure sale. The lender also has the right to evict the tenant.

SECOND MORTGAGES

A second, or third, or fourth mortgage is basically the same as a first mortgage. The primary difference is that the second mortgage is second in priority of claim to the proceeds of a foreclosure sale. The holder of the first or senior mortgage has first claim, after taxes and expenses of the sale, and any remaining funds go to the second mortgage holder. The second mortgage holder does not receive any funds if the sale fails to bring an amount sufficient to pay claims above the junior lien. The holder of the second mortgage may sue on the promissory note to collect the debt. The junior lienor may foreclose but the action does not disturb the first mortgage and a buyer of the property takes it with the first mortgage.

The foreclosure of the first mortgage will terminate the junior mortgage if the holder of the latter is joined as a party to the action. The junior mortgagee may take steps to protect the second lien, such as making payments to the first mortgage holder, or buying out the interests of the mortgagor or the first mortgagee.

Junior mortgages may, in addition to the usual provisions in any mortgage, have clauses designed to serve a special purpose. Two such clauses are the lifting clause and the default in prior mortgage clause.

The lifting clause permits the borrower to lift the first mortgage and replace it with another one without changing the junior status of the second mortgage. The clause protects the borrower by keeping the second mortgage in a junior position of priority; otherwise, when the senior mortgage is paid off or refinanced, the junior mortgage would be raised to the senior position. It may be difficult or impossible for the borrower to obtain new financing if the junior mortgage becomes a first mortgage, since most institutional lenders are legally required to lend only on first mortgages. The junior mortgage should also require that the amount of a new first mortgage should not exceed the amount of the original first mortgage.

The default in prior mortgage clause protects the lender on the second mortgage. It provides that if the borrower defaults on the senior lien the junior mortgage holder may pay the defaulted items, add the amount to the second mortgage, and foreclose on the junior mortgage. The senior mortgage is of importance to the junior mortgage holder since the latter may be wiped out if the senior loan is foreclosed.

REVIEW AND STUDY QUESTIONS

1. Distinguish between a mortgage and a promissory note and explain why the two instruments are usually used together in real estate financing.
2. Distinguish between: (A) title theory vs. lien theory, and (B) equity of redemption vs. statutory redemption.
3. What are the essential elements of any mortgage in order to have a valid instrument?
4. Explain how the mortgage is affected by: (A) the Statute of Frauds, and (B) the Statute of Limitations.
5. With reference to the interest rate on mortgages, what is: (A) the annual percentage rate, and (B) usury?
6. Explain the following provisions of mortgages: (A) prepayment; (B) assignment; (C) subordination; and (D) hazard insurance.
7. What is meant by the "recording" of a mortgage? Where is a mortgage recorded?
8. Explain the following aspects of mortgages and the possible effect of each on the parties to a mortgage: (A) extension; (B) satisfaction; and (C) merger.
9. Distinguish between the "assumption" of an existing mortgage, and buying a property "subject to" an existing mortgage.

10. Explain each of the following: (A) default and acceleration; (B) strict fore-closure; (C) voluntary deed; (D) power of sale; (E) legal foreclosure; and (F) receiver.
11. What is a second or junior mortgage? What two special clauses might be found in such mortgages?

FURTHER READINGS AND REFERENCES

Dykstra, Gerald O., and Lilian G. Dykstra, *The Business Law of Real Estate.* New York: The Macmillan Company, 1956.

Grange, William J., and Thomas C. Woodbury, *Manual of Real Estate Law and Procedures,* Second Ed. New York: The Ronald Press Company, 1968.

Hebard, Edna L., and Gerald S. Meisel, *Principles of Real Estate Law.* Cambridge, Mass.: Schenkman Publishing Company, 1967.

Kratovil, Robert, *Real Estate Law,* Fifth Ed. Englewood Cliffs, N.J.: Prentice-Hall, Inc., 1969.

Lusk, Harold F., *The Law of the Real Estate Business.* Homewood, Ill.: Richard D. Irwin, Inc., 1965.

Osborne, George E., *Handbook on the Law of Mortgages.* St. Paul, Minn.: West Publishing Co., 1951.

Semenow, Robert W., *Questions and Answers on Real Estate,* Seventh Ed. Englewood Cliffs, N.J.: Prentice-Hall, Inc., 1972.

Tiffany, Herbert Thorndike, *The Modern Law of Real Property.* New Abridged Edition by Carl Zollman. Chicago: Callaghan and Company, 1940.

FOUR

Permanent Financing

Permanent mortgage, or end mortgage, financing encompasses the entire spectrum of the mortgage lending process. Permanent mortgage financing can and does apply to junior mortgages as well as first mortgages. Major institutional lenders may issue permanent second mortgage loans, especially on commercial property. Oftentimes this is a result of gap financing but just as often it is strictly for the purpose of establishing additional financing which is secured by a second mortgage lien.

The lending activity begins with the lender finding a party desiring funds and ends when the loan is paid in full. The steps in the process as applied to the individual loan are: (1) solicitation; (2) application; (3) processing and underwriting; (4) closing; and (5) servicing. The process also involves market activities concerned with groups of mortgages rather than an individual loan: (1) portfolio management; (2) warehousing; (3) sale of mortgages to investors; and (4) the private and governmental secondary mortgage markets.

SOLICITATION

Solicitation is the function of finding applicants for mortgage loans. Financial institutions, such as savings and loan associations, commercial banks, and life insurance companies obtain mortgage business through their regular customers and contacts in the business and real estate community. Mortgage bankers and mortgage brokers actively solicit business from real estate brokers and developers. Business is obtained from calls directly from persons needing real estate loans, such as developers and home buyers.

The mortgage solicitor is a salesman who secures applications for loans. He is often said to be in "production," meaning his job is to produce loan applicants. Solicitors are paid on a salary or commission, or a combination of the two plans. The solicitor in Florida must be licensed under the Mortgage Brokerage Act.

APPLICATION

The loan application process is an essential element in mortgage lending. An understanding of its nature and use involves consideration of the following factors: (1) definition of the application; (2) reasons for use of an application; (3) the preliminary or informal interview; and (4) the formal application.

Definition

The loan application, in a practical sense, is a request from a prospective borrower to a lender for a loan in a specified amount and on certain terms. The applicant provides data and information to support the request. In a legal sense it is an offer from the borrower, which, if accepted by the lender, becomes a contract. It is doubtful whether either party would attempt to enforce the application as a contract.

Reasons for Use

The basic reason for a lender having a loan application is to obtain, in an orderly and complete manner, information about the borrower and about the property which will serve as the physical security for the loan. The information will assist the lender in determining whether a loan should be made to the applicant and on what terms and conditions.

The application becomes a part of the loan file and serves as a source of information for servicing of the loan. Mortgage loan servicing starts with the initial contact between borrower and lender.

The application gives the lender an opportunity for a personal interview with the applicant. He can observe responses to questions, note answers that lead to other questions, and make a judgment as to the attitude of the borrower toward the purpose of the loan and his ability and willingness to meet obligations, known as the moral hazard. The borrower is able to receive information about the lender's policies and have an opportunity to discuss the proposed transaction with the lender.

The application benefits both lender and borrower. Analysis of the information will assist a borrower in obtaining a loan within his ability to repay and the lender in making a loan that will not lead to foreclosure.

Preliminary Interview

The initial contact between the prospective borrower and lender is a preliminary interview or informal application. The purpose of the interview is to determine whether the loan needs of the applicant can probably be met by the lender and a formal application taken. If an applicant obviously does not qualify for a loan (the lender may not make the type of loan requested or on the terms the applicant wants), the initial interview gives the lender an opportunity to explain the reasons for declining the applicant, and saves the time and expense of a formal application. The interview will give the lender an opportunity to suggest alternative financing plans.

The preliminary interview is important to both the lender and the prospective borrower. Information is gathered by each party for decision making and first impressions are formed. The interview is conducted by a person who has a complete knowledge of the lender's policies and procedures as well as an understanding of the real estate finance business. It is necessary to be able to deal effectively with people and maintain their confidence, goodwill, and cooperation. The attitude of the interviewer reflects the image of the lender. A personal interview should be conducted even if the application comes through an outside source, such as a real estate broker or mortgage broker.

Formal Application

The formal application provides detailed information about the borrower and the property. There is no standard form and each lender has developed or uses a form that has proven most useful in its operations.

Any form must be used by a skilled interviewer for maximum effectiveness.

The formal application should be completed by the interviewer. This person understands questions on the form and can explain them to the applicant and record answers. The form is detailed and the interviewer explains the charges for the application and the importance of complete and accurate information.

Lenders request essentially the same information in formal applications. A typical form includes questions about the applicant (assets and liabilities, income and expenses), the property, and the particulars of the requested loan. Information may be classified as follows:

1. Formal request for a loan, including amount and terms.
2. Location of the property; description of the improvements and neighborhood.
3. Encumbrances, mortgages, and other liens against the property.
4. Financial and credit information.
5. Biographical data, such as full and correct name, age, family, employment, and residence.
6. Appraisal report.
7. Signature of the applicant.
8. Comments of the interviewer.
9. Decision of the lender.

PROCESSING AND UNDERWRITING

The request for a loan and the supporting information from the interview and formal application must be processed and underwritten, or evaluated, by the lender, and a decision made on the granting, rejection, or modification of the request. The procedure is detailed but basically includes the following: (1) appraisal of the property; (2) credit check including an analysis of the borrower; (3) title analysis; (4) analysis of the risk in the loan amount and terms requested; and (5) decision on the application.

Property Appraisal

The appraisal of the property is ordered as one of the initial functions in processing the application. The lender must have an evaluation of the physical security to determine: (1) the value on which to base the loan amount; and (2) whether the type and location of the property meets the standards of the lender and regulatory agencies.

Credit

A credit investigation and analysis is essential for a sound loan. A borrower must have the financial ability and desire or willingness to repay a loan. Loan delinquency, default, and foreclosure are expensive to both borrower and lender. The lender needs to know as much as possible about the credit of the applicant.

Credit information comes from three sources: (1) the application form; (2) commercial credit bureaus; and (3) interviews with persons who have had personal or business contact with the applicant. Information consists of data about the applicant's income, employment, assets, debts, promptness in paying obligations, family and dependents, and credit references. Verification and analysis of the factual data is intended to: (1) determine the applicant's management of his financial affairs, including his attitude toward money management; (2) discover any personal or domestic traits and habits which influence ability and willingness to repay the loan; and, (3) estimate the risk in the loan requested in relation to the results of the credit analysis.

Title Analysis

Title examination is a function performed by qualified legal talent. It may be done by the lender's legal department, by outside independent attorneys, or by a title company. A title binder, or title report, is ordered by the lender and shows the nature of the title, the legal description, liens and encumbrances, and other exceptions. The title report specifies items which must be performed in order to clear the title or to have the title insurance company issue a policy. The regulated institutional lender must have a marketable title and first lien on the property.

Loan Terms

An element of risk in mortgage lending is in the amount and terms of the loan. A low downpayment loan, with a long maturity, increases the risk. Analysis of the borrower, and the property, may indicate a need for modification of the required loan terms.

Decision

The decision as to whether to approve a loan application is made by a loan committee of the lender. A complete and properly processed application with recommendations from mortgage officers should enable the committee to perform its function efficiently. If the loan is approved, the applicant is notified in writing by means of a "loan commitment" setting forth all contingencies. The lender commits itself to grant the loan under specified terms and conditions. The borrower is advised of the credit costs of the loan.

CLOSING THE LOAN

Loan closing, or loan settlement, includes all of the activities, after approval of the loan, to complete the transaction and disburse the money to the borrower. It is a detailed process involving legal considerations and instruments. It is also a time to maintain and enhance goodwill and confidence between the lender and borrower. A loan is closed at the office of the lender or an escrow agent, such as a title insurance company. A borrower should retain an attorney to represent his interests in the transaction.

Documents

The legal instruments, documents, and papers used in a loan closing are prepared by the lender and his representatives in advance of the closing date. The content and purpose of the forms are explained to the borrower at the closing, the forms are executed by the parties, and given to the appropriate persons. Forms used vary with lenders, the nature of the transactions, state laws, and customs and procedures in the locality. The papers listed below are not necessarily used in every transaction but are representative of the documentation found in conventional loan closings on existing single-family houses.

1. Promissory note and mortgage.
2. Title insurance binder, showing a marketable title.
3. Hazard insurance policies, with statement that borrower selected his own insurance agent or company.
4. Application form of borrower.
5. Loan closing, or loan settlement, statement showing disbursement of loan and fees and charges.
6. Affidavits.
7. Disclosure statements.
8. Contracts.
9. Inspection reports.
10. Warranties.
11. Commitments.
12. Deeds.

13. Photographs.
14. Physical survey plat.
15. Releases of prior liens.
16. Waivers of mechanic's liens.
17. Property tax statements.
18. Payment book.

Closing Costs

A borrower must be fully informed in writing of all charges and costs, including discounts, that he will be required to pay in connection with the loan. Further, there are items of prepayment, and initial deposits into an escrow account. Some of the fees and charges are deducted from the loan proceeds and some are paid in cash. The borrower must be prepared to pay these charges and costs at closing and the lender should have given notification of the amount prior to the closing date.

Lenders provide the borrower with a loan closing, or loan settlement, statement. The statement itemizes all loan costs, disbursements, and prorations. The signature of the borrower on the form acknowledges receipt of the statement and authorizes disbursements of funds as shown on the statement.

SERVICING

Loan servicing begins with the initial interview with the applicant and ends when the loan is fully repaid to the lender. Some lenders classify all activities prior to closing as "processing" and activities after closing as "servicing." The objective of loan servicing is to generate a safe and sound loan that is paid in accordance with the terms and conditions of the loan agreement. The interests of both lender and borrower must be protected, and good servicing policies and procedures assure that protection. If a good loan is made initially, it is the function of servicing to maintain that quality.

Mechanics

The mechanics of loan servicing involve the collection of payments from the borrower for principal, interest, and escrow account items, such as for property taxes and hazard insurance premiums, according to the terms of the note and mortgage, and remittances to investors. Further, there are operational procedures involving the loan, such as accounting, tax and insurance payments and records, private mortgage insurance, loan payment followup, delinquent loan followup, and loan analysis. Files must be maintained for all loan accounts. Servicing, in some types of lending institutions, handles loans paid off, assumptions, assignments, prepayments, participations, loan adjustments, additional advances, and refinancing, in addition to the usual loan collection operations.

Delinquency

Delinquency occurs when a borrower fails to make a payment when due. Prevention of delinquency starts with the application when a loan is made only to applicants whose information indicates a reasonable expectation of capacity and willingness to repay the loan. Delinquencies are a result of several causes: domestic difficulty; loss or decline of income; overextension of financial obligations; loss of pride in property ownership; and family illness or death. It is not possible for a lender to prevent delinquencies completely, since the causes may not be present or evident when the loan is made and it is impossible to foresee them.

Various techniques are used to prevent and cure delinquencies. Proper loan terms and amount are made at the inception of the transaction. The borrower is encouraged to consult the lender for assistance before a delinquency occurs. Loan adjustments are worked out between the parties. Periodic inspections of the property and its neighborhood will indicate potential changes which weaken the loan security. Grace periods are permitted borrowers to cure the delinquency. Prompt reminder notices and collection procedures are essential to delinquency prevention.

PORTFOLIO MANAGEMENT

The mortgage portfolio is the total or overall composition or combination of loans which make up the holdings of a lender. The management of the portfolio is concerned with the development of lending policies which maximize profits with safety and within a regulated framework of flexibility to meet loan needs of an area and take advantage of new lending situations.

Lenders follow a variety of portfolio policies, some of which are required by law and some a result of the lender's own decisions. Risk in the portfolio is controlled by diversification of mortgages as to amounts committed on each mortgage; the regional geographic and neighborhood areas in which the mortgaged properties are located; the periods of time in which the loans are made; loan maturities and repayment dates; types of mortgages; individuals or companies to whom loans are made over a period of time; and terms granted in the loans, such as prepayment, open-end borrowing, and interest rate. Diversification helps the liquidity of the portfolio and keeps it from incurring serious loss in the event of a major change in an area, such as the closing of a military facility or a manufacturing plant.

The portfolio needs a steady flow of funds and liquidity, that is, the ability to convert the portfolio into cash without undue delay or costs. Institutional lenders, such as savings and loan associations and commercial banks, obtain their flow of funds from five sources: (1) savings; (2) repayments of loans, such as through monthly payments and prepayments; (3) retained earnings of the lender; (4) borrowed money; and (5) sale of loans and loan participations to other lenders and investors. The flow of funds can be controlled through a sound system of projection, including an evaluation of changing economic conditions, the money market, and long-run changes in demand and supply in the housing market. Sound management of the portfolio requires that the lender have definite policies to achieve specified objectives. There must be procedures to implement the policies.

MORTGAGE WAREHOUSING

The primary function of a mortgage banker is to originate, close, and service mortgages for permanent investors, such as life insurance companies. The mortgage banker uses temporary funds for working capital, termed "interim financing," to originate and process loans, such as construction loans and regular mortgages, before delivering a completed mortgage with the final borrower to the permanent investor for purchase. The period of time between the origination of a mortgage and its purchase by a permanent investor can vary from two months to a year. The selling of the loans may be individually or in blocks and it is often necessary to maintain an inventory. The commercial bank grants the interim funds to the mortgage banker and the funds are secured by mortgages in the portfolio of the mortgage banker.

Types of Warehouse Loans

Warehousing transactions vary and there is no standardized arrangement. Typical practices, however, involve two kinds of loans: (1) committed, and (2) uncommitted.

Under the committed warehouse loan, the commercial bank extends credit on the basis of pledged mortgages which have a firm commitment for purchase from a permanent investor. This type of loan has the lower risk to the bank and is the one commonly used with mortgage bankers.

Under the uncommitted warehouse loan, the collateral consists of mortgages which are not supported by a firm purchase commitment from a permanent investor. There are several reasons why a mortgage banker makes mortgages without a prior purchase commitment: (1) accommodation to a customer who needs a loan closed before the mortgage banker has had time to obtain a firm commitment; (2) temporary withdrawal of a permanent investor from the market and need for the mortgage banker to hold or inventory some loans; (3) maintainance of an inventory of loans to meet changing needs of the permanent investors and to be ready to supply new investors; and (4) maintainance of an inventory of loans to take advantage of shifts in the mortgage market, such as the possibility of a higher price for the mortgage. In all of these instances the mortgage banker may need an uncommitted warehouse loan to carry the mortgages until they are sold to a permanent investor. If the loan is not sold before the expiration of the warehouse loan, and the warehousing loan is "with recourse," the mortgage banker must take over the mortgage and carry it with his own funds or arrange other sources of financing for it. Such arrangement is basically a line of credit with mortgages as collateral. Or, if the warehousing credit is "without recourse," the commercial bank may purchase the pledged mortgage, usually at a discounted price.

Mortgages made by a mortgage banker without a firm commitment involve risks to both the mortgage banker and the commercial banker who accepts them as collateral for temporary or interim warehousing credit. While an inventory of such loans gives the mortgage banker flexibility in serving investors and mortgage market participation, changes in the market can occur quickly and the mortgages in the portfolio become unattractive to investors and hence unmarketable. Additional considerations from the viewpoint of the commercial bank include: (1) the size of the mortgage banker, its management and experience in making uncommitted mortgage loans, and its ability to take a loss; (2) experience of the commercial bank with the mortgage banker; (3) financial status of the mortgage banker relative to the amount of requested uncommitted warehousing credit; (4) nature and number of investors used by the mortgage banker and experience in the disposition of uncommitted loans; and (5) projections as to demand and supply in the capital and mortgage markets.

Standby Commitment

A standby commitment from an institutional lender is "a contract to accept delivery of a mortgage or group of mortgages within a specified period of time at a fixed price, usually considerably under market price, and requiring a commitment fee payable in advance. Loans may or may not be delivered under the commitment. There is no obligation to deliver loans to an investor under this type of commitment."[1] The investor issuing the commitment does not expect to acquire the mortgages because of the below market price offered, but the investor stands ready to take the mortgages if they are presented for purchase. The mortgage banker uses the standby commitment to obtain a warehouse loan and then seeks to obtain another commitment with better terms. Mortgage bankers benefit from standby commitments in three ways: (1) they can obtain a warehouse loan; (2) have time to shop for a more favorable commitment; and (3) provide a floor or minimum price at which the mortgages may be sold. Three factors of risk are considered by the commercial bank: (1) the strength of the institution issuing the commitment; (2) terms of the commitment; and (3) ability of the mortgage banker to obtain more attractive commitments, at their below market purchase prices, so that the standby will not have to be exercised.

A commercial bank may issue both the standby commitment and the warehouse loan. Such an arrangement occurs when the uncommitted warehouse loan is made without recourse and the commercial bank is obligated to take the mortgage if it cannot be sold to a permanent investor.

Institution Warehousing

Another type of warehousing arrangement is designed to assist the permanent investor rather than directly assist the mortgage banker. An investor may want to commit itself to acquire mortgages, but defer the ultimate purchase for a considerable period of time, such as a year. Such a procedure gives the investor a degree of flexibility in the management of its mortgage portfolio. The investor, for instance, may want to take advantage of a particularly attractive mortgage market but not be in the market on a continuing basis. The investor needs the funds from the commercial banks because its own funds are not adequate for the extra investment in mortgages.

[1] J. I. Kislak Mortgage Corporation, "Kislak Mortgage Glossary."

Purchase and Repurchase Agreement

Under a purchase and repurchase agreement, a commercial bank purchases mortgages from a permanent investor. The investor commits itself to repurchase them at a later date. The bank, under this arrangement, is not making the investor a loan with mortgages as collateral and therefore the investor does not have to show a large loan on its financial statement.

Impact

Mortgage warehousing has benefits to the mortgage banker, the commercial banker, the institutional permanent investor, and to the economy. The specific impact on each varies with the nature of the warehousing arrangements.

The mortgage banker obtains a needed source of funds for its operations and the maintenance of a flexible portfolio policy. The commercial banker earns an attractive yield on its warehouse loans in addition to income from related business generated from the warehousing service, such as compensating balances and new business generated from referrals by the borrower and investor. The permanent investor is able to maintain a more flexible mortgage portfolio policy and have a balanced program of investments. The economy benefits by having an improved availability and flow of funds into the mortgage market and the construction industry.

SALE OF MORTGAGES

Lenders sell mortgages to institutional investors and frequently retain the servicing. Investors seek the best possible yields consistent with a sound loan. One of the primary factors in determining whether the lender, or middleman, will sell the investor on a loan package is the quality of the presentation to the investor.

Mortgage Presentations [2]

The mortgage banker sells loans to investors. The selling of the loan requires a presentation to the investor of the facts about the loan package and the merits of the investment. A presentation may be a telephone

[2] Stephen F. Weiner, "Four Major Ingredients for Mortgage Presentations," *The Mortgage Banker*, February, 1973, pp. 48–52.

call or a complete documentation of the investment. Every mortgage presentation is composed of four ingredients: (1) product knowledge; (2) sound experience; (3) proven expertise; and (4) meaningful communication.

Product knowledge means an understanding of the mechanics of putting a project together and satisfying the investment needs of lenders. The mortgage banker knows factors of risk in the market and is able to match the suitability of a project to the portfolio requirements of lenders. Proper structuring of a loan requires product knowledge. Investors know the value of projects and the mortgage banker must match this knowledge.

Sound experience means the ability to detect and interpret factors about an investment which might otherwise cause a good loan to be rejected. Broad experience is needed in economic analysis, planning, financing, and construction. Exposure to both successful and unsuccessful loans enables the mortgage banker to spot and correct weaknesses in a presentation before the borrower and investor are adversely affected.

Proven expertise is skill that is developed over the years to serve the best interests of borrower and investor effectively. Such skill includes the ability to: (1) select the right lender; (2) make a seemingly unworkable loan into a bankable transaction; and (3) keep perspective and respond to a changing business environment.

The above three factors must be tied together with the ingredient of meaningful communication. A presentation must include facts and documentation along with a clear explanation of the investment. The presentation must demonstrate that the mortgage banker has accurately examined the worthiness of the loan applicant and the economic viability of the project, and has structured the loan to the mutual advantage of lender and borrower.

SECONDARY MORTGAGE MARKET

A lender originates or makes a mortgage loan, holds the loan in its portfolio as an investment, and collects the payments of principal and interest during the term of the loan. If the lender sells the loan to another lender, or investor, or governmental agency, the transaction is said to take place in the secondary mortgage market. It is a market of lenders and investors and governmental agencies who buy and sell mortgage loans which have already been originated. It is a resale market for existing loans. Lenders operate to a large extent in both the originating or primary market and the secondary market. A secondary market transaction is based on a mortgage that is already in existence at the time of the transaction. Sales and purchases based upon prior commitments from the ultimate investor are not classified as secondary market transactions.

Reasons for the Market

The secondary mortgage market provides the lender with a source of liquidity for its mortgage portfolio. It is a market in which a lender can sell loans and obtain funds for making further loans, or for other uses.

The secondary mortgage market is intended to create a national market for mortgages and provide a smooth interregional flow of funds. Lenders in areas having a surplus of mortgage funds may purchase mortgages as an investment from lenders in areas needing additional mortgage funds.

The secondary mortgage market gives a lender an element of flexibility in portfolio management. Further, there is an element of confidence when a lender has reasonable expectation of a market for a loan.

Limitations

There are limitations to the development of an effective national secondary market. The mortgage instrument is not standardized and is governed by state laws. Lenders are not permitted by law to make mortgage investments of certain types or to operate in all geographic areas. There is lack of uniformity and standards for risk evaluation of a borrower and a property. Real estate itself lacks standard terminology and readily available accurate and complete market information.

The secondary mortgage market for residential mortgages is comprised largely of Federal government agencies. The most important are the: (1) Federal National Mortgage Association, known as "Fannie Mae"; (2) Government National Mortgage Association, known as "Ginnie Mae"; and, (3) Federal Home Loan Mortgage Corporation, known as "Freddie Mac."

Federal National Mortgage Association

The Federal National Mortgage Association (FNMA), also referred to as Fannie Mae, was chartered by Congress in 1938 to encourage investors to participate in the Federal Housing Administration program which had been enacted in 1934. Its charter was changed in 1954 so that the agency became a selfsupporting corporate entity in the U.S. Department of Housing and Urban Development (HUD). It later became a government-sponsored private corporation.

The primary objectives and functions of FNMA were: (1) to provide a secondary market for FHA insured home mortgages; and, under the Charter Act of 1954 (2) to manage and liquidate its mortgage portfolio as of October 31, 1954; and (3) provide a special assistance program of direct financing to special segments of the housing market, such as urban renewal, low-income housing, housing for the elderly, and military housing. Only FHA-insured mortgages were initially eligible for purchase, but eligibility was extended in 1948 to include VA-guaranteed mortgages.

FNMA was reorganized in 1968 and divided into two corporations. The Government National Mortgage Corporation (GNMA) was created to take over the federally financed Management and Liquidating Function and the Special Assistance Function of FNMA. The privately financed secondary market function remained with FNMA. The Corporation later became privately owned and managed by its stockholders and five persons appointed by the President of the United States. FNMA is now permitted to deal in conventional loans.

FNMA Debt Financing Structure [3]

FNMA, as a privately owned, federally-chartered corporation, must obtain funds to pay costs of operations, maturing debt issues, and for mortgages it purchases. The funds are obtained in the market through several means: (1) short-term discount notes; (2) debentures; (3) subordinated capital debentures; (4) convertible capital debentures; (5) mortgage-backed bonds; and (6) sale of common stock to mortgage originators who deliver mortgages under commitments. FNMA also charges fees for the use of its facilities. Further, it has established lines of credit at some banks.

The credit standing of FNMA is enhanced by the fact that it has a "backstop" of the U.S. Treasury. The Treasury is authorized to buy up to $2.25 billion of FNMA securities if FNMA is unable to market its debt securities in the regular capital markets.

The discount notes, with maturities of 30 to 270 days, provide short-term flexibility while the debentures constitute the long-term segment of the debt structure. The total amount of debt issued and outstanding at any time is set by the Secretary of Housing and Urban Development and is subject to change. The debentures and notes are sold through dealers, rather than directly to the public. There have been some direct

[3] "FNMA Explains Debt Financing Structure," *The Mortgage Banker*, August, 1973, pp. 43–46.

private placements of debentures and mortgage-backed bonds to local and state governments.

The mortgage-backed bonds are general obligations of FNMA backed by a pool of mortgages in the portfolio of FNMA and held in trust by the corporation. The principal and interest on the bonds is guaranteed by the Government National Mortgage Corporation (GNMA) and the guarantee is backed by the full faith and credit of the U.S. Government.

Government National Mortgage Corporation

The Government National Mortgage Corporation (GNMA), also referred to as Ginnie Mae, was created by Congress in 1968, and is a government corporation under the Department of Housing and Urban Development. GNMA conducts the management and liquidation function and special assistance function of FNMA.

GNMA also provides a program for mortgage-backed securities. Securities are issued by private lenders against pools of government-backed mortgages, such as FHA and VA, with full principal and interest guaranteed by the full faith and credit of the U.S. Government. The new type of security is intended to provide greater liquidity to the mortgage market and an additional method of financing its operation. Investors receive an attractive yield and the program gives lenders an opportunity to tap new sources of capital, such as private and governmental pension funds, which have not invested in mortgages due to lack of specialized personnel and managerial talent to make direct mortgage investments. The security is a pass-through participation type whereby the issuer, or lender, pays or passes-through to the investor its proportionate share of the principal and interest on the pool of FHA and VA mortgages. The lender retains the servicing of the mortgages for a fee and GNMA guarantees the performance of the servicing agent.

GNMA also issues a bond-type security in which principal is paid at maturity and interest is paid semiannually. Issuers of the bonds, due to the risks involved and the large minimum size of an issue, have been limited to FNMA and FHLMC. Both the bonds and pass-through securities are traded in the financial market.

Conventional Secondary Market

The Emergency Home Finance Act of 1970 gave the Federal National Mortgage Association (FNMA), and the Federal Home Loan Mortgage Corporation (FHLMC) authority to purchase conventional mortgages on owner-occupied, single-family residences, under specified conditions. The objective was to provide liquidity in the conventional mortgage market. High ratio conventional mortgages of up to 95 percent are now accepted for purchase by FNMA, with private mortgage insurance required if the loan is over a certain percentage. In addition to the governmental market, there is also a private conventional secondary market.

FNMA, or Fannie Mae, issues conventional commitments through its bi-weekly free market system auction. Commitments are of two types: (1) 4-month, and (2) convertible standby. The 12-month standby commitment for proposed construction may be converted to a regular 4-month commitment at a yield equal to the average yield at the latest conventional auction. The convertible standby permits an originating lender to work more effectively with developers and also helps him in periods of changes in the cost of money. FNMA also has a "prior approval" program in connection with the 12-month convertible standby commitment on existing or proposed construction. Approved lenders may receive prior approval of the property and credit approval of an individual borrower.

Institutional lenders, such as mortgage bankers, commercial banks, savings and loan associations, insurance companies, and mutual savings banks, apply to FNMA to become an "approved seller-servicer" in the conventional loan program. Appraisers must also be acceptable to FNMA. The approved lender submits a loan package to FNMA for evaluation and underwriting by the FNMA conventional mortgage staff, and a determination of its acceptability. FNMA seeks to purchase mortgages which meet the usual standards of private institutional lenders. Efforts are being made to standardize mortgage documents, such as the promissory note, mortgage application, and property appraisal form. Some forms are already used by both FNMA and FHLMC.

The FNMA conventional mortgage program has been successful and continues to show growth and increasing flexibility in its obligation to provide mortgage financing for high quality loans. An executive of FNMA, speaking to a National Mortgage Banking Conference, presented by the Mortgage Bankers Association of America, cited the below challenges facing the conventional secondary market in future years:

1. Variable interest rates will be studied more thoroughly during the years ahead, and a workable system could eventually affect the commitment policies of FNMA in the conventional program.
2. The present trend of activity away from FHA mortgages toward conventional financing will continue only if home purchasers

find acceptable financing through conventional mortgages from primary lenders and the secondary markets.

3. The Uniform Land Transaction Code, if adopted by individual states, would greatly reduce the legal documentation required in originating and liquidating mortgage investments, thereby encouraging interest in mortgages as an investment instrument. FNMA fully supports the American Bar Association Committee working on this code.

4. Usury statutes, extremely antiquated in several jurisdictions, will almost certainly come under close legislative scrutiny, and laws will be changed to encourage the origination of mortgages by the primary and secondary markets in periods of credit stringencies.

5. Private mortgage insurance, still a new industry, will go through an evolutionary process over the next few years and, through self-regulation or legislation creating regulation, will continue as a reliable insurer of mortgage risks. FNMA has approved some dozen private mortgage insurance companies for the conventional program. We also expect several new PMIs to begin operations this year and we have recently received requests for approval from others.[4]

Federal Home Loan Mortgage Corporation

The Federal Home Loan Mortgage Corporation (FHLMC), also referred to as Freddie Mac, was created in 1970 and is a subsidiary of the Federal Home Loan Bank Board (FHLB). FHLMC is authorized to purchase FHA and VA mortgages from the originating lender, combine the mortgages into pools, and issue bonds, secured by the mortgages and guaranteed by FNMA, for sale to the public. FHLMC has the authority to buy and sell conventional mortgages for its portfolio and can issue bonds backed by conventional mortgages, though they would not be guaranteed by GNMA.

FEDERAL HOME LOAN BANK SYSTEM

The Federal Home Loan Bank System (FHLB) was established in 1932 and serves as a source of liquidity for its member institutions, who are primarily savings and loan associations. It does not buy and sell

[4] Russel B. Clifton, "FNMA Conventional Program Shows Dramatic Growth," *The Mortgage Banker*, July, 1973, pp. 51–54; 56; 58.

mortgages but accepts them as security for advances to its members. It enables savings and loan associations to obtain funds to meet demand for mortgage money in their local areas, or to meet demand for withdrawals from savings accounts, or for cash needs for operations. Members also have a line of credit at their regional bank. FHLB is similar to the Federal Reserve System for commercial banks in that it is essentially a pool of credit or a credit reserve system providing one source of liquidity for its members. The System regulates and supervises its members. It does not make direct loans to home buyers but is an indirect source of funds for the home mortgage market.

REVIEW AND STUDY QUESTIONS

1. What is "permanent" financing, and what are the steps in the lending process: (A) as applied to the individual loans; and (B) as involved with market activities concerned with groups of mortgages rather than the individual loan?
2. What is a mortgage "solicitor" and how is he compensated?
3. Define a loan application. Give the reasons for its use and distinguish between the informal and formal applications.
4. What basic steps are involved in loan processing and underwriting?
5. What is meant by "loan closing"? What documents and loan closing costs are involved in closing a conventional single-family home loan in your local area?
6. Define "loan servicing" and its objective.
7. What is meant by a mortgage portfolio and its management? Give several ways by which the element of risk in a mortgage portfolio is controlled?
8. Define: (A) mortgage warehousing, and (B) the types of warehouse loans.
9. What are the four ingredients of every mortgage presentation?
10. Describe the secondary mortgage market and the reasons for its existence. Include in your discussion the operations of FNMA, GNMA, and FHLMC.

FURTHER READINGS AND REFERENCES

American Institute of Banking, *Home Mortgage Lending*. New York: American Institute of Banking, 1963.

American Savings and Loan Institute, *Lending Principles and Practices*. Chicago, Ill.: American Savings and Loan Institute Press, 1971.

Beaton, William R., *Real Estate Investment*. Englewood Cliffs, N.J.: Prentice-Hall, Inc., 1971.

Bryant, Willis R., *Mortgage Lending*, Second Ed. New York: McGraw-Hill Book Company, 1962.

De Huszar, William I., *Mortgage Loan Administration*. New York: McGraw-Hill Book Company, 1972.

Kinnard, William N., Jr., and Stephen D. Messner, *Industrial Real Estate, Second Ed.* Washington, D.C.: Society of Industrial Realtors, 1971.

Maisel, Sherman J., *Financing Real Estate*. New York: McGraw-Hill Book Company, 1965.

Pease, Robert H., and Lewis O. Kerwood, *Mortgage Banking*, Second Ed. New York: McGraw-Hill Book Company, 1965.

FIVE

Construction Financing

Buildings and other improvements on land are usually financed by means of a construction loan. This type of financing is short-term, the money is disbursed by the lender in installments as construction progresses rather than in a lump sum at the date of the loan, the interest is usually charged only on the money that is actually being used by the borrower, and the lender expects that the loan will be repaid in full in a lump sum upon completion of the construction. Construction financing, and the construction mortgage, has features which distinguish it from permanent or end financing, yet the two types of financing are interrelated since the availability of one often depends upon the availability of the other.

RISKS

Construction financing has risks which are unique to it. A construction loan is made upon a proposed project, that is, an improvement that is not yet a physical reality. The loan is based upon an estimated value arrived at from plans and specifications, a projected market for the proposed building upon its completion, an estimated construction cost, and a reliance upon the managerial and financial ability of the builder to complete the building on schedule. Many adverse events can happen between the date of the loan and the completion of the building. Among such factors are: (1) delays due to weather, unavailability of skilled labor, labor strikes, or unavailability of materials; (2) increase in construction costs; (3) environmental legislation, such as construction moratoriums; (4) change in the market demand for the building; and (5) inability of the builder to complete the project. Further, there are the risks of competition and of disposition or sale of the loan and the project.

SOURCES OF FUNDS

Money for construction loans comes primarily from commercial banks, savings and loan associations, and real estate investment trusts. Other types of institutional lenders (such as pension funds) and individual lenders occasionally make construction loans. Mortgage bankers also provide construction money and then seek a permanent loan through a variety of possible arrangements. Joint ventures and syndications provide both equity and mortgage combinations.

INTEREST RATES AND FEES

Interest rates on construction mortgages are usually higher than on permanent mortgages because of the greater risk in construction lending. The interest is usually charged only on the money actually disbursed to the borrower. The rate quoted may be fixed, such as 8 percent, or it may be quoted as "prime plus so many points, such as '1, 2, 3, points over prime,' plus 2 percent for the deal, and 1 percent for the mortgage broker." The "prime" is the interest rate charged by large commercial banks for business loans to their best customers. The points over prime vary with the lender's evaluation of the risk in the particular loan and money market conditions. The percentage "for the deal" is the fee charged by the lender making the loan. The percentage for the mortgage broker will vary and is his fee for structuring, packaging, and placing the loan. The interest rate will also vary according to whether there is a "take out" or commitment from a lender for the permanent financing.

Rates may be lower if a permanent lender has already agreed to issue a loan upon completion of construction.

Higher of Prime or Commercial Paper [1]

Some real estate investment trusts (REIT's) engaged in short-term lending on construction mortgages have developed a dual base technique for their base interest rates on construction loans. The base rate is "the higher of" the commercial bank prime rate or a specific commercial paper rate. Commitments are made at a rate that floats at a certain percent, such as 2 to 5 percent, above the higher of prime or commercial paper.

REIT's engaged in construction lending obtain a substantial portion of their short-term funds through the sale of commercial paper, which is similar to a corporate IOU or promissory note. The interest rate paid for this borrowing is set in the market and normally is less than the commercial bank prime rate. The market rate, however, can increase considerably in periods of tight money.

REIT's normally use the commercial bank prime rate as a base rate for construction loans. When this rate is controlled by government and kept at an artificial rather than a market level, as has been done on occasion, REIT's making construction loans can be put in a profit squeeze. Loans were being made at a rate based on the prime rate, which was held down by controls and distorted. The cost of money to the REIT from the sale of commercial paper, whose rate was set in the free market, was increasing substantially. The pegging of the construction lending rate to the higher of prime or commercial paper was an effort by some REIT's to meet the profit squeeze problem.

The dual base rate of pricing construction loans is not used by all REIT's and some tried it but encountered borrower resistance and were not successful. The technique could, however, become standard practice, and there are four factors supporting a more frequent and widespread use: (1) builders want to borrow out with 100 percent financing for their projects and generally are willing to pay the necessary borrowing costs for a no equity transaction; (2) REIT's will probably increase their use of commercial paper to raise short-term funds and use the dual base technique; (3) government, having controlled the prime rate for a short time, may make other attempts, perhaps in a more forceful way; and (4) tight money will enable REIT's to use the dual base technique as standard practice regardless of the attitude of government toward rates.

[1] Trevvett Matthews, "Construction Loans Float with Commercial Paper." *The Mortgage Banker*, August, 1973, pp. 26–32.

TYPES OF LOANS

Construction financing may be arranged in several ways. Developers, contractors, and builders with a proven "track record," that is, a history of successful experience in their business, are often able to obtain a line of credit with a lender, such as a commercial bank. The bank makes straight business loans to them for construction purposes and there is no individual mortgage for each project, such as houses in a subdivision. Or, a large developer may use his own funds entirely or in combination with line of credit funds. Suppliers of building materials also provide credit.

The most commonly used instrument and technique for construction financing is the construction mortgage, with the property under construction serving as security for the loan. A promissory note usually accompanies the specific lien of the mortgage, though in some loans the lender may not require personal liability of the borrower. Release from such liability is by means of an "exculpatory" clause. The construction mortgage may be combined with a land acquisition and development loan (A&D loan); or it may be combined with a permanent mortgage; or all three types of financing may be included in one arrangement or package. Separate lenders may provide each type of financing or all of the funds may come from a single lender.

The combination loans offer benefits to both developer and lender. The developer or builder is able to obtain all of his funds from one source with the resulting saving in time and the expense of several loans from different lenders. The borrower may also receive better and quicker service since the lender knows him and has lending and inspection control over the entire development process of the developer. Lower charges may also be available because of the combination arrangement. The lender benefits by receiving the income from the additional loans and by having more complete control over the developer's operations.

CONSTRUCTION LOAN AGREEMENT

The parties to a construction loan, the lender and borrower, and in some instances the general contractor, title company, and disbursing consultant, enter into an agreement setting forth the terms, rights, duties, and obligations of the parties along with the terms of the loan. Such agreements vary among lenders but the following items are typical of provisions found in such documents, though all are not necessarily found in a single transaction.

PURPOSE. States date of agreement; identifies parties; states purpose of loan, namely, to erect improvements upon land in a specified manner; amount of loan applied for and interest rate.

TITLE. States nature of borrower's title to the land—fee simple, lessee, etc.

PERMANENT COMMITMENT. Borrower acknowledges receipt of a "Permanent Mortgage Commitment" in a minimum amount from a specified permanent lender, acceptable to the construction lender; the permanent first mortgage is to be funded upon completion of the buildings and improvements.

CONSTRUCTION COMMITMENT. Lender acknowledges that it has issued a Construction Loan Commitment setting forth the terms and conditions of the construction loan and such commitment is incorporated into the Construction Loan Agreement.

CONSIDERATION. Includes a statement of consideration for the agreement, such as above premises or recitations and other good and valuable considerations; a non-refundable commitment fee, if any; and the promissory note secured by a first mortgage on the security, both of which are executed simultaneously with the agreement. Mortgage will be recorded; also recorded, if required by state statute, is the Notice of Commencement.

TITLE COMPANY. Designates the title company which parties agree will serve as title insurer for the transaction.

NOTICE OF COMMENCEMENT. The notice must be recorded with the appropriate authority at least one day after the recording of the mortgage. No disbursements are made by the lender until assurance is received of the posting of this notice as required by statute.

REPRESENTATIONS AND WARRANTIES OF THE BORROWER. (1) Documents furnished in support of the loan are true and accurately set out the facts; (2) financial statements provided in support of the loan request are complete and correct and in accordance with good accounting practice; (3) no legal actions, suits, or proceedings are pending against the borrower; (4) the corporation borrower has valid existence and power to enter into and carry out the terms and conditions of the construction loan agreement; (5) there are no outstanding and unpaid judgments against the borrower which would have a materially adverse effect on the borrower; also, the borrower is not in default of any regulation or order of a governmental agency; and (6) there is no visible commencement of construction before execution and recording of the note and mortgage.

DISBURSEMENT OF LOAN FUNDS. The lender disburses the loan fund to the borrower according to a Schedule of Disbursements set forth in the Construction Loan Agreement. The borrower must deliver to the lender certain documents before the start of disbursements, such as: (1) the executed note and mortgage, and (2) a title insurance binder or commitment, assignable without additional cost to the permanent lender and providing, among other things, full coverage against mechanic's liens, and (3) a policy of hazard insurance.

The lender may disburse the funds to the borrower through a title insurance agency, mortgage company, or other third party, such as a disbursing consultant. The lender also may disburse directly to subcontractors, materialmen, and laborers. Interest accrues on each disbursement from the date it is made until the loan is fully paid. Requisitions for disbursements are made on a form provided by the lender.

FUND DEFICIENCY. If there is a deficiency in the loan fund, that is, the amount of monies remaining undisbursed is less than the amount required to complete the improvements, the lender may demand that the borrower deposit an amount equal to the deficiency.

ARCHITECT. The borrower provides a supervising architect acceptable to the lender to inspect the premises during the course of construction. The architect also executes a certificate to the lender with each requisition from the borrower for a draw or advance from the construction loan fund. The certificate states that work reported by the borrower as being completed to date has actually been completed according to plans and specifications.

PROGRESS REPORTS. The borrower delivers to the lender a report of the progress of the proposed improvements, the costs of the improvements compared to estimates or contracts, the promotion and merchandising efforts for the sale of the property, and current sales reports. Information is furnished on a monthly basis.

COMMENCEMENT AND CONTINUITY OF WORK. Development and construction of improvements are to commence within a specified number of days from date of agreement and shall be carried on continuously, diligently, and with dispatch, and shall be completed not later than a specified date. Borrower recognizes that the commitment of the permanent mortgage lender to purchase the mortgage is conditioned upon the completion of the improvements by a specified date. Borrower recognizes that the lender may be substantially damaged in the event the improvements are not completed by the specified date.

DEVELOPMENT AND CONSTRUCTION WORK CRITERIA.   The buildings and improvements are to be erected in accordance with the plans and specifications and are to comply with all restrictions, conditions, ordinances, codes, regulations, and laws of governmental agencies and departments having jurisdiction over the security. The borrower also will comply with requirements of the Federal Housing Administration, Veterans Administration, any lending institution which has committed itself to a permanent first mortgage loan on the property, and any political subdivision.

No extra work or materials or change in plans and specifications are to be ordered or authorized by the borrower without written consent of the lender. If the lender consents, the borrower deposits the additional cost with the lender for disbursement upon completion of the extras or changes. The permanent mortgage lender must give written approval of the extras or changes.

INSURANCE COVERAGE AND APPLICATION OF PROCEEDS.   The interest of the lender at all times is to be protected by adequate Builder's Risk Insurance, completed value on a non-reporting form. All policies are written to cover the building against such hazards, including Other Perils, in amounts required by the lender, and in companies acceptable to the lender. Loss under policies is payable first to the lender to the extent of its interest. Original policies are kept in possession of the lender. Proceeds from any loss covered by the insurance are, at the option of the lender, applied to the replacement of the loss, or toward the repayment of the loan.

TAXES, ASSESSMENTS, AND DEBTS.   The borrower agrees to promptly pay taxes, assessments, or indebtedness upon the property which may become due or be payable during the existence of the construction loan. The lender has the right to pay unpaid taxes, assessments, and debts, and include them under the security of the first mortgage lien.

LENDER'S REMEDIES.   The lender has the right and option, upon default by the borrower on any provision of the construction loan agreement, to take certain actions. Such actions may include one or all of the following:

1. Cancel the agreement by written notice to the borrower.
2. Sue for specific performance.
3. Withhold further advances.
4. Declare default on the mortgage and institute foreclosure proceedings.
5. Appoint a receiver to take charge of the property and complete construction of the buildings and improvements, or to act as

custodian of the property. All expenses of such action are charged to the borrower and enforced as a lien against the property.

NON-ASSIGNABLE BY BORROWER. The borrower may not assign the agreement without written consent of the lender. Further, the borrower may not encumber the property with a mortgage or other liens without permission of the lender. Also not permitted without written consent of the lender is a change in contractors, subcontractors, parties furnishing labor and materials, or title company.

EVENTS OF DEFAULT. There are certain events which constitute a default of the construction agreement and the note and mortgage. Among the events are: (1) failure to pay principal and interest when due; (2) violation of any term, condition, or representation in the agreement, note, and mortgage; (3) development or construction work being substantially discontinued without cause for a specified period of time; (4) filing of a voluntary or involuntary petition in bankruptcy against the borrower, the borrower making assignment for the benefit of creditors, or being insolvent; (5) foreclosure action against the property, or the filing of a lien which is not removed of record, bonded, or dismissed with a specified number of days after filing; (6) changing general contractor, architect, or title company without permission of lender; (7) breach of any provision or covenant of the construction loan agreement, or of the note of mortgage; and (8) any condition or situation which the lender determines to constitute a danger or impairment to the security of the loan, and is not remedied within a specified number of days after written notice.

NO AGENCY RELATIONSHIP. The lender is not the agent or representative of the borrower and is not liable to materialmen, contractors, subcontractors, craftsmen, laborers, or others, for goods or services delivered by them upon the property. There is no contractual relationship between the above parties and the lender, and the persons are not intended to be third-party beneficiaries under the construction loan agreement.

TITLE INSURANCE. The borrower provides, at its own expense, title insurance in the standard ALTA form, issued by a title insurance company acceptable to the lender. Title policy is to be issued without exceptions, except such as are acceptable to lender, insuring lender's mortgage as a valid lien. The lender may, at its option, accept a title binder issued by an acceptable title company in lieu of the ALTA standard form policy.

FINANCIAL STATEMENT. The borrower furnishes to the lender a

quarterly unaudited statement of financial condition, and profit and loss statement. Also furnished is an audited annual statement.

CONDEMNATION. The borrower assigns to the lender any condemnation award affecting the property. The lender is given authority and power to collect and receive the proceeds of such award and to apply the amount toward the payment of the note and mortgage.

SURVEYS. The borrower agrees to deliver to the lender, from time to time, surveys of the property, showing the improvements and their location. The surveys support requests for advances and are inspected and certified by the title company to the effect that no condition exists which affects the title coverage under the title company's binder, commitment, or title policy.

PARTIAL RELEASES. The lender agrees to release from the mortgage lien any unit, lot, parcel, or other portion of the property in accordance with an agreed upon Release Schedule. Payments made for such releases are applied to reduction of note and mortgage principal and are credited against the next ensuing payment to become due.

DISBURSEMENT OF LOAN

Construction loans are disbursed by the lender to the borrower as construction progresses. There are numerous plans for the amount and timing of the disbursements, also known as advances, draws, progress payments, or pay-outs.

Disbursement Schedules

One schedule of advances, used by a commercial bank on commercial property loans, provides that the borrower has the right, subject to a specified final payment and holdback, to draw each month a specified percentage of the amount represented by work completed since the previous requisition for a disbursement. A final payment is made, including the holdback percentage, upon completion of the work and submission of all lien waivers and certificates required by law.

Disbursements for loans on single-family houses are made according to stages of construction. A schedule might call, for example, for funds to be disbursed in four stages: (1) foundation and enclosure of the structure; (2) exterior and interior rough work; (3) plastering, exterior and interior finishes and trim; and (4) improvements and house ready for occupancy and all bills paid, with proper affidavits and assurances of no mechanic's liens.

Invoices for materials and labor may be paid directly by the builder after submission to the lender for approval. Or the invoices may be paid by the lender, or through a disbursing agent.

Holdbacks

Lenders may withhold from payment to subcontractors a specified percentage of the contract amount, such as 10 or 20 percent. The purpose of the "holdback" is to assure that work is promptly completed according to plans and specifications. The holdback is disbursed upon completion of the subcontractor's work and its approval by the architect and lender.

Inspections

Lenders regularly inspect the property during construction. The purpose of the inspection is to verify that construction is progressing as scheduled and that the work is being done in an acceptable quality of workmanship and according to plans and specifications. The initial inspection is of the site to verify that no work has been started or materials delivered. It is important that no mechanic's liens or other liens are on the property which may have priority over the construction mortgage. The number of inspections during the course of construction varies with lenders. Inspections typically are tied in with the schedule of advances and are made before each advance. The final inspection is made after the building and improvements are completed and ready for occupany.

Objectives

A disbursement system must have an efficient and effective method for inspections and payouts for profitable construction lending. The system must provide for assurances that: (1) the borrower authorizes all advances from the construction loan fund; (2) funds in the account are always sufficient to complete the construction; (3) completed work is equal to the funds paid out; (4) plans and specifications are being followed; (5) funds are actually being used on the designated project and are not drawn in advance of actual construction or delivery of materials; (6) construction costs are in line with original estimates by the builder; and (7) changes and extras are approved in advance and funds are available for the added costs.

BONDING OF CONTRACTOR

The lender may require that the general contractor be bonded. If bonding is not required, a specified percentage of all progress payments may be withheld by the lender until the final payment is due and all required affidavits and certificates are received by the lender. Bonding may not be required of a contractor with a proven "track record" of successful projects and with an established record of financial strength. Or deposits or other collateral may be accepted by some lenders.

The purpose of bonding is to give the lender an assured source of funds to complete the project in the event the contractor is unable to do so. Two types of bonds used in construction lending are of interest to the lender: (1) the performance bond, and (2) the completion bond. The performance bond guarantees the contractor will fulfill the existing contract, that is, the completion of the building and improvements. If the contractor defaults, the surety or insurance company protects the policyholder against loss up to the bond penalty. The completion bond insures the owner that there will be a direct finishing of the project free of liens.

COMMITMENTS

A commitment is a written promise from a lender stating that it will make a loan under specified terms and conditions set forth in the commitment letter or agreement. Several types of commitments are used in construction lending: (1) conditional; (2) firm; (3) take-out; and (4) standby.

Conditional

The FHA issues a conditional commitment to an operative or speculative builder. The builder applicant is requesting only an FHA appraisal of the proposed property and has no particular borrower-occupant in mind. The conditional commitment deals only with the property and not with any borrower. The FHA agrees to insure a mortgage on a specified property, when the construction is completed, in a specified amount and terms, provided the person who buys the house is an acceptable borrower to the FHA. The builder is accepting the market risk of finding an acceptable buyer. The builder makes application for the conditional commitment through a private lender who is an FHA-approved mortgagee and pays an application fee. The lender sends the application and fee to the regional FHA office. The office has the proposed property appraised, processes the application, and either issues the conditional commitment or a reject report. Reasons for rejection may be satisfied and the application submitted again without charge within a specified period of time. A seller of an existing house may also obtain a conditional commitment so as to know the FHA valuation of the property for sale purposes.

Firm

Under a firm commitment the FHA agrees to insure a mortgage on a property, upon its completion, in the amount and on terms in the commitment, and with a specified borrower. The ultimate borrower or mortgagor is known at the date of the application. The conditional commitment is for a property appraisal while the firm commitment is for both appraisal and borrower or mortgagor approval.

The operative or speculative builder may have the firm commitment issued in his name as permanent mortgagor, with a provision converting it to an approved owner-occupant as mortgagor upon sale of the property and specifying the loan terms. The amount of the owner-occupant loan commitment is usually greater than the amount received by the builder. This variation of the firm commitment is known as "dual commitment." The lender is accepting the marketing risk in that he is taking on the builder as a permanent mortgagor or has confidence in the ability of the builder to sell the property. The firm commitment or dual commitment assists the operative builder in obtaining construction financing since the interim or construction lender is assured of a permanent loan being available to pay off the construction loan.

The lender submits an application to FHA, when the borrower or mortgagor is known, for credit approval of the borrower, and for a firm commitment. The application is accompanied by required documents, such as the credit report, verification of deposit, verification of employment, contract of sale, working wife's statement, interest rate letter, and estimated loan costs. Additional documents needed if the commitment is for the construction of a home are blueprint plans, description of materials, estimated construction costs or builder's contract, and restrictions on the property.

The FHA provides forms for the application and processing of its loans. A package of bound forms with instructions is used for the conditional and firm commitments. FHA, as well as VA, loan processing is a detailed procedure and requires knowledgeable and experienced personnel.

Take-Out

A take-out commitment from an institutional investor, such as a life insurance company, is issued to a construction lender. The lender is assured that the investor will take over mortgages as construction projects are completed. The lender making the construction loans may be a mortgage banker who uses the take-out commitment, or take-out letter, as a basis for borrowing funds from a commercial bank to provide the construction financing for a builder. The lender must be certain it can comply with any contingencies in the commitment.

The take-out commitment is basically a commitment to issue a permanent loan which will take out the construction lender. The take-out commitment can be either a firm commitment or a contingent commitment.

Standby

The standby commitment is used to permit an owner to obtain construction financing. It is an agreement from an institutional lender that it will accept delivery of a mortgage or group of mortgages within a specified period of time at a fixed price, usually under market price, and requiring a commitment fee payable in advance. Loans may or may not be delivered under the commitment. There is no obligation to deliver loans to an investor. (Definition from J. L. Kislak Mortgage Corporation, "Kislak Mortgage Glossary.")

A standby commitment may be issued to a seller of real estate. It is a contract from a lender to process and close loans at a fixed price for a given period of time, with a further provision to pay to the seller of the real estate any price received for the mortgage over the fixed price after the mortgage has been sold to a permanent investor. (Definition from "Kislak Mortgage Glossary.")

Other Classification

Commitments may also be classified as described below. The same concept is involved regardless of the label given to a particular arrangement.

1. Forward—takes effect sometime in the future, usually later than 90 days from the time of issuance.

2. Immediate—funded within 90 days.
3. Allocation—an allocation of funds to a mortgage company to lend out for a lender according to his pre-set criteria within a specified period of time.
4. Direct—made on a particular property either directly to the mortgage company or directly to the borrower through the mortgage company, relating, in either case, to a specified property.
5. Firm—one which is absolute as is any other contract without any stipulated contingencies.
6. Contingent—a contract as is any other contract which must be executed by all parties so long as none of the pre-stated items of contingency arise.

PROTECTING LOAN COMMITMENTS [2]

The loan commitment is a legal document and should be properly drafted to aid in insuring full control or enforceability. Many lender commitments, according to a special study, are carelessly drafted and difficult to interpret, particularly as to what happens upon default of the borrower.

The two principal documents which define the obligations of borrower and lender are the commitment and the buy-sell agreement. It is recommended that combination construction loan-permanent loan papers be used to, in effect, "pre-close" the long-term mortgage. Further, the subcommittee making the special study offers the following suggestions.[3]

The Commitment

The subcommittee report made suggestions as to how the mortgage banker could protect its interest in the commitment. Among the considerations covered were: (1) protection of the mortgage banker as a conduit in commitments, which run from permanent lender to mortgage banker or directly to borrower; (2) conflicting provisions in the application and the commitment; (3) date for execution of a buy-sell agreement between borrower, mortgage banker, permanent lender, and construction

---

[2] Lawrence J. Melody, "Protecting Loan Commitments," *The Mortgage Banker*, June, 1973, pp. 28–34; 42–44. This article is the report of a project of a special subcommittee established by the Income Property Finance Committee of the Mortgage Bankers Association of America to study proper documentation to protect loan commitments. The author of the article was the chairman of the subcommittee.
[3] *Ibid.*

lender; (4) clear intention of borrower, construction lender, and permanent lender to close and fund the permanent loan; and (5) expiration of commitment; purpose and disposition of fees, such as origination or placement fee, non-refundable fees paid to permanent lender, and "good faith" or "standby" fee held by permanent lender.[4]

Combination Construction Loan-Permanent Loan Papers

The subcommittee recommended the use of combination construction loan-permanent loan papers. The suggestions supporting this recommendation are: (1) better control if use of combination papers is required in the commitment of the permanent lender; (2) pre-approval by permanent lender of loan documents to be used by construction lender before recording and funding of construction loan; (3) execution of documents before recording and first disbursement of combination construction-permanent loan so construction lender can assign and deliver documents to permanent lender without borrower having to execute additional documents upon completion of construction; (4) transfer of permanent papers to construction lender by an unrecorded assignment of the mortgage and an endorsement of the note, to expedite delivery of mortgage to permanent lender upon completion of construction; no need for construction lender to record mortgage back to mortgage banker or permanent lender; and (5) expedition of approval by construction lender and permanent lender of all documents and items necessary to allow the construction lender to make an initial funding. Such action will eliminate any claim by the borrower that delays or inaction by the lender contributed to a default or nullified the commitment.[5]

Buy-Sell Agreement

Subcommittee suggestions were as follows: (1) the buy-sell agreement may be triparty among the construction lender, permanent lender, and the borrower. Or, the agreement may be four-party among the above three parties plus the mortgage banker. In either case the exact role and liability of the mortgage banker should be made clear; (2) even where a mortgage banker is the construction lender, a buy-sell agreement has an advantage of further obligating a borrower to assist in delivering the permanent loan; (3) it should be made clear that the purpose of the buy-sell agreement is to spell out reciprocal duties and obligations of the parties; further, the document is for the mutual benefit of the construc-

4 *Ibid.*
5 *Ibid.*

tion lender and the permanent lender and not for the benefit of the borrower, who executes it solely to demonstrate his agreement to assume certain obligations; (4) intent of parties to accomplish assignment and delivery of loan from construction lender to permanent lender upon satisfaction of all terms of the permanent loan commitment is clear; (5) documents should be drawn on forms of permanent lender, pre-approved by the permanent lender, and be satisfactory to the construction lender; any changes by one party need prior approval by other party; (6) delivery of documents from construction lender to permanent lender should be accomplished without further action by borrower; (7) permanent lender retains a reasonably limited right and option to extend date of commitment or waive conditions by giving notice to borrower; (8) borrower acknowledges intention to exercise due diligence to satisfy commitment conditions, assist and cooperate in closing and funding of permanent loan, and delivery of loan documents to the permanent lender; further, borrower agrees to proceed promptly with construction and immediately cure all defaults in any agreement; (9) obligation of permanent lender to purchase the loan should be specifically spelled out under all contingencies; (10) remedies of permanent lender in event of default, such as monetary damages, option to require specific performance of borrower and construction lender to deliver the loan and assign all loan documents should be clear; and (11) right of construction lender to cure certain non-monetary defaults by the borrower, take over borrower's position, and deliver loan to permanent lender if all conditions of the permanent loan commitment are met should be spelled out.[6]

FRONT MONEY

Developers of large projects need money to get the project planned and under way. An investor commit funds prior to the start of construction or the obtaining of tenants and buyers for the proposed project. The developer commits his construction ability and the lender provides the money.

MECHANIC'S LIEN

A mechanic's lien is created by state statute and exists in favor of persons who have supplied materials to or performed labor on a property. The lien, when properly filed and recorded, attaches to both

[6] *Ibid.*

land and building and is enforced by foreclosure. Protection against such liens is a major concern of construction lenders. Forms and procedures are developed to insure that invoices for materials and labor are properly paid and that the construction mortgage and all advances retain a first priority position.

TYPICAL PATTERN

The procedures followed in making a construction loan vary with lenders and with the nature of the loan, such as conventional, FHA, VA, and with the type of property, such as single-family house or a large commercial project. There are, however, certain items and steps a lender goes through with any construction loan. The pattern below outlines these minimum considerations.

Origination

1. Application
   A. Legal description
   B. Plans and specifications
   C. Plat of survey; subdivision plat, if available.
   D. Financial condition of applicant and ability to complete a project.
   E. Builder's contract or cost estimate.
2. Construction Loan Agreement
3. Credit report
4. Appraisal of the land and proposed building and improvements.

Processing and Closing

1. Processing and submission of forms to any government agency, such as FHA and VA.
2. Review of application by appropriate committee; approval or rejection.
3. Handling of title matters.
4. Issue commitment setting forth terms and conditions of loan.
5. Obtain builder's risk insurance policy or binder.
6. Execution of loan documents and affidavits.
7. Inspection of building site to make certain no work has started or materials delivered.
8. Recording of mortgage.
9. Notice of Commencement filed after recording of mortgage.

Disbursement of Funds

1. Inspections and advances of funds as construction progresses.
2. Final advance after completion of property and submission of proof of no outstanding liens.
3. Waiver of liens.

REMINDERS

There are many factors to consider in making construction loans. Expertise in the field comes from knowledgeable experience. Some lenders have, in addition to a formal procedure manual, a checklist of things to remember, points to watch, or reminders, in making construction loans. The items below are practical points from the experience of construction lenders:

1. A lender should have a policy and procedure manual or, at a minimum, an outline for construction lending so that employees follow the same procedures. The material might be considered elementary and something done daily. Mistakes and poor performance, however, are often the result of habits and taking things for granted. Certain functions must be performed and they should be done promptly, efficiently, and with courtesy and sincerity.
2. Lenders should keep their eyes open for good new builders.
3. Each employee should do his or her job properly so there will never be a comeback to that person.
4. Documentation for a loan should be in proper form, complete, accurate, and recorded where necessary.
5. An inspection should precede each disbursement. Inspections should be as frequent as necessary to insure the proper completion of the building.
6. Money in the construction loan fund should always be adequate to complete the job.
7. The Waiver of Lien instrument, signed by the contractor and subcontractor, should be accepted before the final disbursement.
8. An owner should enter into an acceptance of the project before occupying the premises.
9. There should be full compliance with the terms and conditions of the commitment from a permanent lender.

ELEVEN WAYS TO LOSE YOUR SHIRT
IN DEVELOPING LAND

The below eleven points were "contributed about 1948 for the enlightenment of homebuilders meetings by Mr. Barney Eddy, formerly Chief, Land Planning District of Columbia Office, FHA." [7] While the dollar figures may be obsolete today, the principles in the article are as applicable as they were in 1948.

1. Rush out and buy the cheapest piece of raw land available to heck-and-gone away from sewers and water and other civilized conveniences.
2. Pick a tract shaped like a jigsaw puzzle with some of the pieces lost. A lot of land will be hard to get unless you can deal with your neighbor.
3. Be sure the land is beautifully wooded with trees too big to uproot and worthless for saw logs and standing on ground where you expect to do some grading.
4. Don't bother to find out what FHA and VA think of the location and development program or what has to be done for sewage disposal and water supply to satisfy the health authorities.
5. Get way out where you can enjoy low taxes and the full impact of working out your own municipal functions such as bus services, garbage removal, police protection, street lighting, and storm water sewers.
6. It helps to pick a tract that's flat and low and saturated with water which has no place to go. You can sink a lot of dough in trying to dry the place up by hauling in dirt and by digging canals and burying a lot of big pipes all over the place clean down to the river.
7. If you like hills, try fooling around with some having plenty of gullies and springs and maybe some underlying rock. It gives the Le Tourneaux a workout and it's interesting to note the variations you can achieve in getting the footings in and bringing the foundations up to the first floor grades.
8. Bulldoze the devil out of everything. Push the top soil into the creek and cover it up with stumps, tree trunks and rubble

[7] Neal MacGiehan, *Construction Financing for Home Builders*. Washington, D.C.: Housing and Home Finance Agency, December, 1953, p. 19.

topped off with some clay subsoil. Or pile the stuff where it will get all churned up with concrete and trash if it doesn't wash away. You only have to buy 537 cubic yards of topsoil per acre to put back 4 inches of growing soil. Buying the topsoil, spreading it around, and grassing it over again nice and pretty will cost right around $2,000 per acre.

9. Never mind the kind of building site the street layout leaves you with. Just put a street along both sides of any stream and cut through the hills. Fit the lots to the streets afterwards and try adding the cost to the sales price. Don't plan. Let the water-boy figure it out.

10. Change the direction of the streets frequently and create plenty of street intersections. That means more culverts and curb inlets. Try some scissor angle intersections, too.

11. Put in the cheapest possible street improvements which go to pieces before the subdivision is sold out. That will slow things down for sure.

REVIEW AND STUDY QUESTIONS

1. Define a construction loan and give the factors of risk associated with such a loan.
2. How are interest rates quoted on construction loans?
3. Describe several ways by which construction loan financing can be arranged, that is, the types of construction loans.
4. List some typical provisions which are found in construction loan agreements.
5. Describe the methods by which a construction loan may be disbursed and the objectives of a good disbursement system.
6. Define a "commitment" and describe several types of commitments used in construction lending.
7. Discuss the ways by which a lender may draft a loan commitment so as to give him the best protection on it.
8. Outline the typical minimum considerations or procedures a lender follows in making a construction loan.

FURTHER READINGS AND REFERENCES

Beaton, William R., *Real Estate Investment*. Englewood Cliffs, N.J.: Prentice-Hall, Inc., 1971.

Casey, William J., *How to Buy and Sell Land*. New York: Institute for Business Planning, Inc., 1962.

————, *Real Estate Investment Planning.* New York: Institute for Business Planning, Inc., 1965.

MacGiehan, Neal, *Construction Financing for Home Builders.* Paperback. Washington, D.C.: Housing and Home Finance Agency, December, 1953.

National Association of Home Builders, *Land Development Manual.* Washington, D.C.: National Association of Home Builders, 1969.

Penny, Norman, and Richard F. Bronde, *Cases and Materials on Land Financing.* Mineola, N.Y.: The Foundation Press, Inc., 1970.

Sokol, Andrew, Jr., *Contractor or Manipulator?* Coral Gables, Fla.: University of Miami Press, 1968.

Urban Land Institute, *The Community Builders Handbook,* Anniversary Ed. Washington, D.C.: Urban Land Institute, 1968.

SIX

Residential Mortgages

The three types of mortgages most commonly used in residential real estate transactions are conventional, FHA, and VA. The conventional mortgage has no governmental backing and is based upon "conventional" lending practices. FHA and VA mortgages have government backing; that is, they are government underwritten.

CONVENTIONAL MORTGAGE

The number of conventional mortgages made each year exceeds the combined total of FHA and VA mortgages, though the annual volume of each type of mortgage varies with money market conditions and other factors which at a given time make one type of mortgage more attractive than the others. Terms and provisions of a conventional mortgage are determined by individual lenders, on an individual transaction basis, and according to state and local area needs and practices. The interest rate is determined by the lender and is a going market rate. The loan-to-value ratio, maturity, escrow, prepayment privilege, appraisal value, and closing costs are determined by the lender. The lender conducts its own analysis and evaluation of the borrower and property and makes the loan decision.

Conventional mortgages on single-family houses have usually been made by institutional lenders, such as savings and loan associations, who held the mortgages in their portfolios as investments. The lack of standardization of the conventional mortgage made it unattractive for sale in the secondary mortgage market. Conventional lending was based largely on tradition and lenders were restricted by numerous regulatory limitations. Lenders were restricted to local geographic areas. Loan-to-value ratios were lower than on government underwritten mortgages. The amount of assets which a lender could invest in conventional mortgages was limited.

Conventional lending has flexibility in that the loan terms may be tailored to fit a given situation. Further, a loan decision may be made in a relatively short time since the mortgage papers do not have to be processed through a government agency.

High Ratio Loans

The loan-to-value ratio on conventional mortgages on single-family homes has typically been low. A ratio of 50 to 60 percent was common in the 1930's. The 1940's witnessed an increase to 66⅔ percent, and then gradually reached a 75 percent ratio through insurance companies in the 1950's and early 1960's. Further, a transition was taking place with the savings and loan associations who were making 90 percent ratio conventional loans, using private mortgage insurance to cover the top 20 percent of the loan. Further, new organizations were formed which purchased second mortgages from developers for up to 15 percent of the value of the property. The mortgage banker closed the first mortgage at a typical 75 percent ratio and the developer accepted a second mortgage from the purchaser for 15 percent, thereby making possible a 90 percent loan. The developer sold the second mortgage to the new investing organization and the purchaser of the house made one payment, covering both mortgages, to the mortgage banker who serviced both the first mortgage and second mortgage institutional investors.

High-ratio conventional loans on single-family houses were also made possible by the "piggyback" method. An institutional lender, such as a savings and loan association, originates a conventional 90 percent loan and provides the usual 75 percent of the funds. The private or noninstitutional investor provides the top 15 percent. The joint loan is insured by a private mortgage insurer and remains in force until the loan is reduced to a normal ratio. Piggyback is essentially junior or second mortgage financing with the originating lender, or primary investor, owning 75 percent of the mortgage and another investor having a 15 percent subordinated or junior participation.[1]

There are variations of the piggyback method. Collateral for the top part of the higher-than-normal loan may be put up by the borrower or by a third party, and the lender may make the entire loan with its own funds. Collateral might be in the form of a passbook loan in which the borrower pledges a savings account for the excess amount of the loan. Or, the excess might be guaranteed by an outside institution.[2]

PRIVATE MORTGAGE INSURANCE [3]

Private mortgage insurance is coverage issued by a mortgage guaranty company to approved mortgage lenders to insure the lenders against loss on conventional mortgages if the borrower defaults on the obligation. The insurance is purchased by the lenders and covers the lender and not the borrower, though the borrower pays the premium. The insurance is called "private" since it is not issued by a government agency, such as the Federal Housing Administration, whose successful mutual mortgage insurance program was largely responsible for the development of a private program. Private mortgage insurance applies only to conventional mortgages and enlarges the government-sponsored markets which deal primarily in government-underwritten residential mortgages. Private mortgage insurers also provide secondary market sales facilities for lenders.

Types of Properties and Loans

The basic program of private mortgage insurers is coverage for high-ratio (90-95 percent) loans on owner-occupied, single-family houses. Many insurers offer special programs for other types of properties and loan purposes: second or vacation homes, modular and double wide dwellings, duplexes, three and four family rental units, permanently attached mobile homes, residential property improvement and repair loans, commercial real estate, such as medical centers, office buildings, shopping centers,

[1] William R. Beaton, *Real Estate Investment* (Englewood Cliffs, N.J.: Prentice-Hall, Inc., 1971), pp. 119–120.
[2] *Ibid.*
[3] The discussion in this section is based upon publications of private mortgage insurance companies. Particularly useful were the Lenders Manuals of the Liberty Mortgage Insurance Corporation of Cincinnati, Ohio, and the Excel Mortgage Insurance Corporation, Bettendorf, Iowa. Operating details vary between insurers but the basic pattern of mortgage insurance is essentially the same.

motels, and multi-unit apartments, condominiums, participation loans, lease guarantee, rural properties, older homes, and proposed construction.

Benefits to Borrower

The borrower is not the direct beneficiary of private mortgage insurance but there are indirect benefits. The home buyer receives the following advantages: (1) reduction in the size of the downpayment; (2) elimination of the need for second mortgage; (3) ability to acquire a larger or more expensive home; (4) ability to acquire a home sooner; and (5) availability of the higher ratio conventional loan at lower cost, faster service, and simpler procedure, than a government-underwritten mortgage. Loan origination and servicing expense is slightly higher than for a conventional loan without insurance.

Benefits to Lender

The lender using private mortgage insurance can benefit from the coverage and the services of the insurer. Among the benefits are the following: (1) broadening of the capacity of the lender without increasing risk exposure, thereby enabling it to offer high-ratio financing needed by home buyers; (2) primary element of risk taken by insurer at no expense to lender; (3) ability of lender to handle unusual loan situations, such as good customer who needs a loan outside of the usual lending pattern of the lender; and (4) availability of private secondary market facilities and services.

Premium Plans and Rates

Insurers offer several types of premium plans and rates for insurance of one- to four-family residential first mortgage loans. The following example is typical, though there will be differences among insurers in specifics.

Apartment Rates

The premium rates stated here are applicable to multi-family dwellings containing five or more units.

ANNUAL PREMIUM PLAN. 1/2 of 1% of the amount of the loan for the first year and 3/8 of 1% of the outstanding principal balance at the beginning of each succeeding year of the five year period.

SINGLE PREMIUM PLAN. 1¾% of the amount of the loan for the first five years of coverage.

Loans Not Exceeding 80% of Value (20% Coverage)

Annual Plans

First year coverage	¼ of 1% of loan
Annual renewals	¼ of 1% of principal

Single Plans

Four years coverage	¾ of 1% of loan
Annual renewals	¼% of principal
Ten years coverage	1¾% of loan
5-Year renewals (2)	½ of 1% of principal for 5-year period.

No appraisal review fee.

Loans Above 80% and Not Exceeding 90% of Value

Annual Plans

First year coverage	½ of 1% of loan
Annual renewal	¼ of 1% of principal

Single Plans

Four years	1% of loan
Annual renewals	¼ of 1% of principal
Ten years coverage	2% of loan
5-Year renewals (2)	½ of 1% of principal for 5-year period.

Appraisal review fee of $20.00.

Loans Above 90% and Not Exceeding 95% of Value (20% Coverage)

Annual Plans

First year coverage	¾ of 1% of loan amount
Annual renewals	¼ of 1% of principal

Single Plans

Five year coverage	1½% of loan amount
Annual renewals	¼ of 1% of principal
Seven years coverage	1¾% of loan amount
Annual renewals	¼ of 1% of principal
Ten years coverage	2¼% of loan amount
5-Year renewals (2)	½ of 1% of principal for 5-year period.

Loans Above 90% and Not Exceeding 95% of Value (25% Coverage)

Annual Plans

First year coverage	1% of loan amount
Annual renewals	¼ of 1% of principal
Each of first three years coverage	½ of 1% of loan balance
Annual renewals	¼ of 1% of principal

Single Plans

Five years coverage	1¾% of loan amount
Annual renewals	¼ of 1% of principal
Seven years coverage	2% of loan amount
Annual renewals	¼ of 1% of principal
Ten years coverage	2½% of loan amount
5-Year renewals (2)	½ of 1% of principal for 5-year period.
Fifteen years coverage	2¾% of loan amount
5-Year renewals (2)	½ of 1% of principal for 5-year period.

Appraisal review fee of $20.00.

The insured may wish to renew the insurance on an annual basis for 3/8 of 1% of the unpaid principal balance of the loan at the end of the fifth year. In order to apply, the insured must make a written request to the insurer at least 30 days prior to the expiration of the original policy period.

A commitment premium of $20.00 must accompany the original application for insurance. This premium is retained by the insurer and is not refunded unless the insurer rejects the application.

Settlement of Claims

The lender may file a claim for loss with the insurer within a specified period of time, such as 60 days, after a clear title has been obtained from the mortgagor. The insurer will, at its option, either:

1. Accept title to the property, free and clear of all liens and encumbrances, and pay to the lender the sum of the following:
   A. Principal balance.
   B. Accumulated interest, excluding penalty interest.
   C. Real estate taxes, and hazard insurance premium advances.
   D. Expense of necessary repair and maintenance during foreclosure.
   E. Statutory disbursements incurred in foreclosure.
   F. Reasonable attorney's fees allowed by court, not exceeding 3% of the total of principal and interest.
2. Or, relinquish all claim to the property and pay to the lender a sum equal to 20 percent of the claim amount shown above.

If the lender has sold the property with the approval of the insurer, a settlement for less than 20 percent may result. The amount of reimbursement in such cases is determined by deducting the net proceeds of sale from the total claim.

Delinquency

Lenders must notify the insurer when a loan is in default for a specified period of time, such as two, three, or four months. Periodic status reports are made to the insurer until such time as the borrower is no longer in default, or title to the property has been obtained by the lender.

Proceedings to obtain title must be started when an insured loan is in default for a specified period of time, such as six or nine months, or earlier if it is determined that a default will not be cured. Title acquisition may be by (1) voluntary conveyance or (2) appropriate judicial or nonjudicial proceedings, such as a sheriff's sale or trustee's sale.

Qualifications of Borrowers

The financial statement and credit rating of the borrower are as important as the physical real estate securing a loan. The borrower's age, dependents, employment stability, and income are important in judging the ability of the borrower to meet the loan obligations. Mortgage payments, including taxes and insurance, should not be greater than 25 percent of the monthly gross income. Monthly time contracts, such as mortgage payments, installment loans in excess of ten months duration, and other obligations should not exceed 33 percent of the monthly gross income of the borrower.

Income of the wife is considered if age and type of employment and "working pattern" are satisfactory. Secondary income is not considered unless evidence shows it to be a future certainty. Self-employed borrowers must submit financial statements from past years as evidence of earning capacity. A credit report must reflect a proper regard for repayment of contractual obligations. Borrowers must be of legal age.

Property Qualifications

Emphasis is placed on neighborhood factors and on items of design which contribute to convenience, livability and performance, as well as the quality of construction, materials, and equipment. Neighborhood factors and trends include:

1. Comparability of price range.
2. Conformity to zoning regulations and possibility of encroachment by commercial or industrial property.
3. Accessibility of schools, transportation and shopping.
4. Availability and accessibility of recreation, parks, swimming pools, etc.
5. Evidence of pride of ownership.
6. Adequacy of public utilities and services.
7. Proper egress and ingress to property.
8. Public and/or private improvements—sewers, water, paving, etc.

Older homes must be modernized as to kitchens, bath, plumbing, and heating, and capable of use during the life of the mortgage. There is no restriction on the amount of land involved in conjunction with the borrower's house, providing at least 67 percent of the total value is actually in the dwelling. There is no restriction on location as long as the house is not going to be subject to excessive depreciation due to building trends or zoning factors. There is no restriction to a farm property as long as the principal income of the borrower is not from farming activities. Suburban or rural properties may be insured if they are not so remote as to make resale difficult.

Assumption of Mortgage

When real estate is transferred to a new borrower and the personal liability of the original borrower is not released by the lender, the insurance coverage remains in force. If the property is sold to a new owner and the original borrower is released, or the mortgage terms are modified without approval of the insurer, coverage terminates. A new application must be submitted showing financial qualifications of the new borrower along with the usual supporting exhibits.

Assignment

A lender may sell a loan and the insurance coverage remains in force. The insurer must be notified if servicing of the loan is also transferred so as to facilitate the billing of renewal premiums.

Change in Status of Loans

Various changes or adjustments may be made in the status of a loan during its life. Some changes need prior approval of the insurer while the insurer needs only to be notified of others. Examples of changes are:

additional advances on open-end loans; refinancing, that is, placing a new mortgage on the same property; and loan modification agreement.

FHA AND VA RESIDENTIAL MORTGAGES

Both the Federal Housing Administration (FHA), created in 1934, and the Veterans Administration (VA), created in 1944, provide government backing for individual residential mortgages. The specific eligibility requirements, conditions, and terms differ between the two programs but both programs are designed to assist the home buyer and to encourage lenders to make loans under specified requirements and standards.

THE FHA INSURED LOAN

The FHA program most widely used is the insured mortgage on the single-family, owner-occupied house, known as a Section 203 (b) loan, referring to the authorizing provision in the National Housing Act of 1934. The money for the loan is provided by a private commercial lender who is approved by FHA, that is, an FHA approved mortgagee. FHA does not lend money or construct houses. FHA insures the lender against loss on the mortgage; the insurance does not protect the borrower although he pays the premium. The lender, as a result of the insurance, is willing to make loans on terms not otherwise possible. The borrower and the property must meet FHA requirements and minimum standards.

Advantages to Borrower and Lender

The FHA insured loan offers a number of benefits to the borrower. Among the attractive features in contrast to conventional mortgages, are the following: (1) a high loan-to-value ratio, with a resulting low downpayment; (2) a favorable interest rate; (3) a longer maturity; and (4) a knowledge that the property has met minimum standards of construction and standard procedures of valuation. The lender finds the FHA insured loan attractive because of: (1) the insurance feature, which reduces the risk of loss to the lender; (2) the existence of a national secondary market; (3) the broadening of the lender's market for making mortgages; and (4) the possibility of a non-risk asset classification.

Effect on Mortgage Market

The FHA resulted in the creation of a national mortgage market for its instruments, that is, the local real estate mortgage with no market was changed into an instrument that was transferable and saleable on a national basis. The primary reason for this negotiability was the mutual mortgage insurance feature of the FHA mortgage. The risk of loss to the lender was not totally eliminated but it was transferred to the government and substantially reduced when the lender was able to exchange a defaulted mortgage for a government backed FHA debenture, or cash settlement. Further, standards as to construction, borrower credit, and financial analysis and appraisal procedures gave the FHA insured mortgage a national acceptance with investors. State regulatory restrictions on lending areas, mortgage terms, and type of permitted investments were reduced or eliminated for the FHA insured mortgage.

FHA, through its standards and requirements, influenced lending practices in the mortgage market, such as interest rates, loan-to-value ratios, amortization plans, loan maturities, and land planning. Improvements were made in housing conditions and standards. More persons were able to acquire housing.

Sale of FHA Insured House

An owner of a house subject to an FHA insured mortgage may sell the property and the buyer may assume or take subject to the existing mortgage, without permission of the lender. The seller remains liable to the lender on the note. The seller is permitted to take back a second mortgage from the buyer as a part of the purchase price.

The seller may want to be relieved of liability to the lender on the note. The lender files a request on the appropriate forms with FHA for consent to substitution of mortgagor after insurance. FHA, if approval is granted, will issue a commitment good for ninety days. The commitment will be submitted for final approval when the transaction is completed with the new borrower. It also requires lender approval.

Prepayment and Late Charges

Prepayments are permitted in any year without penalty. A lender is authorized to make a charge for late payments. The charge is 2 percent of the total monthly payment for delinquency of more than 15 days.

Truth in Lending

The Federal Truth in Lending Law requires the lender to disclose to the borrower the "annual percentage rate" (APR) on the loan. The APR for FHA loans is the stated or contract interest rate plus the mutual mortgage insurance premium of 1/2 of 1 percent. The premium is included because it is required of the borrower, is paid by the borrower, and is of no direct benefit to him. Also included are discount points. Charges excluded from the APR computation include the appraisal fee, title examination, title insurance, preparation of legal instruments, and credit report.

Monthly Payments

The FHA loan is repaid on a monthly basis with payments due on the first of each month. The lender must apply each payment as follows: (1) mortgage insurance premiums; (2) taxes and hazard insurance escrow; (3) interest; and (4) principal.

Defaults

A lender must notify FHA within 91 days of a default. A payment which is 30 days late is considered a default. If the delinquency extends to six monthly payments, FHA must be given another notice of default, with additional reports every sixty days as to the status of the default.

If a default is for reasons beyond the control of the borrower, the lender may enter into a forbearance agreement with the borrower. The agreement permits the lender to grant relief in cases of hardship, such as death in the family or loss of employment, and give the borrower temporary assistance and time to cure the delinquency. Regular payments are reduced or suspended for a period of time and a temporary new payment plan is worked out to bring the loan current.

A lender must, at any time within one year of a default, acquire marketable title to the property by means other than foreclosure, or must institute foreclosure proceedings. The lender may accept a voluntary deed from the borrower in lieu of foreclosure or the borrower may deed the property directly to FHA. If the default is due to circumstances beyond the control of the borrower, the lender may assign the note and mortgage to FHA and apply for the insurance benefits.

Foreclosure may be started by the lender at any time after the initial default report to FHA. After foreclosure the lender may, within thirty days, convey the property to FHA for settlement under the insurance fund. Claims are paid in cash or debentures and include the loan balance plus certain expenses of the lender resulting from the foreclosure.

The lender has the option of holding the property and attempting to sell it to satisfy the debt. The decision on whether to sell or convey to FHA depends upon the market, the value of the property, and the costs involved in acquiring and disposing of the property.

Discounts or Points

The maximum FHA interest rate is set by the Secretary of the Housing and Urban Development; it is a fixed or "pegged" rate. The rate is frequently not competitive with the market rate of interest on conventional mortgages; it is usually lower. Lenders invest money where it will earn the best rate of return, whether it is in mortgages or stocks and bonds.

When the FHA interest rate is lower than the market interest rate, a lender may make up the difference or spread by charging a discount or points on the loan. The discount, which is paid by the seller, increases the effective interest rate on the FHA mortgage so that the yield to the lender is the same as the market rate. There are two instances where the seller does not pay a discount: (1) the refinancing of an existing FHA mortgage; and (2) where the individual has a house built on a lot he owns. There is, in reality, no seller in each case.

Mutual Mortgage Insurance

FHA charges the borrower an annual insurance premium of one half of one percent on the declining balance of the principal of the mortgage. The premium is paid monthly as a part of the mortgage payment. The lender, once a year, forwards the annual premium to FHA. The accumulated premium reserves are used to pay operating costs and losses for the insurance system.

Commitment

The lender sends a completed application to FHA for processing and approval and issuance of a commitment for insurance. If the property is acceptable to FHA, a conditional commitment is issued. When the borrower is approved, a firm commitment is issued, which gives the terms of the loan. Both commitments, on existing property, are good for six months, and for twelve months on proposed construction.

Application Cost

An application for an FHA loan is made through an approved mortgagee, such as a mortgage banker or other institutional lender. The cost is $40.00 for existing properties and properties which are under construction and were not approved prior to beginning of construction. The cost is $50.00 for proposed construction.

Appraised Value

The term "value," as used by FHA, means the estimated total price of the property, including estimated closing costs incidental to the transaction. Payments for prepaid expenses, such as taxes and insurance, are excluded from the estimate.

Maturity

The maximum term on new construction is 35 years, which is allowed only where the borrower is unable to afford a 30 years payment. The maximum term on existing construction is three-fourths of the estimated remaining economic life of the property, but never more than 30 years.

Interest Rate, MIP, and Escrow

The maximum interest rate on FHA mortgages is subject to change. The borrower must add to the interest rate the FHA mortgage insurance premium (MIP) of 1/2 percent. The monthly payment must also include 1/12 of the annual cost of real estate taxes and hazard insurance to be held in escrow. Also included are assessments and water charges, if a lien. A loan is repaid in basically equal payments throughout its term. The insurance premium is computed on the average balance to be outstanding in the current year. It declines slightly from year to year but is averaged out so that it stays the same for a year.

Maximum Loan—Owner Occupied

The maximum loan on an owner-occupied single-family house is $45,000. The maximum on a 2- or 3-family house is $48,750, and $56,000 on a 4-family house. These amounts are for approved new construction, approved existing construction less than one year old, and existing construction over one year old.

Downpayment—Owner Occupied

The downpayment schedule on an owner-occupied residence is as follows: 3% of first $25,000 of appraised value; plus 10% of next $10,000; plus 20% in excess of $35,000. Figures are adjusted to $50,000 multiples. This schedule is for approved new construction, approved existing construction less than one year old, and approved existing construction over one year old.

EXAMPLE. Appraised value of house is $30,000. The downpayment is $1,250, with a maximum loan of $28,750, computed as follows:

3% of 1st $25,000	=	$ 750
10% of next $5,000	=	500
Downpayment		$1,250
Loan		$28,750

THE VA LOAN

The Servicemen's Readjustment Act of 1944 provided benefits for veterans of World War II. Title III of the Act is concerned with the financing of housing. Lenders were partially guaranteed against loss on loans made to veterans on terms specified by law and by the Veterans Administration. The terms were more favorable than would ordinarily be available in the market. The guaranty feature removed some of the risk and encouraged the lender to make the loan. The VA loan program has been continued by Congress since its inception and eligible veterans include, in addition to World War II personnel, those from later wars and military actions. The discussion below is concerned with the standard VA program for one to four family, owner-occupied residences.

Guaranty

The guaranty feature covers the lender against loss in the event the borrower defaults on the loan. The Veterans Administration, on a home loan, reimburses the lender for a percentage of the defaulted balance, namely, up to 60 percent of the loan amount, or $17,500, whichever is less. The amount of the guaranty declines in proportion to reduction in the debt. The veteran may have his entitlement reinstated if: (1) he is involuntarily transferred to another geographic area of employment; or (2) he is required to move due to health reasons.

Insurance

A loan may be guaranteed or insured at the option of the borrower and lender. If insurance is elected, and the Veterans Administration is properly notified by the lender of the choice, the lender's insurance account is credited with 15 percent of the loan amount, with a maximum limited to the guaranty amount. In the event of default, the lender may receive his net loss after disposition of the security, assuming the lender has sufficient credit in the insurance account. The insurance feature of the VA loan program is seldom used by borrowers and lenders.

Lenders

Lenders under the VA program are classified as supervised and non-supervised. Supervised lenders include lenders subject to supervision and examination by an agency of the Federal or state governments, such as commercial banks, life insurance companies, savings and loan associations, and mortgage companies. A supervised lender can make a VA loan without prior approval of the Veterans Administration. A nonsupervised lender must obtain approval for each loan; the guaranty is not automatic.

Buyer Eligibility

The applicant for a VA loan must have been on active duty in the armed forces for ninety consecutive days. Eligibility may be certified by evidence of honorable discharge or by a Certificate of Eligibility issued by the VA. The following veterans are eligible for guaranteed or insured loans:

1. A veteran who served at any time between September 16, 1940, and July 25, 1947, and was discharged under conditions other than dishonorable after at least 90 days active service (or for service-incurred disability in less than 90 days).
2. A veteran whose entitlement was derived from active service between June 27, 1950, and January 31, 1955, inclusive. The minimum term of active service for veterans of the Korean conflict is the same as that required for World War II veterans,

i.e., 90 days or discharge by reason of a service-connected disability.

3. Widows of men who served during either of the periods referred to above and who died as the result of service.

4. Any member of the Women's Army Auxiliary Corps who served for at least 90 days and who was honorably discharged therefrom for disability incurred in the line of duty rendering her physically unfit to perform further service in the Women's Army Auxiliary Corps or in the Women's Army Corps. (This applies only to persons so discharged from the Women's Army Auxiliary Corps prior to the integration of that corps into the Women's Army Corps, pursuant to Public Law 110, 78th Congress.)

5. Certain United States citizens who served in the Armed Forces of a Government allied with the United States in World War II.

The following are eligible for guaranteed loans, but are not eligible for insured or business loans (unless they also were eligible based on World War II or Korean conflict service, and such entitlement has not been used):

1. Veterans who served on active duty for 181 days or more, any part of which occurred after January 31, 1955, and who were discharged or released under conditions other than dishonorable, or were discharged or released from active duty after such date for a service-connected disability.

2. Servicemen who have served at least 181 days in active duty status, even though not discharged, while their service continues without a break.

3. Widows of the above-described eligible persons who died as the result of service.

4. The wife of any member of the armed forces serving on active duty who is listed as missing in action, or is a prisoner of war and has been so listed for a total of more than 90 days.

Income and Credit

Lenders may use a 4 to 1 or 5 to 1 ratio of debt to income as one of the guides in estimating the amount of loan for a borrower. For example, an applicant with a monthly income of $1,000 could carry a monthly mortgage payment of $250, including taxes and insurance, under the 4 to 1 ratio.

VA will accept, for income computation, the income of a working wife in full in the loan if the wife has at least two consecutive years of employment and steady income. VA credit analysis of both the husband and wife is concerned with their ability to manage their finances, their financial habits, and their payment record. Ability to pay the loan is not necessarily the deciding factor; an applicant may have the income ability to pay but not the willingness.

Loan Terms

There is no limit on the dollar amount of a VA loan, except as the lender may impose. Maximum maturity is thirty years. The maximum interest rate is set by law and no increase is permitted during the term of the loan. The loan is amortized in equal monthly payments. There is no penalty for prepayment. The lender may impose a late charge of 4 percent of any installment paid more than 15 days after its due date.

Sale of Property

The owner of property subject to a VA mortgage may sell the property to anyone, including a non-veteran, without VA approval. The veteran remains personally liable to the government for any amount the VA pays the holder of the mortgage in event of default and foreclosure.

The veteran may request the VA for release from liability upon assumption of the mortgage by the buyer of the home. Three conditions must be met: (1) the loan must be current; (2) the purchaser must qualify as an acceptable credit risk; and (3) the purchaser must assume the obligations and liability of the veteran, including the indemnity obligation of the veteran, evidenced by an agreement in writing in such form as VA may require. The lender does not have to release the veteran from liability but if he does the guaranty is still valid to the lender.

Reasonable Value and Sales Price

The sales price of a home is permitted to exceed its reasonable value as determined by VA. The loan amount, however, must not exceed the reasonable value. If the sales price is more than the reasonable value, the veteran must certify that he paid the difference in cash from his own resources. No borrowing is permitted for the difference.

Reasonable value is defined by VA as "that figure which represents the amount a reputable and qualified appraiser, unaffected by personal interest, bias, or prejudice, would recommend to a prospective purchaser as a proper price or cost in the light of prevailing conditions." The VA appraises the property and issues a Certificate of Reasonable Value (CRV). The lender then checks to see whether the value figure is what is needed, what the terms of the loan will be to the borrower, and what repairs are needed to the property.

Closing Costs

A lender may charge the veteran closing costs customary for the locality. An example of closing costs are the following: title insurance, recording fees, state intangible tax, state documentary tax, application fee, appraisal fee, credit report, plat of physical survey, abstract continuation fee charged to buyer, origination or servicing fee (1%), and prepaid items for escrow. The annual percentage rate (APR) includes any item that is amortized, such as the contract or stated rate of interest, origination fee, discount, and interest to end of month.

Direct Loans

The VA makes direct loans to veterans under certain conditions and limitations. Under a direct loan, the veteran borrows the money directly from the VA and not from a private lender. The purpose of the direct home loan program is to provide home financing to eligible veterans in areas where private financing is not generally available. Such areas are designated by VA as housing credit shortage areas and are generally rural areas and small cities not near the metropolitan or commuting areas of large cities, and areas where VA loans from private institutions have not been and are not presently available to veterans. Designated credit shortage areas are subject to change depending upon the availability of VA loans from private lenders.

The maximum loan amount generally is $21,000. The interest rate may vary with changes in law and regulations. The VA may not make a loan for more than the reasonable value of the property. If the veteran agrees to pay more than the reasonable value, the difference must be paid in cash from the veteran's own resources. Closing costs must also be paid in cash.

Closing costs are approximately the same as on a VA guaranteed loan. The VA also charges an origination fee of $50.00, or one percent of the loan, whichever is greater, and the fee is used to pay for the appraisal, credit report, and loan closer's fee. If the direct loan is used to finance construction of a home, the origination fee is $50.00 or two percent of the loan, whichever is greater.

Purpose of Loan

A VA loan may be obtained for several purposes. Depending upon the eligibility of the veteran, the loan may be obtained to:

1. Buy a home.
2. Buy a residential unit in a condominium project.
3. Build a home.
4. Repair, alter, or improve a home.
5. Refinance an existing home loan.
6. Buy a mobile home.
7. Buy a farm, livestock, equipment, supplies, or for working capital.
8. Construct a farmhouse or other buildings on a farm.
9. Repair, alter, or improve farmhouse or outbuildings.
10. Improve farm land or equipment.
11. Conduct farming operations.
12. Purchase stock in a cooperative association where the purchase of such stock is required by Federal law in connection with obtaining a farm loan.
13. Buy a business.
14. Buy a building or land for business purposes.
15. Buy business supplies and inventory.
16. Buy machinery, tools, and equipment for operating a business.
17. Construct, repair, or improve a business building or personal property.
18. Obtain working capital for a business.

Multiple Units

A veteran may obtain a VA loan to buy or construct a residential property containing more than one family unit. The total number of separate units cannot be more than four if one veteran is buying, and one additional family unit may be added to the basic four for each participating veteran. One veteran, for example, could buy four units and two veterans could buy six units.

Mobile Homes

A veteran may obtain a loan for financing the purchasing of a mobile home, lot acquisition, and site preparation, The loan is obtained from a private lender.

Foreclosure and Claims [4]

The lender, upon determining that a default is incurable, acquires title to the property either by voluntary deed or by foreclosure. The lender may choose to cancel the VA guaranty without filing a claim. The lender retains the property and assumes any profit or loss from its ultimate disposition.

The lender may decide not to cancel the guaranty, and file a claim with VA. The VA has two options: (1) make a cash settlement with the lender for the full amount of the partial guaranty, and the lender keeps the property; or (2) pay a claim to the lender for the full amount of the guaranteed debt, including the entire unpaid principal balance plus interest, advances, and allowable foreclosure expenses, and the lender ordinarily conveys the property to the VA which then has full responsibility for its eventual disposition. If the lender prefers to retain the property, it may do so by "buying" the property from the VA for the "specified amount" or "credit figure" or "upset price" established by the VA.

COMPARISON OF FHA AND VA

The FHA and VA are both designed to assist qualified persons in acquiring real estate under attractive terms. Both programs provide the private lender with a form of reimbursement for loss due to the default of the borrower. There are, however, several basic differences between the two programs.

1. The FHA program is one of 100 percent insurance for which the borrower pays a premium. The VA is a program of partial guaranty to the lender for which no charge is made to the veteran.
2. Both VA and FHA pay lender's claims in cash. FHA, however, has the option to pay in either cash or debentures. The debentures, because of market and other factors, could result in some loss to the lender.
3. There is a difference between the two programs in allowances for foreclosure expenses. VA gives a 100 percent allowance for

[4] *FHA-VA Foreclosure and Claims Procedure* by Thomas J. Melody and Leonard J. Giblin. A manual edited by a special subcommittee of The Loan Administration Committee, Mortgage Bankers Association of America, March, 1967.

reasonable attorney's fees and other foreclosure expenses. The maximum attorney's fee, however, may not exceed $250, which may be low in some areas. FHA pays two-thirds of all reasonable foreclosure costs, including attorney's fees, and there is no specified upper limit.

4. VA regulates and supervises the foreclosure process. FHA leaves the process primarily up to the lender.
5. VA will actively seek a deficiency judgment against a defaulted borrower. FHA does not pursue such a judgment.
6. FHA requires a marketable title to foreclosed property and that the property be vacant. VA will accept title even though the redemption period has not expired. Further, VA does not require that the property be vacant.

EVALUATION OF FHA AND VA PROGRAMS

The FHA and VA programs, in addition to the specific benefits accruing to the individual borrower (such as low downpayment, long maturities, assurance of minimum standards of construction quality, and good appraisal and underwriting practices), have been strong influences in the national economy and mortgage markets. The impact and accomplishments of the two programs include the following: (1) improved housing standards, living conditions, and land planning and utilization; (2) improved flow of mortgage funds because the mortgages are traded in a secondary mortgage market; (3) housing available to a greater number of persons and expanding home ownership; (4) improved lending practices as to analysis of the borrower, appraisal of the property, and servicing of the loan; (5) reduction of risks and costs in mortgage lending; (6) contribution to the growth of the construction industry and the mortgage banking business; and (7) ability of more lenders and investors to participate in the mortgage business.

The programs have been successful though they have weaknesses and there is disagreement as to their impact. Among the criticisms or questioning of the programs are the following: (1) the FHA seeks to meet both economic and social objectives which, in certain cases, leads to unsound loans; (2) the fixed or pegged interest rates lead to the practice of discounting and rates should be free to seek their market level; and (3) the programs were intended to meet objectives and serve needs existing at the time of their enactment and were not to be permanent. The programs have been a strong but a varying influence in the home mortgage market in recent years.

REVIEW AND STUDY QUESTIONS

1. Describe the basic features of each of the three types of mortgages most commonly used in residential real estate transactions.
2. Explain the use of "piggyback" financing and private mortgage insurance in the making of high-ratio conventional mortgage loans.
3. Explain the basic features of the: (A) FHA insured home loan, and (B) VA guaranteed home loan.
4. Explain the use of "discounts" or "points" and their effect on the mortgage interest rate.
5. Give an example of the closing costs on an FHA and a VA loan in your local area.
6. What is the current interest rate on FHA and VA mortgages? Is this rate the same as the current rate on conventional mortgages in your local area?
7. Briefly explain the VA foreclosure and claims procedure.
8. Evaluate the FHA and VA programs from the point of view of their accomplishments and their limitations or criticism.

FURTHER READINGS AND REFERENCES

Beaton, William R., *Real Estate Investment*. Englewood Cliffs, N.J.: Prentice-Hall, Inc., 1971.

Hoagland, Henry E., and Leo D. Stone, *Real Estate Finance,* Fourth Ed. Homewood, Ill.: Richard D. Irwin, Inc., 1969.

McMichael, Stanley, and Paul T. O'Keefe, *How to Finance Real Estate,* Third Ed. Englewood Cliffs, N.J.: Prentice-Hall, Inc., 1967.

National Association of Home Builders, *The New Mortgage Market,* Revised. Washington, D.C.: National Association of Home Builders, April, 1971.

Pease, Robert H., and Lewis O. Kerwood, *Mortgage Banking,* Second Ed. New York: McGraw-Hill Book Company, 1965.

Penny, Norman, and Richard F. Broude, *Cases and Materials on Land Financing*. Mineola, N.Y.: The Foundation Press, Inc., 1970.

Practising Law Institute, *Real Estate Financing: Business and Legal Considerations*. Real Estate Transcript Series No. 1. Herman M. Glassner and Kurt W. Lore, Chairmen. Jim McCord, ed. New York: Practising Law Institute, 1968.

Pugh, J. W., and William H. Hippaka, *California Real Estate Finance*. Englewood Cliffs, N.J.: Prentice-Hall, Inc., 1966.

SEVEN

Leases

The long-term lease is a financing instrument that is widely used in land and business property transactions. Negotiations for such leases can be lengthy and complex. Professional guidance is needed from real estate brokers, tax experts, and legal counsel. The lease instrument is both a contract and a conveyance. It is governed by law, such as the law of landlord and tenant, but the wording of the lease also determines the legal rights and duties of the parties and is the basis for the income tax treatment of the parties. The discussion below covers leaseholds, sandwich leases, rent, income tax factors, lease guaranty insurance, and sale-leaseback.

LEASEHOLDS

A leasehold is the interest of the tenant under a lease; it is an estate for years and consists of the right of the tenant to the possession, use, and quiet enjoyment of the leased premises. The tenant or lessee can borrow money or can mortgage the leasehold estate, assuming there are no lease, deed, or other restrictions against such financing. The leasehold serves as security for the mortgage and the mortgage is known as a leasehold mortgage.

The leasehold mortgage is subordinate to the fee interest of the property owner or the lessor. A default by the tenant on the leasehold mortgage does not directly affect the lessor. The lender acquires the tenant's interest in the leasehold, such as through foreclosure. The lender is, however, concerned in the event of default by the tenant on lease payments or rent to the lessor. The leasehold mortgage, which is subordinate to the interest of the lessor, could be wiped out if the tenant defaulted in the payment of rent and the lessor terminated the lease.

A loan upon a leasehold has more risk to the lender than a loan upon a fee simple interest. Some lenders do not make leasehold mortgages either as a matter of management policy or because they are legally restricted from making them. Or, if they do make them, certain rights and safeguards are written into the loan agreement, such as the right of the lender to take over the tenant's interests under the lease and cure any defaults, such as in the payment of the rent.

GROUND LEASES

Leasehold mortgage financing, as described above, is usually used in connection with long-term leases on land, known as ground leases. Such leases usually require the tenant or lessee to erect a building on the site or replace an existing one. The rent is net to the property owner or lessor, that is, the tenant pays taxes, insurance, maintenance, and operating costs of the property.

Benefits to Owner

The owner of land, for any number of reasons, may not want to, or be able to, sell the land. Or the owner may not have the ability to develop it personally. Or the value of the land may have reached a value level too high for a person both to buy the land and develop it. The ground lease offers attractive benefits to the land owner, which may solve these problems.

Among the possible advantages are the following: (1) proper capital improvements made by the tenant enhance the value of the land; (2) proper capital improvements also give greater security to the lessor because the tenant has spent money to erect the building and would hesitate to lose it through foreclosure—there is a greater incentive to retain the investment; (3) there are possible saving in income taxes since rental income is distributed over a period of years rather than coming all in one year with a sale; (4) there is no capital investment on the part of the owner—the tenant makes all new capital expenditures; (5) the owner has no problem of reinvesting funds from a sale of the property; (6) the tenant assumes the management of the property; (7) proper improvements to the land make the fee more financeable and salable; and (8) the amount of the principal is fixed for the period of the lease.

Benefits to Tenant

The tenant or lessee is usually a developer and builder. The possible advantages to the tenant include the following: (1) acquisition of land, perhaps high-valued, with a minimum of capital outlay; (2) release of funds for use in development or business; (3) no need for a large loan to acquire the land; (4) deductible ground rental for income tax purposes as a business expense; (5) acquisition by developer of an asset, namely the leasehold, which can increase in value and be sold later at a profit or used as security for a loan; and (6) in effect, acquisition of a "loan" by the developer of the land from the owner with rent being paid instead of interest payments. Further, the loan-to-value ratio of a conventional mortgage loan would be less than the full value of the property. The developer, with a subordinated ground lease, has in effect acquired a 100 percent loan on the land value. Also, the ground lease, as a technique of financing, can generate a higher return on equity to the tenant or developer as compared to conventional mortgage financing of the fee.

SUBORDINATION

Leasehold loans are either "subordinated" or "unsubordinated". In an unsubordinated leasehold mortgage the owner of the land has not permitted his fee interest to be placed in a junior or subordinate position to the lender's mortgage. The rights of the fee owner are superior to the rights of the lender.

A "subordinated" ground lease, or subordinated fee, is one in which the lessor or land owner has agreed to place his interest in a junior or subordinate position to that of the lender's mortgage. The lessor is cooperating with the lessee in helping the latter to obtain construction financing by agreeing to join in financing the improvements. The lessor permits the construction mortgage to include the land as well as the building as security for the loan. The effect to the lender is to create a fee mortgage rather than a leasehold mortgage. The land owner signs the mortgage but not the promissory note and thereby limits any loss in the event of foreclosure to the value of the land.

Subordination can be attractive to both the land owner and developer. The owner may capitalize fully on the value of his land. He may negotiate for higher rentals or other lease features in exchange for granting subordination. The developer may be able to obtain a larger loan with subordination since the lender has greater security. Subordination may permit a developer to obtain a loan which would not otherwise be available because of restrictions of some lenders against the making of leasehold loans without subordination.

VALUATION

A fee simple estate which is leased is divided into two sets of property rights—the leased fee estate and the leasehold interest. The owner of the leased fee estate is entitled to the contract rental income for the term of the lease and the right to recover the property at the end of the term, called the reversion. The tenant, as owner of the leasehold interest, has the right of possession, use, and enjoyment of the property over the term of the lease. There are usually no reversionary rights in the leasehold estate and all rights of tenancy are terminated upon expiration of the lease.

The value of the leased fee estate is the discounted present worth of the future income stream plus the present worth of the reversionary rights. The value of the leasehold interest is the discounted present worth of the income stream earned by the interest. If the market or economic rent exceeds contract rent, the value of the leasehold is equal to the discounted present worth of the difference between contract rent and economic rent over the remaining term of the lease.

The terms and covenants of the lease instrument must be analyzed as to their impact on the income stream. An accurate projection of income to each of the lease interests is necessary for a proper valuation of the interests. The values of a leased fee and a leasehold interest are directly related to the terms and covenants of the lease. Lease values can be affected by provisions that are unreasonable or unduly restrict the rights and duties of the parties.

Rental provisions make the lease either gross or net. The lessor under a gross lease must pay some of the property expenses, such as taxes and maintenance. The earnings to the leased fee estate needed to be reduced by the amount of these expenses. In a net lease the tenant pays these expenses and the income to the leased fee estate is net, with the leasehold estate's earnings correspondingly reduced in amount. Further, the amount of rent can vary as to whether it is fixed, graduated, declining, or a percentage arrangement.

Reasonable repair and maintenance clauses can help retain property value by requiring the tenant to keep the improvements in good repair and giving the lessor permission to make neglected repairs and charge them to the tenant. Other provisions which can affect the attractiveness of a lease and hence its value include: subordination, assigning and subletting, control by the lessor over use of the property by the tenant, condemnation, and damages caused by hazards such as fire.

Contract rent is the rent called for in the lease agreement. Economic rent is current market rent, that is, what the property would rent for if placed on the market. When the contract rent is less than market rent, the leasehold estate has an advantage because the fee estate has given up some of its benefits. If the contract rent is greater than the market rent, the fee estate has an advantage and encroaches upon the leasehold interest. Attention must be given to these advantages and disadvantages where they exist and their influence on the owner and tenant.

Once the income stream is determined, the discounting process requires the selection of a proper rate of capitalization. Leased fee estates and leasehold interests are valued individually according to their respective market values created by the lease agreement. The sum of the two interests do not equal the value of the fee simple estate if different capitalizations are applied, as should be the case, to the different interests. The property rights created by the lease may be valued at a discount or at a premium in relation to the value of the fee simple estate. The degree of risk involved with each interest is different and capitalization rates will vary with the degree of risk assumed by each interest. The leased fee estate has first claim on the income from the property and the risk is based on the credit of the tenant and the terms of the lease agreement. The leasehold interest has a greater risk since it involves an obligation to pay the rent. A subtenant, or sandwich lease interest, involves greater risk than the original leasehold. The proper capitalization rates, applied to the future income streams of the respective interests, give the discounted present worth of the lease benefits, or its market value.

Tri-party Agreement

A tri-party agreement is used between the permanent lender, the interim lender, and the borrower. It usually provides for the joint use of loan documents by the two lenders, assignment of the loan documents by the interim lender only to the permanent lender, and assignment of the loan to the permanent lender within a specified period of time after the terms of the commitment have been met.[1]

The agreement facilitates the closing of the loan. It also protects the permanent lender between the date of the commitment and the payout of the loan. The permanent lender seeks to be assured of receiving the loan and wants to be sure that the interim lender does not sell the loan to another party.[2]

Leasehold Lending Policies

Lender's policies as to the making of loans on leaseholds vary. The below factors, however, give an example of some considerations by lenders in making such loans.[3]

1. Leasehold loan term must not exceed a certain percentage of the unexpired ground lease term, such as 75 or 80 percent.
2. Preference is shown for leasehold loans on high-grade, well-located, income-producing properties, such as office buildings, shopping centers, apartment projects, and industrial properties. Single-family dwellings may be acceptable if residential leaseholds are customary in the locality.
3. The amount of the mortgage loan is limited to a percentage of the value of the leasehold estate, such as two-thirds or three-fourths.
4. The lender has the right to cure default on the ground lease and, if necessary, to sell the property upon default and foreclosure.
5. The ground lease must permit lessee to mortgage the leasehold and to assign it freely.
6. A condemnation award must be paid first to the lender who may apply it to the mortgage.

SANDWICH LEASE

The sandwich lease is a result of two transactions. The first transaction is the making of a lease between the lessor and lessee. The second transaction is a sublease from the original lessee to a third

[1] William R. Beaton, *Real Estate Investment* (Englewood Cliffs, N.J.: Prentice-Hall, Inc., 1971), p. 107.
[2] *Ibid.*
[3] Charles P. Flanagan, "Financing of Leasehold Estates," *The Appraisal Journal,* July, 1968, pp. 383–392. Also, see William R. Beaton, *Real Estate Investment* (Englewood Cliffs, N.J.: Prentice-Hall, Inc., 1971), Chapter 6, "Commercial Leasehold Financing."

party. The original lessee is now both a tenant and a landlord. The sublessee has occupancy, use, and control of the property. The original lessee is now the owner of a sandwich leasehold. He receives rental payments for the term of years stated in the sublease. He pays rent to the original lessor. The difference, if any, between these payments—the underlying rent paid and subleasehold rent received—is a series of marginal income streams which represent a capital value.[4]

The sandwich leasehold is valued by capitalizing the marginal income stream in the same manner as valuation of a leased fee and a leasehold estate. The entire property is appraised and value is allocated among the three interests, namely, leased fee, sandwich leasehold, and subleasehold. The below computation illustrates this method of valuation.[5] Assume:

A leases to B for $12,000 per year net.
B subleases to C for $15,000 per year net.
C constructs a new building; net income of $36,000 per year.
Remaining term of lease is 42 years.
Land value, if vacant and unimproved is $300,000.

Step No. 1—Value Land and Building as a Unit

Net income before depreciation	$36,000
Return on land, 6% × $300,000	18,000
Net to building	$18,000
Capitalize @ 8½%	
(6% return and 2½% recapture)	$211,765
Value of building, say	$212,000
Land	$300,000
Total	$512,000

Step No. 2—Allocate Total Value to the Three Lease Interests

Leased Fee Estate

PW of $12,000 per year at	
5½%, 42 years (Inwood factor = 16,623)	$195,156
PW of land reversion at	
$300,000, 42 years, @5½% (Inwood factor = .1055)	31,650
Total	$226,806

Sandwich Leasehold

PW of $3,000 per year marginal rent	
at 6%, 42 years (factor = 15.225)	$45,675

[4] Robert L. Free, "The Appraisal of Sandwich Leases," *The Appraisal Journal,* July, 1958, pp. 354–59.
[5] *Ibid.*

Subleasehold

PW of $21,000 per year margin of rental ($36,000 net less
$15,000 paid out) at 8½%, 42 years (factor = 11.382) $239,022

Total All Three Interests $511,503

RENT

The contract rent on a lease may be paid in a number of ways. It may be a fixed or flat amount for the entire term of the lease, such as $125.00 per month for 10 years. Such a lease can work to the disadvantage of the lessor when the market rent becomes greater than the contract rent. Or the lease may provide for rent on a graduated or step-up basis, whereby the rent is increased at scheduled periodic intervals. Or the lease may be a reappraisal one whereby the amount of the rent is based on a reappraisal of the property at specified intervals. An index lease or escalation lease ties the rent to changes in a given index, such as the Cost of Living Index. All such leases are designed to give the lessor a degree of protection for increases in costs and expenses due to inflation and the general increases in the value of the leased real estate.

Another major form of rental payment is the percentage lease whereby the rental is computed as a percentage of the sales volume of the business in the leased property. There are many variations of this kind of lease but probably the most common is the one in which a minimum rental is paid regardless of the sales volume and then a percentage is applied to the sales volume to determine the total rent. For example, the minimum rent might be $10,000 per year, with a 5 percent on sales volume of $300,000. The annual rent is $15,000. If the sales volume is $150,000 per year, the rent is $10,000. The minimum rent should be sufficient to pay carrying charges, such as taxes and insurance, and provide the lessor with a reasonable return on his investment.

There are wide variations in the percentage rate used for different types of tenants, such as department store, jewelry store, super market, and barber shop. The factors used in determining the rate are numerous but there are established ranges for given types of businesses.[6] Factors to be considered include the margin of profit of the tenant and his ability to pay; location of the property; size of the city; tenant's sales volume and costs of closing business; the competitive situation for that type of business and area; economic features of the trading area; physical

[6] See National Institute of Real Estate Brokers, *Percentage Leases*, Chicago, Illinois.

aspects of the property, such as design and flexibility of use; management, policies, and merchandise of the tenants; and lease provisions, such as maintenance, store hours, advertising, and tenant's accounting for his sales volume.

INCOME TAX FACTORS

Income tax factors are a major consideration in the drafting of leases. The wording of the lease can have a significant influence on the tax impact on the parties. Some of the major tax considerations in leases are discussed below.

Improvements by Lessor

A property may already have improvements on it, or the lessor may erect improvements as a condition of the lease. The lessor may depreciate these capital expenditure improvements over their useful life. The tenant may have a lease obligation to restore the premises to their original condition at the expiration of the lease. This obligation to restore should exclude ordinary wear and tear or the lessor may lose his depreciation deduction. The tenant may deduct expenditures for the restoration in the year paid.

Improvements by Lessee

Where a tenant makes improvements to leased property, their cost may be depreciated over their useful life or amortized over the remaining term of the lease, whichever is shorter. Accelerated methods of depreciation may be used where the estimated life of the improvements is equal to or shorter than the remaining lease term. Where the life of the improvements is longer than the remaining lease term and the improvements are amortized over the life of the lease, only the straight-line method may be used.

Effect of Lessee's Improvements on Lessor

Improvements made by the lessee are not considered as income to the lessor, either upon construction or at the termination of the lease, unless the improvements are deemed to be a substitute for rent. If the improvements are intended to be a substitute for rent, the lessor realizes income to the extent of the market value of the improvement when it is made. The lessee may then deduct the cost of the improvement as rent. For example, land is leased for nominal rent with a lease provision that the lessee construct a $20,000 building on the land. The building will be considered as an improvement in lieu of rent and is income to the lessor. Such a situation could be avoided if a reasonable rental was specified and there was no indication of intent that the improvements were to be considered as a substitute for rent.

Plan for Improvement

It may be advisable for a lessor to permit the tenant to make improvements, in exchange for a reduced rent. For example, assume the cost of the improvements is $5,000 and the rent is $25,000. If the lessor made the improvements and was able to deduct their cost—which he is not permitted to do, being forced to depreciate them—the net rent would be $20,000. An alternative is to reduce the tenant's rent to $20,000 and have him make the improvements. The net result to the tenant is the same from a tax aspect since he is giving up a portion of the deduction for rent in exchange for an amortization of the improvement costs. The lessor also gets the same net result, namely, $20,000 of income. Further, the lessor has improvements which probably increase the value of the property and which do not constitute income at the termination of the lease. The improvements are reflected in the selling price of the property when it is sold but the gain is a capital gain.

Renewal Options

A renewal option in a lease affects the deduction for depreciation or amortization of improvements made by the tenant after July 28, 1958. If the life of the lease at the date of the improvement is less than 60 percent of the useful life of the improvement, renewal periods must be taken into account in determining the period of amortization—that is, the tenant must add the term of renewal to the period of the original lease. For example, assume a building constructed by the tenant has a useful life of 35 years. The lease has a remaining term of 20 years, with a renewal option for 10 years. Sixty percent of 35 years is 21 years. The remaining 20 years of the lease is shorter than 21 years, so the building must be amortized over 30 years, that is, the remaining lease term (20 years) plus the renewal option (10 years).

The above 60 percent rule may not apply to the tenant if he can show that it is more probable that the lease will not be renewed than that it will be renewed. Such a determination is based upon the facts and circumstances of each situation.

If a lease is made between "related parties," the tenant must depreciate improvements over their useful life. There is no option to use the remaining life of the lease as a shorter period. Examples of related parties are: husband and wife, related corporations, and a fiduciary and beneficiary of the same trust.

Option to Purchase

The lease with option to purchase is simply a typical lease until exercise of the purchase option. Upon exercise of the option the arrangement is a purchase transaction. The lessor has rental income and the lessee has rental deductions. When the option is exercised, the option price is the cost basis for the purchaser (lessee) and the receipt of the option price is the seller's (lessor) proceeds of the sale.

The purchase option and the amount of the rent must not be arranged by the parties so that the Internal Revenue Service may construe the lease to be a conditional sales contract or a deferred purchase of the property rather than a lease. The tenant must not, through his rent payments, be building up an equity in the property or the lease will be considered as a sale and the rents not deductible. If the payments were disallowed as rent, the tenant would have to capitalize them as cost of the property and take deductions as depreciation, which could be a lesser amount than the payments.

Several factors may be considered in determining whether a lease is a conditional sales contract instead of a lease—that is, whether the lessee is acquiring an equity in the property. Some of the factors are as follows: (1) option price is small in relation to the market value of the property; (2) lease permits lessee to apply all or part of past rental payments to a reduction of the option price; and (3) total rental payments exceed the market value of the property.

Assignment and Subletting

If the tenant assigns his leasehold to another person the transaction is treated as a sale or exchange. The gain is capital gain if the leasehold was not used in the tenant's trade or business. If the tenant sublets for less than the full term of the leasehold, the income from the sublease is considered to be ordinary income.

Cancellation of Lease

Several different situations may occur in the cancellation of a lease, and the tax consequences differ in each case. If the lessor pays the tenant a bonus to surrender the lease, the tenant treats such payment as proceeds from the sale or exchange of a lease and any amount in excess of the cost of the lease to him may be capital gain. A loss is recognized if the tenant's basis for the lease exceeds the proceeds. The lessor deducts the bonus payment over the remaining term of the surrendered lease since the payment is considered to have been made to obtain the property for the remainder of the lease term. The payment is a capital expenditure and is part of the lessor's basis in the property. If the lease was surrendered so that the lessor could erect a new building on the property, the bonus is added to the cost of the new buildng. If the lessor cancels the lease in order to sell the property, the bonus is added to his basis in the property to determine his gain or loss.

A payment by the tenant to the lessor to cancel a lease is deductible by the tenant in the year of cancellation. The payment is reported by the lessor as ordinary income in the year of receipt.

Security Deposits

It is important to distinguish between an advance rental and a security deposit. An advance rental received by the lessor is taxable income to him in the year of receipt. The tenant does not take a deduction until the year for which the advance rentals are applicable.

A security deposit is an amount deposited with the lessor to insure the performance of the tenant's obligations under the lease. They are not taxable income to the lessor while they are held by him as security. The tenant may deduct the deposit at the same time that the lessor's obligation to hold it ends. If the security deposit is to be held as payment of the last month's rent, it is deemed to be an advance rental and the lessor must report it as income in the year of receipt. The tenant is entitled to a deduction at the same time.

Acquisition Costs

A lessor will incur expenses to procure a lease, such as legal fees and brokers' commissions. Such expenses are considered to be part of the lease cost and must be capitalized and spread or amortized over the life of the lease. When the lessor sells the property, the unamortized costs of the expenses are added to the lessor's basis of the property. The tenant also adds the unamortized costs to his basis. If a lease is not agreed upon, the expenses may be deducted by the lessor or tenant in the year incurred or paid.

Real Estate Taxes

A lessor may deduct real estate taxes in the year paid. If the lease provides that the tenant is to pay the taxes, such as under a net lease, the payment is taxable income to the lessor. The lessor may, however, deduct the payments from his income taxes as if he had made them himself.

LEASE GUARANTY INSURANCE

Lease guaranty insurance is issued to a commercial or industrial landlord and protects him against loss when tenants fail to make rental payments. The landlord is guaranteed a stable income stream from the leased premises. This guaranty also means that the mortgage lender is protected from default on mortgage payments resulting from lack of rental income to the landlord.

Eligibility

Tenants eligible for coverage include retail, service, and light manufacturing firms. Eligible properties include retail stores, shopping centers, industrial parks, light manufacturing structures, warehouses, service buildings, and office buildings. Ground leases may also be covered by lease insurance.

Benefits

Lease insurance offers benefits to landlords, tenants, and lenders. Benefits to the landlord include the following: (1) greater latitude in selection of tenants; and (2) ability to obtain more favorable mortgage financing terms or a larger loan because with the lease insurance there is less risk to the lender. Tenants benefit by having an improved credit standing which gives them a stronger competitive position to secure desirable locations and to compete with larger firms. Further, the tenant may be able to negotiate better rental terms with the landlord. Lenders benefit by having increased security for their loans.

Policy Term and Limits

The minimum policy term of an insurable lease is 5 years and the maximum is 20 years or the term of the lease, whichever is shorter. Both the insurer and the tenant may elect to guarantee less than the full term of the lease and less than the full amount of the rent due.

Premium Rates

A commitment premium or fee, such as $100 or $300, must accompany the application for insurance. A single premium for the entire policy period is paid at the time of issuance of the policy. There are no renewal premiums. The policy may not be canceled by either the tenant or land-lord. No portion of the policy premium is refundable. The dollar amount of the premium is computed by multiplying the total aggregate rental during the policy period by the appropriate percentage indicated below.

Policy Period (in years)	Premium as a Percent of Total Guaranteed Rental
5	5.4%
6	5.4
7	5.2
8	4.8
9	4.4
10	4.0
11	3.7
12	3.4
13	3.1
14	2.9
15	2.8
16	2.8
17	2.8
18	2.8
19	2.8
20	2.8

Rent Escrow Deposits

In addition to the advance payment of premium, a deposit equal to three months guaranteed rent must be placed in escrow with the insurer. If there is no default in rent payments, the escrow fund plus annual inter-est of 4 percent is returned to the lessor or tenant at the termination of the lease. The insurer may, in lieu of the escrow arrangement, elect to issue a policy with a 90-day deductible feature.

Default and Payment of Claims

If a tenant is 30 days in arrears on his rental obligations, the landlord must notify the insurance company. The landlord must use his best efforts to minimize rent losses and cure the default. He must, with the approval of the insurer, remove the tenant from the premises, restore the premises to rentable condition, and attempt to locate a new tenant. Once the landlord has fulfilled these obligations, he submits a claim for the rent loss resulting from the default. Claims are paid first from the escrow funds and then from the resources of the insurer. It should be pointed out that lease guaranty insurance does not guarantee all provisions of the lease but only rental loss.

SALE-LEASEBACK

Under the sale-leaseback arrangement of financing, an owner-user of real estate, either land or building or both, will sell the property to another party. At the same time, and as a part of the same transaction, the buyer leases the property back to the seller for a specified period of years. The arrangement is also known as a purchase-leaseback and a liquidating lease. The lease provides a rental sufficient to yield a given return on the investment and liquidate the principal over the lease term.

The buyer under the sale-leaseback is usually a financial institution, such as a life insurance company, a pension fund, or a university endowment fund. In recent years large investors and syndicates have engaged in this type of financing. Sellers are usually organizations with excellent credit and prime real estate, such as retail buildings, industrial corporations, office buildings, hotels, and motels. The arrangement, however, is flexible and need not be limited to the above high credit and prime property situations, but can be used with smaller institutions and smaller properties.

Lease terms and provisions are negotiable and, in fact, a great deal of skill and technical competence is needed in the creation of a satisfactory sale-leaseback transaction. The rent is usually based on the market value purchase price. The lease is long term—20, 40, 50, 75 years—and usually contains renewal options or a purchase option. Care must be exercised in drafting a purchase option so that a tax court does not construe the transaction to be a mortgage instead of a lease. Under the sale-leaseback the lessee deducts the entire rental from his income tax. If the transaction were a mortgage, only the interest would be deductible and not amortization. The Internal Revenue Service could rule that the sale-leaseback was simply a 100 percent loan, and many leasing companies hesitate to include a repurchase option in the lease. The lessee may, however, want a cancellation provision in case he wants to change locations. The lessor may grant a cancellation privilege for specified intervals in exchange for the agreement of the lessee to repurchase the property at the time of cancellation. The lessor may either sell the property or keep it and permit cancellation of the lease. The sale price would be set so as to result in a profit to the lessor. The price might, for example, be the amortized value of the original purchase price of the lease to the lessor plus a small premium. Such an arrangement is not a definite purchase option because the lessor has the right to decline the lessee's offer to purchase.

REVIEW AND STUDY QUESTIONS

1. Explain a leasehold mortgage and why a loan upon a leasehold has more risk to the lender than a loan upon a fee simple interest.
2. What is a ground lease and what are its benefits to: (A) the owner, and (B) the tenant?
3. Explain the concept of subordinated and unsubordinated leasehold mortgages.
4. Explain how lease interests are valuated.
5. Explain the tri-party agreement and its use.
6. List some factors or considerations given by lenders in making leasehold loans.
7. What is a sandwich lease and how is one valued?
8. What are several ways of setting rents on a lease?
9. Discuss the income tax aspects of leases with regard to the following: (A) improvements by lessor; (B) improvements by lessee; (C) renewal options; (D) option to purchase; (E) assignment and subletting; (F) cancellation of lease; (G) security deposits; (H) acquisition costs; and (I) real estate taxes.
10. Discuss lease guaranty insurance and its use.
11. Describe the sale-leaseback arrangement.

FURTHER READINGS AND REFERENCES

Beaton, William R., *Real Estate Investment,* Chapter 6, "Commercial Leasehold Financing," Englewood Cliffs, N.J.: Prentice-Hall, Inc., 1971.

Entreken, Henry T., Jr., "Case History of An Unsubordinated Leasehold," *The Real Estate Appraiser,* January-February, 1972, pp. 31-36.

Foglesong, Charles W., "The Computations of Yields on Sale Leaseback," *The Appraisal Journal,* January, 1964, pp. 39-49.

Ground Leases, Sponsor, Byron W. Trerice, Jr. Chicago, Ill.: National Institute of Real Estate Brokers, December, 1965.

Gunning, Francis P., "A Primer For Mortgageable Ground Leases," *The Mortgage Banker,* March, 1967, pp. 35-41.

McMichael, Stanley L., and Paul T. O'Keefe, *Leases-Percentage, Short and Long Term,* Fifth Ed. Englewood Cliffs, N.J.: Prentice-Hall, Inc., 1959.

O'Keefe, Raymond T., "The Why and How of Making Mortgages on Leaseholds," *The Mortgage Banker,* June, 1962, pp. 31-33.

Yeager, Philip J., "The Sandwich Lease—A Creative Selling Tool," *California Real Estate Magazine,* October, 1971, pp. 22-24. Published by the California Real Estate Association, Los Angeles, California.

EIGHT

Residential Property Valuation

The basic concepts and principles of real estate valuation are applicable to all types of real estate. The emphasis in this chapter is on their meaning, significance, and application with reference to single-family residences which are being appraised for long-term mortgage loan purposes.

The lender on real estate needs an appraisal of the value of the property which is to serve as the physical security for the loan. The value estimate is: (1) a legal requirement in most loans, such as those made by government-regulated institutional lenders; and (2) an underwriting factor in all loans. Loan-to-value amounts are based upon the appraised value of the property. Value factors such as location, neighborhood and site conditions, and condition of the site improvements directly affect the risk in the loan and therefore influence such factors as interest rate and maturity. The mortgage lender should be able to interpret and understand an appraisal report and the process behind it.

THE APPRAISER

An appraiser estimates the value of property as of a given date and under specified conditions. An appraisal is only as good as the ability of the person who makes it and his judgment in evaluating the available facts. Value is made by people in the market and the appraiser seeks to reflect in the appraisal the results of the market actions of buyers and sellers.

Staff and Independent Appraisers

Lenders utilize their own salaried staff appraisers or they may use the services of independent, self-employed appraisers who work on a fee basis. Institutional lenders, such as savings and loan associations, usually have appraisers employed full-time on their staff, who make appraisals only for their institution. The Federal Housing Administration utilizes its own appraisers and uses independent appraisers in periods when the FHA appraisal volume is too heavy for the regular staff. Mortgage bankers and mortgage brokers often utilize both staff and independent appraisers, depending upon the size of the company and the complexity of the appraisal.

Regulatory and Personal Qualifications

A real estate appraiser who accepts fee assignments must be licensed in some states, such as Florida, as a real estate broker or salesman. Staff appraisers who do assignments only for their employer need not be licensed.

Appraisers for lenders need to be familiar with the needs of lenders, investors, and government agencies as to the required documentation and type of information wanted in appraisal reports. Complete, well prepared, and fully documented appraisal reports are essential for loans which are to be sold in the secondary mortgage market.

Personal qualifications of a good appraiser include: (1) current and workable knowledge of valuation theories, concepts, principles, and techniques; (2) practical experience in the market; (3) sound, objective judgment; (4) common sense; (5) analytical ability; (6) attention to detail; (7) hard and thorough work; and (8) integrity.

Professional Organizations and Ethics

There are professional groups in the field of real estate appraising dedicated to maintaining high standards of work and ethics. Both staff and independent appraisers are eligible to apply for membership in the organizations and, if qualified, to work toward a professional designation. Two of the groups and their professional designations are as follows:

1. American Institute of Real Estate Appraisers
   MAI—Member, Appraisal Institute
   RM—Residential Member
2. Society of Real Estate Appraisers
   SREA—Senior Real Estate Analyst
   SRPA—Senior Real Property Appraiser
   SRA—Senior Residential Appraiser

ETHICS. Professional appraisal organizations have codes of ethics governing the conduct of their members. The codes are excellent guides for the professional conduct of any appraiser.

Provisions of the codes are essentially the same for each organization. Basic items covered include the following: (1) minimum contents of an appraisal report; (2) confidential nature of findings; (3) personal interest of appraiser in subject property; (4) proper and adequate opinion of value; (5) statement as to affiliation with the professional organization; (6) fees; (7) experience for an assignment; (8) acceptance of an assignment contingent upon reporting a predetermined value estimate; (9) report documentation; (10) fractional appraisals; (11) use of approaches; (12) competitive bidding for assignments; (13) relations with fellow members; (14) advertising and solicitation of assignments; (15) court testimony; and (16) discipline of members.

APPRAISAL REPORTS

The completed work of an appraiser is presented in an appraisal report. The report may be oral but is more likely to be written. The written report usually takes whatever form is desired by the client or employer of the appraiser. A one-page letter or certificate is sometimes used and simply reports the value estimate with no supporting documentation.

Lenders more commonly use: (1) a narrative, or (2) a printed form type of report. The narrative report presents a complete analysis and discussion of the steps the appraiser took in making the appraisal. Techniques used in the appraisal are explained along with the reasoning of the appraiser in each step of the appraisal process. The same appraisal process, analysis, and reasoning support a printed form appraisal report except that the report does not contain a narrative discussion of each step. The form report gives the lender and investor using it regularly a consistent classification and arrangement of data and information. Further, it is easy to use and gives the appraiser a check list of items to be considered in the appraisal. One type of form report is shown on pages 139–142.

THE APPRAISAL PROCESS

The appraisal process is an orderly and logical series of steps which the appraiser takes in arriving at an estimate of value. The steps are a commonly recognized procedure in the appraisal field. The discussion which follows is based upon the HUD Handbook 4150.1, *VALUATION ANALYSIS FOR HOME MORTGAGE INSURANCE*, April, 1973, which provides an excellent and comprehensive coverage of the subject.

Definition of the Problem

The appraiser must have a clear understanding of the exact nature of the assignment. Five steps are involved in this definition: (1) identify the property to be appraised, both by its physical location and by its legal description; (2) specify the property rights and interests to be appraised; (3) state the purpose of the appraisal, namely, the type of value to be estimated and the function it is to serve; (4) give the date of the value estimate; and (5) give the definition of the value to be estimated.

Data Program

The appraiser must make a preliminary survey of his assignment to estimate the nature and scope of the work required to complete it. The appraisal must be planned and scheduled and data collected in an orderly

[1] This example was prepared by Financial Federal Savings and Loan Association, Miami Beach, Florida. Acknowledgement and appreciation is extended to the association, and to Dennis Kleinman, William B. Smith, and Dennis G. Wilson.

RESIDENTIAL APPRAISAL REPORT [1]

ADDRESS ___94XX S. W. 57 TERRACE, MIAMI, FLORIDA___

LEGAL ___LOT 10, BLOCK 8, DARLINGTON MANOR___

PLAT BOOK ___35___ PAGE ___4___ TOWNSHIP ___54___ RANGE ___40___ SEC. ___28___

OCCUPANT ___BELL___ PURCHASER ___NEWHOUSE___ PROPERTY RIGHTS APPRAISED ___FEE SIMPLE___

					Good	Av	Fair	Poor
Location	☐ Urban	☒ Suburban	☐ Rural	Adequacy of shopping	☒	☐	☐	☐
Built Up	☒ Over 75%	☐ 25% to 75%	☐ Under 25%	Convenience to Schools	☒	☐	☐	☐
Growth Rate ☒ Fully Dev.	☐ Rapid	☐ Steady	☐ Slow	Quality of Schools	☐	☒	☐	☐
Property Values	☒ Increasing	☐ Stable ☐ Weak	☐ Declining	Recreational Facilities	☐	☒	☐	☐
Demand/Supply	☐ In Balance	☒ Shortage	☐ Over Supply	Level of Taxes	☐	☒	☐	☐
Marketing Time	☒ Under 3 Mos.	☐ 4–6 Mos.	☐ Over 6 Mos.	Adequacy of Utilities	☐	☒	☐	☐
Present Use 95 % 1 Family ___% 2-4 Family ___% Apts. 5 %Condo.				Neighborhood Compatibility	☒	☐	☐	☐
Change in Use ☒ Not Likely	☐ Likely	☐ Taking Place		Protection from Adverse Influence	☒	☐	☐	☐
Predominant Occupancy ☒ Owner	☐ Tenant	☐ %Vacant		Police and Fire Protection	☐	☒	☐	☐
Price Range $35,000 to $ 50,000 Predominant Value $40,000				General Appearance of Properties	☒	☐	☐	☐
Age 15 yrs to New yrs Predominant Age 10 yrs				Appeal to Market	☒	☐	☐	☐

Condominium ☐ Rec. Facilities ☐ Rec. Lease ☐ Management Agreement ☐ Full Ownership ☐

Comments: DESIRABLE RESIDENTIAL LOCATION NEAR MAJOR EXPRESSWAY ENTRANCE AND LARGE REGIONAL SHOPPING CENTER.

Dimensions ___ x 87 x 100 x ___ = 8700 Sq. Ft. ☐ Corner ☐ Water Front

Zoning RU 1 ___ Highest and Best Use: ☒ Present Use ☐ Other ___

	Public	Comm.	Individual	Street ☒ Public ☐ Private		Good	Av	Fair	Poor
				Surface ASPHALT	Topography	☐	☒	☐	☐
Elec.	☒	☐	☐	☒ Storm Sewer	Size & Shape of Lot	☒	☐	☐	☐
Gas	☐	☐	☒	☒ Curb and Gutter	Drainage	☐	☒	☐	☐
Water	☒	☐	☐	☒ Sidewalk	View Amenity None				
Sanitary Sewer	☐	☐	Septic Tank ☒	☐ Street Lights	Easements See Survey				
			Cess Pool ☐	☐ Alley	Encroachments None				

☐ Underground Utilities

☐ Fences (type) ___

☒ Driveway (surface) ASPHALT

Flood Conditions Good

Adverse Influences None

Comments: Placement of home on lot good. Lot coverage not excessive.

PHOTOGRAPH	Lot Location Sketch including the plotting of the location of any adverse influences:

GOLF COURSE

Hidden Valley Townhouses

N

--SW 94 Ave.

☒--Subject

S.W. 57 Terrace

▨(shopping)

Miller Dr.(S.W. 56 St.)

VALUATION LAND $___ BUILDINGS $___ TOTAL $___

Recommended for Maximum Mortgage ___ % Maximum Term___ years

Amount of Loan ___ Term ___ Interest Rate ___

Association Service Charge ___

Required Items: Waivers of Lein ___ Sales Contract ___ Credit Report ___

Roof Inspection ___ Termite Inspection ___ Other ___

ADDRESS: 94XX S. W. 57 TERRACE, MIAMI, FLORIDA

139

	☒ Existing (approx. yr. blt.) 19_58_	☒ Detached	Dwelling Units _1_	Design Rambler, Split Level, etc.)	Exterior Walls
	☐ Proposed Construction	☐ Semi-detached	Stories _____1	**RAMBLER**	**CONCRETE BLOCK**
	☐ Under Construction	☐ Row			

Roof (Type)	Gutters	Windows (Type)	☐ Screens	Insulation
TAR & GRAVEL	NONE	AWNING		☐ Ceiling ☒ Roof ☐ Walls

Foundation (Type)
REINFORCED CONCRETE   ☐ Crawl Space   ☒ Slab on Grade

	Basement Level	First Level	Second Level	Third Level			
					Floors: ☐ Hardwood ☒ Carpet Over _____ ☒ Terr. ☐ Sm Conc		
Entry	☐	☒	☐	☐	Walls: ☒ Drywall ☐ Plaster ☐ _____		
Living Room	☐	☒	☐	☐	Trim & Finish ☐ Good ☒ Average ☐ Fair ☐ Poor		
Dining Room ...	☐	☐	☐	☐	Bath Floor: ☒ Ceramic ☐ Composition ☐ _____		
Dining Alcove ..	☐	☒	☐	☐	Bath Wainscote ☒ Ceramic ☐ _____		
Kitchen	☐	☒	☐	☐	Special Features: None Fireplaces (List Other)_____		
No. of Bedrooms	—	3	—	—			
Family Room ...	☐	☒	☐	☐	Car Storage, Garage _____ Yes _____ Carport _____ No		
_____	☐	☐	☐	☐			
_____	☐	☐	☐	☐	# Cars _1_ Adequate _Yes_ Condition _Average_		
Full Bath(s)	—	2	—	—	Porches _Yes (1)_ Screened _Yes_ Enclosed _No_		
¾ Bath (s)	—	—	—	—	Pool _15 x 30_ Condition _Good_		
Half Bath(s)	—	—	—	—			

Kitchen			Good	Av	Fair	Poor
☒ Range/Oven	Heat: Type Central Forced Air	Quality of Construction (Materials & Finish)	☐	☒	☐	☐
☐ Dishwasher	Fuel: ☐ Gas ☐ Elec ☒ Oil ☐ Coal	Condition of Improvements	☒	☐	☐	☐
☒ Fan/Hood	A.C.: ☐ Central ☒ Other Wall Units	Rooms size and layout	☐	☒	☐	☐
☐ Disposal	☒ Adequate ☐ Inadequate	Closets and Storage	☐	☒	☐	☐
☒ Refrigerator	☒ Washer ☒ Dryer	Plumbing — adequacy and condition	☐	☒	☐	☐
☐ Trash Masher	Other Equipment (List) None	Electrical — adequacy and condition	☐	☒	☐	☐
☒ Dbl.Sink	_____	Compatibility to Neighborhood	☒	☐	☐	☐
Cabinets	_____	Overall Livability	☒	☐	☐	☐
☒ Adequate	_____	Appeal and Marketability	☒	☐	☐	☐
☐ Inadequate		Effective Age _5_ Yrs. Estimated Remaining Economic Life _45_ Yrs.				

COMMENTS (Special features, functional or physical inadequacies, repairs needed, modernization, etc.)
Double Sink, Kitchen Bar, Sliding Glass Door, 2 Vanities, 1 Shower Enclosure, Window Shutters
Clean or do minor roof repair, little other deferred maintenance.

BUILDING SKETCH

BASIC LIVING AREA RATE **3/2 Base**	$14.60	
FOUNDATION **Reinforced Concrete**	-	
WALLS **Concrete Block & Stucco**	-	
FLOOR **Terrazzo**	-	
ROOF **Tar & Gravel**	-	
SASH **Awning**	-	
FOOTAGE ADJUSTMENT	-1.00	
PERIMETER ADJUSTMENT	+ .20	
CUSTOM OR PROJECT	-	
QUALITY	-	
AREA ADJUSTMENT	-	
EXTRAS: **Double Sink, Kitchen Bar, Sliding Glass Door, Vanities, Shower Enclosure, Window Shutters**	+ .40	
ADJUSTED COST PER SQ. FT.	$14.20	

Square Footage Computation:

26.3 X 1.7 = 44.7 S.F.
56.5 X 25 = 1412.5 S.F.
1457.0 Square Feet

Footage Adjustment: Base House 1120 S.F.@ $14.60=
$16,352

1457 S.F.
-1120 S.F.
337 S.F.
X$8.50
$ 2865 Total Cost of Square Footage Excess over Base

$16,352
+ 2,865
$19,217

$19,217 ÷ 1457 S.F. = $13.18
$14.20 - 13.18 = $1.02 (Round down to$1

	SQ. FOOTAGE	SQ. FT. COST	UNIT COST
LIVING AREA TOTAL	1457	$14.20	$20,689
CARPORT			
GARAGE **21.5 x 15.2**	327	7.00	2,289
UTILITY **In Garage**			
ROOFED AREA **Entry 5 X 8.7**	44	4.40	194
Overhang & Porch 47 x 5.5	257	4.40	1,131
BASIC COST			$24,303
PROFIT AND OVERHEAD		15%	3,645
BASIC IMPROVEMENT COST ESTIMATE			$27,900
ACCRUED DEPRECIATION:			

PHYSICAL INCURABLE _____ % Per Year **10** % $2800

PHYSICAL CURABLE: List Repairs and cost to cure.
Clean Roof. Other minor deferred maintenance.

_____   400

FUNCTIONAL INCURABLE: Describe items & estimate loss in value.

FUNCTIONAL CURABLE: Describe items & estimate net cost to cure.

ECONOMIC: Describe cause.

TOTAL ACCRUED DEPRECIATION:	$3,200
DEPRECIATED IMPROVEMENT COST ESTIMATE	$24,700

IN PLACE VALUE OF EXTRAS: Consider after depreciation based on fucntion, age and condition.
Describe and estimate:

POOL, EQUIP., & DECK AREA **15 x 30 Pool**	$4000
PATIO **Around Pool**	500
SCREEN ENCLOSURE **47 x 21.3 = 1001 @ $1.00**	1000
KITCHEN EQUIPMENT **Range & Oven, Hood & Fan (Nominal Utility)**	0
AIR CONDITIONING **2 Wall Mounted Air Conditioners**	300
HEATING **Central Forced air**	300
OTHER	
LANDSCAPING & DRIVES	500
TOTAL DEPRECIATED VALUE OF EXTRAS:	$ 6,600
IMPROVEMENT VALUE ESTIMATE	$31,300
LAND VALUE AND JUSTIFICATION	8,700

LOCATION AND COMMENTS ON COMPARABLE LAND VALUES
Comparable lots in comparable areas have been selling for approximately $100 a front foot, say - $8,700 .

REPLACEMENT VALUE ESTIMATE	$40,000

Time Adjustment 1% per month. Footage Adjustment $10 per Square Foot.

Address	Subject 97xx SW 57 Ter	93xx SW 57 Terr.		59xx SW 94 Court		59xx SW 95 Court		59xx SW 96 Ave.		95xx SW 56 Terr.	
Proximity to Subj.		#1		#2		#3		#4		#5	
	DESCRIPTION	DESCRIPTION	+(-)$ Adjustment	DESCRIPTION	+(-)$ Adjustment	DESCRIPTION	+(-)$ Adjustment	DESCRIPTION	+(-)$ Adjustment	DESCRIPTION	+(-)$ Adjustment
Sale date (Time adj.)	1/74	9/73	+1400	9/73	+1400	12/73	+400	11/73	+1000	1/74	0
Site and Location	87 x 100	75 x 105	+1000	75 x 106	+1000	75 x 100	+1000	75 x 105	+1000	76 x 100	+1000
Design and Construction	CBS	CBS	C	CBS	C	CBS	C	CBS	C	CBS	C
Age and Condition	1958 Average	1960 Poorer Cond.	+1000	1960 Better Cond.	-500	1969 Newer & Better	-2000	1971 Newer & Better	-4000	1969 Newer & Better	-2000
Room Count Total / B-rms / Baths	6 / 3 / 2	6 / 4 / 2	-500	6 / 3 / 2	C	7 / 4 / 2	-500	6 / 3 / 2	CC	6 / 3 / 2	C
Livable Area (1) Sq. Ft.	1457	1415	C	1512	-500	1972	-5500	1500	C	1471	C
Functional Util.	Good	Good		Good		Good		Good		Good	
Basement & Bsmt finished rooms	None	None		None		None		None		None	
Garage/Car Port	1 Car Gar.	1 Carporte	+1000	1 Car Gar.	C	None	+2000	1 Car Gar.	C	1 Car Gar	C
Porches, Patio Pool, etc.	Screened Pool and Patio	Screened Pool and Patio	C	Screened Patio Only	+4000	Screened Patio Only	+4000	Screened Pool & Patio (Better)	-1000	None	+5500
Air Conditioning	2 Wall Units	Units	C	Central	-500	Central	-500	Central	-500	Units	C
Landscape	Average	Average		Average		Average		Average		Average	
Financing	Conventional	Conventional		Conventional		Circular Drive -500 Conventional		Chain-Link Fnc. -500 Conventional		Conventional	
List or Sales Price	$40,000	$36,000		$35,000		$41,900		$45,000		$36,000	
Net Adj. + (-)		+ 3,900		+4,900		-1,600		-4,000		+4,500	
Indicated Value of Subject		$39,900		$39,900		$40,300		$41,000		$40,500	

Cost Approach $40,000

Market Approach $40,000

Income Approach Not Applicable

CORRELATION OF ESTIMATES: Cost approach shows replacement cost of $40,000.
Market range: $39,500 to $41,000. Most probable selling price
between $39,500 to $40,500: Say - $40,000.

CONDITIONS OF APPRAISAL: No Non-realty items included in this estimate of market value.

(If Applicable). Fair Market Rent $_____ /MO. x Gross Rent Multiplier _____ = $_____.

Multiple Correlation Analysis:
Valuation suggested by use of multiple correlation analysis with a span of 2-8 denoting a
95% market sale occurrence is $38,500 to $ 42,750.

REMARKS: Conforming Single Family Residences in Attractive Quiet Neighborhood.

Date January 16, 1974

Appraiser _____

Appraiser _____

MARKET VALUE $ 40,000

PURPOSE OF APPRAISAL: To estimate Market Value.
DEFINITION OF MARKET VALUE: The highest price which the property will bring contemplating the consummation of a sale and the passing of full title from seller to buyer by deed, under conditions whereby: buyer and seller are free of undue stimulus and are motivated by no more then the reactions of typical participants, both parties are well informed or well-advised and act prudently each for what he considers his own best interest; a reasonable exposure is given in the open market; and payment is made in cash or on terms reasonably equivalent to cash assuming typical financing terms available in the community for similar property.

I certify, that to the best of my knowledge and belief, the statements made in this report are true and I have not knowingly withheld any significant information that I have personally inspected subject property, both inside and out; that I have no interest, present or contemplated, in subject property or the participants in the sale, that neither the employment nor compensation to make said appraisal is contingent upon my value estimate; and, that all contingent and limiting conditions are stated herein (*). Title is assumed to be good and marketable.

manner. The data is of two types: general and specific. General data is information about the surroundings of the subject property, namely, its location within a region, a city, and a neighborhood. Information and analysis is concerned with elements outside of the property which affect its value. Specific data is information about the property itself, namely, the title, the improvements, and the site.

Location Analysis

Location analysis for single-family residential property is concerned with the stability and quality of the neighborhood of the subject property. The appraiser must identify factors which affect the marketability of the site. He must appraise the present influence of these factors on value as well as their potential future influence. An understanding of trends and the principle of change is essential to location analysis. Value is created, maintained, and modified by changing social, economic, and governmental forces.

Location analysis requires that each location element of the subject site be compared with the same element in competitive locations of similar accommodation and price range. A location should be related to the needs of its occupants and to available alternatives in other competitive locations. Location elements considered include: (1) present and future land use patterns; (2) physical and social attractiveness, such as hazards and nuisances; natural physical features and condition, style, and conformity of neighborhood structures; (3) quality and accessibility of churches, recreation areas, shopping centers, and other such facilities; (4) adequate transportation facilities to places of employment, shopping areas, social and civic centers, and adjacent neighborhoods; (5) adequate utilities and neighborhood services, such as fire and police protection, electric, gas, telephone, garbage disposal, sewage disposal, and the like; and (6) the relative effect of the tax burden and special assessments upon the desirability of the location.

Property Analysis

Property analysis involves an analysis of the site and its physical improvements. Analysis of the site is made to determine the extent to which the site is suitable for the existing or proposed improvements. Further, value elements of the site must be identified for use in estimating its market value. The physical improvements are analyzed to determine their utility and desirability as factors in making a final estimate of value and in evaluating the mortgage risk.

SITE. Site analysis requires the gathering of specific data about the subject site. Such data includes the legal description and information concerning zoning, taxes, easements, restrictions, and encroachments. Further, analysis must be made of the highest and best use of the site; topography; soil and subsoil condition; access; relation to land pattern; availability of adequate water and sewage disposal facilities; and off-site improvements adjoining the subject property, such as curbs, sidewalks, driveways, and street surface. Such improvements as the latter, while not within the legal boundaries of the site, enhance the use and livability of the property and its market acceptance. The subject property is compared with the immediate neighborhood to determine the primary off-site improvements demanded by the market.

IMPROVEMENTS. The appraiser must make a careful inspection of the physical improvements and evaluate the condition and functional adequacy of all property components, including mechanical equipment. Existing improvements are inspected to determine whether repairs, alterations, or additions are needed.

A property should have good design which blends its structural, functional, and decorative elements into a whole. Property components should be in harmony and the property as a whole should be in harmony with its site and surroundings. Good design is recognized and desired by the market and is reflected in the economic life of properties and neighborhoods and prices paid for them.

In addition to harmony of design, other property-neighborhood relationships and their effect on marketability need to be analyzed. The type of structure should conform to others in the neighborhood (i.e., single-family houses should not be located in areas where highest and best use is for multi-family structures).

The functional characteristics of a residential dwelling, that is, its living facilities, should conform to typical standards for the neighborhood. Placement of the house upon the site should conform with the accepted or customary placement in the neighborhood. The size and shape of the site and its topography should be typical for the area. The number, arrangement, and size of rooms in the dwelling should conform to preferences in the neighborhood, such as a preference for four large bedrooms and three baths. A dwelling with three small bedrooms and two baths could have limited marketability in such an area.

Cost Approach

The steps in the cost approach are: (1) estimate the value of the site; (2) estimate the reproduction cost, new, of the improvements at the date of the appraisal; (3) estimate the past or accrued depreciation of the improvements; and (4) correlate these estimates into an indication of value. The value of the land is added to the depreciated reproduction cost of the improvements. The estimate of reproduction cost includes all items of expense which a typical prospective owner would incur in acquiring a property and duplicating its improvements upon an equivalent site.

SITE VALUATION. The appraiser must estimate the market value of a comparable site. The market comparison method should be used whenever possible, and will carry the greatest weight when sufficient market sales data is available. If data for market comparison is inadequate or inconclusive, land value may be estimated by other techniques.

The market comparison or market data method involves gathering, comparing, weighing, and relating sales data to the subject site. Prices presently being paid in the market for sites offering similar utility and amenities provide a reliable basis for a value conclusion. Consideration is given to all factors, both favorable and unfavorable, recognized by the typical informed purchaser in the market.

IMPROVEMENTS. An estimate is made of the direct and indirect current costs of reproducing the dwelling, new. Costs estimation methods include the quantity survey method, unit-in-place method, and the square foot and cubic foot method. Once the costs factors are estimated, accrued depreciation on the improvements must be deducted to arrive at the depreciated value of the improvements.

The actual depreciation existing in a dwelling at a given date is known as accrued or past depreciation. It is loss in value which has already occurred up to the date of the appraisal. The amount of accrued depreciation in a property at a given time is the difference between the replacement cost, new, of the improvements at the date of the appraisal and the market value of the improvements as of that date. It is a deduction from the cost of reproducing, new, at the date of the appraisal.

Accrued depreciation comes from three sources: (1) physical deterioration; (2) functional obsolescence; and (3) economic or environmental obsolescence. Physical deterioration is the result of normal wear and tear and action of the elements. Functional obsolescence is the result of the dwelling being inadequate or superadequate to serve its expected functions, such as an obsolete heating system or a poor floor plan. Economic obsolescence is loss in value due to forces outside of the property which adversely affect it and lessen market demand for the property.

COMPUTATION. Once the site value and depreciated reproduction cost of the improvements have been estimated, the two amounts are added together. The value indication by the cost approach may be presented as in the below format.

Reproduction cost, new, of building, including direct and indirect costs.
Less: Depreciation
    Physical deterioration
    Functional obsolescence
    Economic obsolescence
Depreciated reproduction cost of improvements
Plus: Land value
    Estimated value by the cost approach

Market Approach

The market or sales comparison approach involves the comparing of market data with the subject property. Significant facts about the sales, listings, and offers on comparable properties are gathered and the data is used to obtain an indication of the value of the subject property.

The market approach, if data is available, is the most reliable method of estimating value because it is based on actions of sellers and buyers in the market. Also, underlying the approach is the principle of substitution which states that a person will not pay more for a property than it will cost to acquire an equally desirable substitute property. The appraiser thoroughly explores the market, much as a prospective well-informed purchaser would do, to determine the price at which comparable properties are being offered and sold. Data is considered from competing similar neighborhoods as well as from the neighborhood of the subject property.

Elements of comparison between properties are: (1) time, (2) location, and (3) physical characteristics. Exact duplicate properties are not usually available so the comparable properties must be reduced to a common basis with the subject property. The process is accomplished by adjusting for the points of differences between the comparable sales and the subject property. Comparable properties should provide equal accommodations, amenities, and livability, such as approximately the same number of square feet, the same total number of rooms, be equally desirable to the same group of occupants, and be within a price range acceptable to typical purchasers. There should also be a sufficient number of transactions used for comparison to establish the present market attitude toward the subject property firmly.

The adjustment process is a detailed comparison of the subject property with the comparables. Lump sum allowances, expressed either as a dollar amount or as a percentage, are made for plus or minus features. The greater the degree of comparability and the fewer the adjustments needed, the more reliable is the approach. An example of the comparison adjustment process is given below. Assume four recent sales of properties reasonably comparable to the subject property.

1. Comparable No. 4 and the subject property are almost identical. The comparable sold for $21,500 which indicates a market value of $21,500 for the subject property.
2. Comparable No. 1 is an exact duplicate of the subject property. It was constructed by the same builder at about the same time as the subject property. The location, however, is less desirable than that of the subject because of its proximity to a busy highway. Comparable No. 1 sold for $21,000. Current market data indicates that properties of this type, in the less desirable locations, sell for $500 less. The indicated market value of the subject property, therefore, would be $21,500, which reflects the better location.
3. Comparable No. 3 has the same location desirability and the same improvements as the subject property but the improvements are in poor condition. It is estimated that the cost of repairs will be $350 to bring the improvements up to the same condition as the subject property. Comparable No. 3 sold for $21,000 which indicates a market value of $21,350 for the subject property.
4. Comparable No. 2 has the same improvements and an equally desirable location. The only difference is that the comparable has a fireplace. The fireplace customarily increases the sales price of properties in the subject neighborhood by $600. Comparable No. 2 sold for $22,200 which indicates the market value of $21,600 for the subject property.

The range of the four adjusted comparable sales is: $21,350 to $21,600. The market value of the subject property is most likely to be $21,500 because comparable No. 1, which is almost identical, sold for that amount.

Income Approach

The valuation of real estate by the income approach is based upon the principle that value is derived from future income from the property. Value is deemed to be the present worth of future benefits.

Gross income from residential property is converted into a value estimate by the use of a monthly gross rental multiplier. The gross rents of comparable properties that have been sold are divided into their respective sales prices and the result is a conversion factor or multiplier. The multiplier is then applied to the rent of the subject property to arrive at an estimate of value by the income approach. Such a capitalization procedure translates future returns from the property into their present worth. The method measures the quantity, quality, and duration of the amenity returns from the property to a typical owner-occupant. The benefits or returns from single-family residential property are primarily in the form of amenities, that is, enjoyment and satisfaction arising from use and occupancy.

A rent multiplier to express the relationship between the monthly rental income and the capitalized value of the property must be carefully derived with accuracy and with pertinent data. The gross rental estimate for both the subject property and for comparables must be justified and supportable. Estimates must not be casual opinions but the results of thorough comparison and investigation of comparables. A small error can have a large impact on capitalized income. A difference of $10.00 in the estimate of monthly rental, for example, will result in a difference of $1100.00 in the final estimate of capitalized value when the rent multiplier is 110. Further, the arbitrary use of a single rent multiplier for all properties in a given area will not give a reliable estimate of value. Rent multipliers vary with areas, properties, economic life, and rental ranges of typical buyers.

Correlation and Final Value Estimate

The value estimates arrived at in the three approaches must be correlated together into a single final estimate of value. The process of correlation runs throughout the appraisal process, starting with the purpose of the appraisal, as each interrelated step is analyzed and coordinated to produce a logical, unified, and convincing conclusion.

Correlation requires the appraiser to make a thorough review of all data and findings. He must determine whether all significant data has been considered and whether proper weight has been given to pertinent factors. Arithmetic should be checked for errors. Land values and building costs are reexamined. Depreciation estimates are checked for reasonableness. Market data is checked and evaluated as to comparability and accuracy of adjustments. Income and expense statements are examined for adequacy and accuracy. Capitalization rates and income multipliers are reviewed. A range of upper and lower indicated value estimates is determined and a critical view is made of all data and approaches to bring the range closer together. A final value estimate will be determined from within the range. The appraiser presents his final value estimate in an appraisal report which should be neat, accurate, readable, understandable, and present the data and conclusions in a clear and logical manner.

MULTIPLE REGRESSION ANALYSIS [2]

In recent years, the appraisal profession has indicated the desire for a more objective method of valuation. To satisfy this desire, inferential statistics has been introduced. The basic market approach as it is practiced currently is a problem in inferential statistics. The appraiser draws a sample of observations from the market and utilizes the sample to infer a value to the subject property.

Multiple Regression Analysis (MRA) as an appraisal tool is not a new concept by any means. However, until the widespread use of computer technology MRA was not a particularly useful tool because of the mathematics involved in its solution.

The process the appraiser must utilize in the market approach is transferred from the selection and analysis of comparable sales to an examination of those factors which seem to influence value. An additional refinement would be the use of stepwise MRA in which the factors are entered (mathematically) as to their importance in explaining value. The subjective dollar determination of comparable sales adjustments vis-à-vis the subject property is completely eliminated and gives the appraiser more latitude in his observation of how various markets seem to be operating. Further, the MRA process indicates how accurate and valid the results are for any particular area.

Since the conceptual framework is most important, no mathematical formulation will be examined.[3] The outcome of the process is in equation form, and allows the appraiser to assign specific value increments to particular factors influencing value (square footage, lot size, income, etc.). It is necessary only for the user to maintain an adequate data base of sales to draw from and the values of the attributes which are deemed to explain the selling prices. The value of any property is calculated by substituting that property's attributes into the appropriate equation.

The value estimates generated using MRA fit the statement of most probable selling price more explicitly, which the appraisal societies are starting to recognize. Rather than a one figure fair market value with

[2] This section was prepared by Professor Terry Robertson of Florida International University.
[3] See Gene Dilmore, *The New Approach to Real Estate Appraising* (Englewood Cliffs, N.J.: Prentice-Hall, Inc., 1971), Chapters 14–16.

an implied probability, MRA output provides a most probable price, expected range, and an associated probability for that range.

The size of an appraisal unit bears a direct relationship to the applicability of MRA within a specific organization. Those units having direct access to large amounts of sales will be more likely to implement this process. Institutions such as savings and loans, tax assessors, and mortgage bankers both have access to the data and need the capability to produce rapid, accurate appraisals.

REVIEW AND STUDY QUESTIONS

1. Discuss the real estate appraiser from the viewpoint of: (A) staff and independent appraisers; (B) regulatory and personal qualifications; (C) professional organizations; and (D) ethics.
2. What are the steps in the "appraisal process"?
3. What steps are included in the "definition of the problem"?
4. What types of data are collected by the appraiser?
5. What elements are considered in the location analysis?
6. What elements are considered in the property analysis?
7. Explain the cost approach.
8. Explain the market approach.
9. Explain the income approach.
10. Explain correlation.

FURTHER READINGS AND REFERENCES

American Institute of Real Estate Appraisers, *The Appraisal of Real Estate,* Sixth Ed. Chicago, Ill.: American Institute of Real Estate Appraisers, 1973.

Babcock, Frederick M., "The Three Approaches," *The Real Estate Appraiser,* July-August, 1970, pp. 5-9.

Friedman, Edith J. (ed.), *Encyclopedia of Real Estate Appraising,* Revised and Enlarged. Englewood Cliffs, N.J.: Prentice-Hall, Inc., 1968.

Holley, Robert S., "A New Look at the Market Approach to Value," *The Real Estate Appraiser,* May-June, 1969, pp. 5-7.

Knowles, Jerome, Jr., *Single-Family Residential Appraisal Manual.* Chicago, Ill.: American Institute of Real Estate Appraisers, 1967.

O'Flaherty, John D., "An Appraiser's Dilemma: The Cost Approach to Value," *The Real Estate Appraiser,* January-February, 1969, pp. 5-15.

Smith, Walstein, Jr., "Market Value: A Rule of Reasoning," *The Real Estate Appraiser,* March, 1968, pp. 40-41.

U. S. Department of Housing and Urban Development, *Valuation Analysis for Home Mortgage Insurance,* HUD Handbook 4150.1. Washington, D.C.: U. S. Department of Housing and Urban Development, April, 1973.

NINE

Income
Property Valuation

Income producing property includes such improvements as stores, shopping centers, apartments, office buildings, warehouses, and industrial buildings. The value of such properties tends to be set by their ability to produce an income stream. The income or economic approach to valuation is based on the premise that the value of income property is the present worth of future benefits, namely, the income stream.

The steps in the income approach follow a logical sequence. The appraiser must: (1) estimate the future potential gross income from the property; (2) make an allowance for vacancy and collection losses, leaving an effective gross income; (3) deduct expenses of operating the property from the effective gross income, leaving a net operating income figure, or a net before depreciation or capital recovery; (4) select a proper capitalization rate; and (5) select a capitalization technique for processing the income stream into a value estimate.

GROSS INCOME ESTIMATE

Gross income or potential gross income is the total income to be realized from a property from all sources during a given period of time. Such income includes rent, concession income, and any services rendered in the property from which income is derived. The appraiser is concerned with economic or market rent, that is, what the space would command in the market at the date of the appraisal. This figure may be different from the contract rent or actual income that the property is currently producing.

The estimate of potential gross income is based on 100 percent occupancy or full utilization of the property. A building is not often fully occupied during its useful life so the appraiser must deduct an allowance for vacancy and collection losses. The percentage figure used will vary with such local factors as the neighborhood, market, and type of property. There is no standard vacancy allowance applicable to all buildings.

Three elements of gross income must be considered in its analysis: (1) quantity; (2) quality; and (3) duration or durability. Quantity refers to the dollar amount of rent collected or earned in a given period of time. This figure is the appraiser's estimated potential gross rent. The estimate should be made carefully and accurately since a small difference in the potential gross income estimate will produce a large difference in the final value estimate.

Quality of the income stream refers to the degree of risk or certainty in collecting it, considering the source of the income. Quality depends upon the financial ability of the tenant—his credit standing—the competitive quality of the building and neighborhood, economic and market trends, and the type and term of any leases on the building. Quality of income is reflected in the capitalization rate. For example, if the source of the income is a rented building in a declining area, the income quality is poor and the risk will be reflected in a higher capitalization rate.

Duration refers to the period of time over which the income stream is expected to continue. Where leases are involved, an analysis of the lease and its term will give an indication of the duration of the income. Duration is also influenced by economic and market trends in the area of the property and the remaining economic life of the improvements. Duration of income, like quality, is reflected in the capitalization rate and has no direct effect on the appraiser's initial estimate of income.

A projected rental schedule should be established on a market comparative basis. The subject property is rated in relation to similar properties in similar neighborhoods where accurate rent data is available, that is, comparable rents in competitive buildings are used. Rental figures provided by an owner may have to be adjusted to reflect potential income under typical and prudent management.

OPERATING EXPENSE ESTIMATE

The third step in the income approach is to estimate the operating expenses of the property for the period of time over which income is to be received. Expenses are not necessarily the same each year. The appraiser needs expense statements covering the property for several years in order to make a reasonable projection of probable future expenses. Further, the expense statements provided by the owner will most likely need to be reconstructed for appraisal use. The statements are usually prepared by accountants and include items that are not real estate operating expenses, such as mortgage charges and income tax payments. The owner's statement also may not reflect proper management fees or reserves for replacements. Adjustments are necessary over the remaining economic life of the property so that the expense estimates reflect operation under typical and prudent management. Operating experiences of similar properties will aid the appraiser in determining whether expenses of the subject property are reasonable.

Operating expenses are usually classified under at least three headings or categories: fixed expenses, operating expenses, and reserves for replacements. Fixed expenses are annually recurring costs and vary little from year to year. They include such items as real estate taxes and hazard insurance. Operating expenses are the actual costs necessary to operate the building and provide services to the tenants. They include such items as utilities, supplies, payroll, maintenance, repairs, management, painting and decorating, administration, and janitorial service. Reserves for replacements refers to the annual prorated amount needed to replace items with a short life, such as refrigerators and furniture, and building parts, such as the roof and elevators.

The first three steps in the income approach involve, in summary, an estimate of the potential gross income with a deduction for estimated vacancy and collection losses, resulting in an effective gross income figure. Operating expenses are deducted from effective gross income, resulting in a net operating income figure. The next step in the income approach is the selection of an appropriate rate of capitalization necessary to attract prudent capital to the income flow.

CAPITALIZATION—SELECTION OF A RATE

Capitalization is a process of converting an income stream into a capital value figure. The process takes the form of discounting the future income by means of a rate. The present worth of the income stream is computed by dividing the income by the appropriate rate. There are four capitalization methods: direct, straight line, sinking fund, and annuity. Before discussing the four methods, however, it is necessary to understand several types of rates.

1. The "discount rate," or interest rate, is the rate of return earned "on" an investment. It is the rate necessary to attract capital to an investment. It does not include any provision for capital recovery or expiration of the income stream. It varies with market forces and with the quality of the investment. The discount rate must include amounts to compensate the investor for: (1) the time element of waiting to receive his money; (2) the relative nonliquidity of the investment; (3) the management of the investment, such as accounting and making mortgage payments; and (4) the risk of loss of the capital investment due, for example, to changes in economic conditions which adversely affect the investment. Several ways of estimating the discount or interest rate will be discussed below.

2. The "capital recovery" rate, or capital recapture rate, is the period of time over which the investor expects to recover or recapture his investment. It is applied only to improvements having a definite and limited economic life. For example, a building with a remaining economic life of 25 years would need an annual capital recovery of 4 percent (100% ÷ 25 years). In mortgage lending, the capital recovery rate of the lender is known as the "amortization rate," which is the rate at which the loan principal is repaid over the term of the loan.

3. The "capitalization rate" is the sum of the discount or interest rate and the capital recovery date. It is used with any income stream having a definite and limited term, such as from building improvements, during which period of time the investor expects to receive a return "of" his capital.

4. An "overall rate" expresses the relationship between the net income and the total value of the property. It includes a

weighted average of the discount or interest rate of the land and the capitalization rate, which includes interest and capital recovery on the improvements. The overall rate is computed by dividing the net operating income by the sales price of the property (NOI ÷ SP). The rate does not compute a direct and separate figure for capital recovery.

Computation of Discount Rate

Capitalization requires the selection of a discount or interest rate to which a rate of capital recovery may be added. There are several methods of computing the discount rate, depending on the availability of data: (1) band of investment; (2) market comparison; and (3) built up.

BAND OF INVESTMENT. The band of investment method of selecting a discount rate is a synthesis of mortgage and equity rates derived from the market for comparable properties. The rate developed is a weighted average which represents the percentage of value of the investment composed of the mortgage and the percentage composed of the equity portion of the investment. For example, assume that the financial structure of a property is as follows: first mortgage of 75 percent at 8 percent interest; equity of 25 percent at 12 percent interest. The discount or interest rate is computed as follows:

	Percentage of Value		Interest Rate		
First mortgage	.75	×	.08	=	.0600
Equity	.25	×	.12	=	.0300
Weighted average					.0900

MARKET COMPARISON. A discount rate may be computed from an analysis of sales transactions in the market. If quality attributes are compared, the appraiser assigns a percentage rating to each of the items, such as stability of value of the property, income and expense ratio, competition, and management. The income quality from comparable properties is rated in order to determine a quality rating for the subject property. For example, assume the actual discount or interest rate on the subject property is 8 percent (NOI ÷ SP). The comparative quality rating based upon an analysis of comparable sales is 95 percent. That is, the quality of the income from the subject property rates only 95 percent in comparison with the ideal quality. The discount or interest rate on the subject property will therefore be higher to compensate for the difference in quality. The discount rate for the subject property will be 8 percent divided by 95 percent, or 8.4 percent. It is obvious that quality comparison is difficult to do and requires proper analysis of very accurate market data. It is probably better to use the same market transactions to compute an overall rate and apply it directly to the net operating income to obtain an estimate of value.

BUILT UP. The built up method is highly subjective and its components are difficult, if not impossible, to estimate with any reliability. Generally speaking, it is not an accepted method of estimating a discount or interest rate. Under this method, a discount or interest rate may be built up by adding together the factors which enter into any composite market rate of interest. These factors were given earlier in this chapter, namely, the riskless or pure interest rate, reflecting the time preference of the investor; the relative nonliquidity factor of real estate; the investment management factor; and the rate for risk of loss of the capital sum. For example, assume a discount rate for a duplex is built up as follows:

Pure or riskless rate	6.0%
Nonliquidity	2.0%
Management	1.5%
Risk	2.5%
Total Discount Rate	12.0%

Computation of a Capital Recovery Rate

The investor wants a return "of" or recovery of his capital investment over a specified period of time. It is estimated on the basis of investors' expectations in the market and may be over the remaining economic life of the property, the remaining lease term, or the holding period of the investment. It is affected by the quality of the income stream and the form and source of the recovery, such as land or land and building. A rate of capital recovery must be computed in all cases where there is a definite period of time over which income is to be received and capital recovery is expected by the investor. The capital recovery rate has an important influence on the final value estimate. Capital recovery is achieved either through straight line, sinking fund, or annuity methods.

STRAIGHT LINE. Straight line capital recovery is in equal annual amounts over the remaining useful life of the building. The rate is computed by dividing the amount to be recovered by the number of years in the projected recovery period. It is applied to the improvements only.

No reinvestment return is assumed on the annual payments so capital recovery payments are largest under this method and total dollar return "on" the investment is the lowest of the three methods of capital recovery. The straight line method assumes that income will decline as the building gets older. The rate of decline may be computed by the formula:

$$\frac{R \times D}{R + D}$$

R is the discount rate and D is the capital recapture rate. For example, assume a discount rate of 8 percent and a capital recovery rate of 4 percent (25 years). The annual rate of decline in net income return "on" the investment is:

$$\frac{.08 \times .04}{.08 + .04} = \frac{.0032}{.12} = .0266 \text{ or } 2.66\%$$

SINKING FUND. Under the sinking fund capital recovery method, the recovery is in equal annual payments which are reinvested by the investor to accumulate at compound interest at the "safe rate," that is, the rate on savings accounts. It applies only to improvements over their remaining economic life. Since the capital recovery payments earn annual compound interest, smaller annual payments are needed to accumulate a total recovery and larger annual dollar amounts are available as return "on" the investment. The income stream is expected to remain constant. The rate of return declines over the recovery period but at a lower rate than in the straight line capital recovery method. The sinking fund capital recovery rate may be expressed as a percentage or as a factor, which is the reciprocal of the rate.

ANNUITY. The annuity method of providing for capital recovery provides for equal annual payments which are reinvested by the investor to accumulate at compound interest at the discount rate. The method is similar to the sinking fund method except that there is no fund into which the recovery payments are made to accumulate. The payments are available to the investor to reinvest as he sees fit. The income stream, as a level annuity, includes both the discount rate and the capital recovery rate which are the same rate. It is usually applied as a factor, namely, the present value of 1 per annum or the Inwood factor. The net income is multiplied by the factor to arrive at the estimate of value ($I \times F = V$). For example, assume a net income stream of $8,000. The annuity factor, from the Inwood table, for 30 years at 9 percent, is 10.274. The value of the income stream, therefore, is $8,000 \times 10.274$, or $82,192. The annuity method of capital recovery may be applied to any income stream—level, declining, increasing, or variable—as long as the income possesses the elements of risk and characteristics represented by the discount or interest rate used.

CAPITALIZATION TECHNIQUES

Capitalization techniques are used for processing net income into a capital value estimate. The techniques are used with one of the methods of decapitalization described earlier in the chapter, namely, direct, straight line, sinking fund, or annuity. The appraiser must choose the proper technique to employ and the selection depends upon the available data, the nature of the property and its income stream, and the form of capital recovery desired by investors in the market. The techniques discussed below are: (1) direct capitalization; (2) land residual; (3) building residual; (4) property residual; (4) mortgage-equity; and (5) Ellwood.

Direct Capitalization

Direct capitalization applies an overall rate directly to the net income from the land and improvements as a whole. There is no breakdown of the parts of the property. The overall rate is derived from market analysis of comparable properties and includes a return "on" and "of" the investment in one rate. For example, if comparable properties were earning 12 percent (net income divided by sales price), the same overall rate would be applied to the income of the subject property to estimate its value ($I \div R = V$).

Land Residual

Residual is net income remaining after a part of the property, either land or building, is first given its share of the total net income. The appraiser is able to estimate the value of one property part independently and the residual goes to the other part to estimate its value. In the land residual technique, the building value is known. The net return earned by the building, including discount or interest and capital recovery, is deducted from the net income earned by the entire property. The residual income is attributable to the land part and is divided by the discount rate to capitalize the land income. The value of the property is the sum of the building value and the value of the land. The method requires that the building be new and represent the highest and best use of the site. The land residual technique is used to value the land part of a property when the land value cannot be estimated by other means. The application of the land residual technique is illustrated below, using the straight line method of capitalization. Assume the following facts:

Building value	$100,000
Discount or interest rate	10%
Remaining economic life	20 years
Property net operating income	$ 18,000

Straight Line

Net operating income		$ 18,000
Income to building:		
Discount rate—10%		
Recovery rate—5%		
15% × $100,000		15,000
Net income to land		3,000
Land Value = $3000 ÷ 10%	$ 30,000	
Add: Building value	100,000	
Property Value	$130,000	

Building Residual

The building residual technique is used in cases where land value can be estimated independently and accurately by other means, such as by market comparison. The land is valued as if it were vacant and a purchaser would put it to its highest and best use. The amount of total net income attributable to the land is computed by multiplying the value of the land by the discount rate. The amount of net income remaining is earned by the building. It is capitalized either by dividing by a capitalization rate (which includes the discount rate and capital recovery rate) or by multiplying by a factor. The sum of the land value and the building value is the total value of the property. The application of the building residual technique is illustrated below, using the straight line method of capitalization. Assume the following facts:

Land value	$30,000
Discount or interest rate	10%
Remaining economic life	20 years
Property net operating income	$18,000

Straight Line

Net operating income		$18,000
Income to land		
$30,000 × 10% =		3,000
Net income to building		$15,000
Discount rate	10%	
Recovery rate	5%	
Capitalization rate	15%	
Building value		
$15,000 ÷ 15% =	$100,000	
Add: Land value	30,000	
Property Value	$130,000	

Property Residual

Under the property residual technique the property is evaluated as a whole and is not divided into land earnings and building earnings. The entire net operating income is capitalized. Such a technique is useful when neither the land or the building can accurately be appraised separately and the use of the land residual or building residual would be inappropriate. Two capitalization methods may be applied in the property residual technique, namely, direct capitalization and annuity. In direct capitalization, a market derived overall rate is applied directly to the net operating income. For example, assume a net operating income of $18,000 and a capitalization rate of 10 percent. The value of the property is $18,000 divided by .10 or $180,000.

The annuity method provides for valuation of the income stream for a given period of years (PW of 1 per annum) and the computation of the value of the reversion (PW of 1) at the end of that period. The technique is particularly applicable to the valuation of long-term leased properties, where the income stream is from the entire lease for a given period and then there is a reversion of the entire property to the lessor.

Mortgage-Equity

The mortgage-equity technique takes into consideration the amount and terms of financing and mortgage factors on a property rather than considering it as free and clear, which is typical of what happens in the real estate market. The technique uses the same basic formula as other means of capitalization, namely, Value is equal to Income divided by the Rate (V = I/R). Property value may be estimated in several ways. First, the overall rate may be computed by the band of investment method. The overall rate is then divided into the net operating income. The loan-to-value ratio of the mortgage is multiplied by the mortgage constant. The amount of equity is multiplied by the rate investors want on the equity part of the investment. Addition of the two results gives the overall rate.

Another way to use the mortgage-equity technique is to value the mortgage and equity parts separately. The equity income or cash flow may be computed when the mortgage loan amount and terms are given. The cash flow is capitalized at the equity dividend rate. The mortgage amount is added to the present value of the equity to compute the total value of the property. The format of this procedure is as follows:

> Gross Income
> Deduct: Vacancy Allowance
> Effective Gross Income
> Deduct: Operating Expenses
> Net Operating Income
> Deduct: Debt Service
> Cash Flow to Equity
> PV of Equity
> Add: Mortgage Amount
> Total Value of Property

It is also possible, under the proper assumptions, to consider the income to the equity as an annuity. Net operating income is computed and debt service is deducted from it. The balance is the income to the equity. The equity dividend rate is used to capitalize this figure. The reversion is computed and its present value is computed by using the equity dividend rate. The present value of the cash flow or income to the equity and the present value of the reversion are added together and the total is the value of the equity. The mortgage amount is added to the value of the equity to compute the total value of the property. The format of this procedure is as follows:

> Gross Income
> Deduct: Vacancy Allowance
> Effective Gross Income
> Deduct: Operating Expenses
> Net Operating Income
> Deduct: Debt Service

Cash Flow to Equity
PV of Equity Income
Add: PV of Reversion
Total PV of Equity
Add: Mortgage Amount
Total Value of Property

It must be pointed out that the mortgage-equity technique is quite comprehensive as a subject and there are many aspects, assumptions, and limitations on its proper use which the appraiser needs to understand. The brief discussion above needs to be supplemented by a deeper study of the subject from courses and real estate appraisal textbooks. The overall rate as illustrated above, for example, does not take into consideration such important factors as equity build-up as a result of reducing the mortgage amount through amortization, nor does it take into consideration changes in property value. "Adjustments" must be made to the overall rate for these factors.

Ellwood

The viewpoint of the Ellwood method is that of the equity investor. Net operating income is computed. It is capitalized into a present value figure through direct capitalization and the use of an overall rate. The formula for the overall rate is:[1]

$$R = Y - MC + \text{dep } 1/s_n$$

or

$$R = Y - MC - \text{app } 1/s_n$$

where:

R = Overall rate
Y = Equity yield rate
M = Ratio of mortgage to total purchase price
C = Mortgage coefficient (provides for the influence of mortgage terms, namely, interest and amortization)
dep = depreciation in market value of the property during the income projection term
app = appreciation in market value of the property during the income projection term
$1/s_n$ = sinking fund factor at the equity rate (Y) for a specific time.

The application of the above formula is illustrated below. Assume the following facts:

[1] L. W. Ellwood, *Ellwood Tables for Real Estate Appraising and Financing*, Third Ed., Part I (Chicago: American Institute of Real Estate Appraisers of the National Association of Realtors®, 1970), pp. 8–16.

1. 75% mortgage at 7% payable in full by level payments in 20 years.
2. Net operating income of $25,000.
3. Equity yield of 10%.
4. Holding period of 10 years.
5. Property depreciation or decline in value at end of 10 years is 20%.

By substitution in the formula, R is found as follows:

$$R = Y - MC + dep\ 1/s_n$$
$$Y = 10\%$$
$$M = 75\%$$
$$C = .0278\ (Ellwood\ Tables)$$
$$dep = 20\%$$
$$1/s_n = .0628\ (Ellwood\ Tables)$$

Therefore:

$$R = .10 - .75 \times .0278 + .20 \times .0628$$
$$= .10 - .02085 + .01256$$
$$= .09171,\ or\ rounded\ to\ .092$$

Value is therefore:

$$\$25,000 \div .092 = \$271,739,\ rounded\ to\ \$271,750.$$

REVIEW AND STUDY QUESTIONS

1. What is income property?
2. What are the steps in the income approach?
3. What are the elements of gross income which must be considered in its analysis?
4. Explain how to analyze and classify operating expenses.
5. Explain the four types of rates.
6. Explain three methods of computing the discount rate.
7. Explain three methods of computing the capital recovery rate.
8. Explain five capitalization techniques used for processing net income into a capital value estimate.

FURTHER READINGS AND REFERENCES

American Institute of Real Estate Appraisers, *The Appraisal of Real Estate,* Sixth Ed. Chicago: American Institute of Real Estate Appraisers, 1973.

Ellwood, L. W., *Ellwood Tables for Real Estate Appraising and Financing,* Part I and Part II, Third Ed. Chicago: American Institute of Real Estate Appraisers, 1970.

Gibbons, James E., "Mortgage-Equity Capitalization and After-Tax Equity Yield," *The Appraisal Journal,* January, 1969, pp. 31-49.

Kahn, Sanders A., Frederick E. Case, and Alfred Schimmel, *Real Estate Appraisal and Investment.* New York: The Ronald Press Company, 1963.

Kinnard, William N., Jr., *Income Property Valuation.* Lexington, Mass.: D. C. Heath and Company, 1971.

North, Lincoln W., *Real Estate Investment Analysis and Valuation,* First Ed. Winnipeg, Canada: Saults and Pollard Limited, 1971.

Ring, Alfred A., *The Valuation of Real Estate,* Second Ed. Englewood Cliffs, N.J.: Prentice Hall, Inc., 1970.

Wendt, Paul F., "Ellwood, Inwood, and the Internal Rate of Return," *The Appraisal Journal,* October, 1967, pp. 561-74.

TEN

Real Estate Investment Trusts

A real estate investment trust (REIT) is a business trust which acts as a passive investor in real estate investments—equity, mortgages, or both—with the objective of realizing income and profit from these investments. The REIT is similar to a mutual fund or closed-end investment company, except that real estate rather than stocks and bonds make up the portfolio, in that the investor has the opportunity to participate, for a small per share cost, in a diversified, professionally managed portfolio of real estate investments. The REIT is a creature of income tax legislation, with its major advantage being that if it distributes at least 90 percent of its taxable income to its shareholders it pays no Federal income tax. A shareholder in a qualified REIT is not subject to the double taxation of stockholders in corporations where profits are taxed to the corporation and again as personal income when distributed to individual shareholders. The REIT may also be considered as a financial intermediary. It serves to improve the flow of funds from savers to real estate investors and developers.

BRIEF HISTORY

The REIT has its origin in Massachusetts around 1850. Massachusetts law, prior to 1912, prohibited a corporation from dealing in real estate or holding it as an investment; it could own real estate needed in its business, such as a manufacturer owning its factory building. Real estate in the 1850's, however, was a common medium for investment of wealth and Boston trustees began to acquire real estate, first, for the portfolios of large investors, and later for smaller investors and the public. The Massachusetts business trust form of organizations was best suited for investing in real estate since it had transferable shares. The trusts originally invested in Boston real estate but later expanded their acquisitions to other cities and geographic regions of the country, such as Kansas City, Omaha, Denver, and Chicago. Business trusts became a popular and profitable form of investment medium for the small investor and provided pools of investment capital for a developing country.

The Federal income tax law was enacted in 1913 but business trusts were exempt from corporate income taxes until 1935. A court decision in that year held that a business trust form of organization was taxable as a corporation. Massachusetts in 1912 had also enacted legislation which permitted corporations to invest in real estate. The combination of factors—loss of income tax exemption, with rates of up to 52 percent of taxable income, and corporations entering the investment field—caused interest in real estate investment trusts to decline, and the number of such trusts dropped to a low point.

Congress, in 1936, permitted business trusts investing only in securities, such as mutual funds and closed-end investment companies, to be exempt from the corporate tax if they distributed at least 90 percent of their annual net income to shareholders. In 1961 the Real Estate Investment Trust Act became law and extended the same tax treatment to real estate investment trusts as existed for mutual funds.

ADVISERS

The REIT is usually organized by a group that serves as its investment adviser since the trust itself must be passive. Advisors are usually commercial banks, life insurance companies, or mortgage bankers. The adviser, who usually operates under contract with the REIT, conducts the daily operations of the trust and recommends investment opportunities to the trustees of the REIT. The adviser is a separate and distinct entity from the REIT and receives fees for its advisory services to the trust. REIT trustees usually include some officers of the adviser.

There are several reasons as to why an institution forms an REIT and serves as its adviser. Among the reasons are: (1) to earn advisory fees; (2) to use the REIT to finance real estate projects of the institution; (3) to enable the institution to expand its real estate financing services and offer complete financing packages; (4) to increase income; (5) to generate business for related activities of the institution, such as deposits for commercial banks; (6) to utilize real estate personnel more efficiently; (7) to gain the prestige factor of a good REIT; (8) to make loans not possible under normal institutional restrictions; and (9) to have the advantage of flexibility in real estate investments, such as participation in either short-term or long-term arrangements, or sale of institutional portfolio loans to the REIT to obtain additional liquidity.

REASONS FOR GROWTH

REIT's are a major source of funds in the mortgage market for long-term equity and mortgage money, land acquisition and development loans, and construction financing. Several factors account for the growth of REIT's in recent years: (1) relative lack of regulation and ability to make loans which traditional institutions were not able to make because of government regulations and restrictions; (2) realization by investors that REIT's have a good safety factor; (3) profitability; (4) tight money and the resulting reduced lending by deposit and thrift institutions, causing investors and developers to look to other sources, such as REIT's, for money; and (5) tight money also causing some institutional lenders to sell some of their loans to REIT's.

TAX QUALIFICATIONS

The income tax regulations governing REIT's are comprehensive and complex. The basic requirements an REIT must meet to qualify for exemption from Federal corporate income tax are:

1. At least 90 percent of its net income must be distributed to shareholders.

2. A minimum of 100 persons must own shares and no more than 50 percent of the shares in terms of value may be owned by five or fewer persons. This requirement means that the trust must not be a personal holding company.

3. At least 75 percent of its gross income must be derived from rents, mortgage interest, and gains from the sale of real property.

4. It must be a passive investor and not an active participant in the operation of trust properties. The trust must be an investor and not a dealer or merchant in real estate. It must be only a conduit for investment income.

5. At least 90 percent of the gross income of the trust must be derived from dividends, interest, rents from real property, gains from the sale of securities and real property, and abatements and refunds of taxes on real property.

6. Not more than 30 precent of the gross income of the trust may be derived from sales of securities held for less than six months, or from sales of real property held for less than four years. This requirement means that the trust must not hold property for sale to customers in the ordinary course of business.

7. At the close of each quarter, the trust must have 75 percent of the value of trust assets in real estate, including mortgages, cash, cash items, and government securities.

TYPES OF REIT'S

There are three types of REIT's: (1) equity; (2) mortgage; and (3) a hybrid or combination of equity and mortgage. Trusts may also be classified according to their investment policy, such as short-term and long-term, the type of property they specialize in, and whether their funds are committed in advance to investment.

The assets of an equity trust are invested primarily in the ownership of real property which may or may not be encumbered by mortgages. The real property may be land, commercial, industrial, or residential. The income of the equity trust is derived primarily from rents. The direct ownership of income property, such as shopping centers and office buildings, gives the equity trust a long-term classification. Equity trusts also may own and lease land or develop properties.

Mortgage trusts invest their assets in mortgages or other liens against real property. Income is derived primarily from interest earned on the mortgage portfolio and from commissions and discounts on purchased mortgages. The trusts invest in both short-term and long-term mortgages. Short-term trusts invest primarily in interim construction and land development loans. Many mortgage trusts invest in long-term mortgages and there are trusts which invest in combinations of the two types of maturities.

The hybrid or combination trust invests its assets in both equities and mortgages. They make a variety of types of investments and have a great deal of flexibility.

There are also trusts which specialize in a particular type of property or operation. Examples are trusts which concentrate on equity or mortgage investments in recreational land and facilities or mobile home communities.

A trust may not have committed its funds to any particular equity or mortgage and the trustees may invest them as they deem best. Such a trust is known as a "blank check" trust and is not permitted in some states, such as New York.

TYPES OF REIT INVESTMENTS

Short-term and long-term mortgage trusts make a variety of types of loans. Included in such loans are: (1) first mortgage construction loans; (2) first mortgage land development loans; (3) combination construction and permanent loans; (4) standby commitments; (5) gap loan commitments; (6) wraparound mortgages; (7) warehousing loans; and (8) conventional, long-term permanent mortgages on income-producing properties.

Equity trusts, including the combination equity and mortgage trusts, acquire ownership of or participation in the ownership of real estate. The equity investment may be in the form of direct ownership, solely or as joint venture or as tenants in common, of income producing property; or in real estate to be developed; or in the form of options to acquire such interest. The interest may be in the stock, stock purchase warrants, or other interests in the entity owning or developing the real estate. The interest may be acquired either independently of or in connection with mortgage loans made by the trust. The equity form includes interest in limited partnerships developing or owning improved property as well as options or commitments to purchase land under improved property with concurrent arrangements to lease such land back to the respective land grantors and to subordinate the trust's interest in the land to the first mortgage.

INTERMEDIATE TERM LENDING [1]

An intermediate term loan has a term of ten years or less, though many REIT's prefer limits of three to five years. Loan amounts are usually in the $500,000 to $5 million range. Prepayment penalties and amortization are flexible. Real estate developers prefer loans with a three to five year maturity on completed projects for two reasons: They can (1) play the market and hope for lower rates in the future on permanent or end loans; and (2) bring a project to operating maturity before negotiating permanent financing with stringent prepayment restrictions, which may be demanded under certain market conditions.

A developer, for example, plans to construct an office building project. He approaches an REIT for an intermediate term loan of three years on the completed project, preceded by a two-year construction loan. The arrangement gives him a two-year period in which to build and rent the project plus an additional period of three years in which to increase rents as leases expire or renew, and to seek permanent financing several years hence on a completed project with established management and demonstrated cash flow. It is a flexible type of financing that can be used with apartment projects, motels, condominium conversions, and simlar projects.

The REIT's find intermediate loans attractive for several reasons. Competition from commercial banks combined with a rapid turnover of short-term loans leads the short-term trusts to intermediate lendings as: (1) a new source of business; (2) a means of reducing the velocity of "roll over" of funds; and (3) an aid to asset growth. The fees of trust managers are based on the assets (loans) of the REIT, and profits are increased by leverage, or the use of borrowed funds. Trusts seek, therefore, to enlarge their portfolio with intermediate term loans and they prefer interest rates which float at 4 to 5 percent over prime.

Intermediate term lending by REIT's gives mortgage bankers an additional source of funds for clients. REIT's are relatively unregulated and loan terms can be negotiated to satisfy individual cases. The mortgage banker has the flexibility to arrange financing tailored to needs of developers of speculative real estate. The mortgage banker can: (1) arrange construction financing; (2) provide for a holding period in which to demonstrate feasibility; and (3) arrange long-term financing on the best possible terms for a project of proven worth.

[1] James E. Liek, "Activity of REIT's In Intermediate-Term Lending," *The Mortgage Banker*, October, 1972, pp. 84, 86–90.

REGULATION

The REIT, in comparison with other financial intermediaries such as savings and loan associations and commercial banks, is relatively unregulated by government. Trusts do, however, have to meet exacting requirements to qualify for income tax exemption. Further, they must meet the disclosure requirements of Federal and state securities laws. Trusts, however, have no governmental restrictions on their lending area, loan amounts, types of properties, amortization period, and loan-to-value ratios.

RISK FACTORS

The REIT, like any entity involved with real estate equity or mortgage investment, has risk factors which investors should consider. Among the risk factors are the following.

COMPETITION. A trust competes for acceptable investments with other financial institutions, including other trusts. The results of future operations of a trust depend upon available yields and the ability of the trust to make desirable investments. An increase in the availability of investment funds might increase competition for investments and reduce their yields. The yields available on investments depend to a large extent on the type of loan, the geographic location of the property, usury statutes, condition of the money market, tax laws, government regulations, and other factors, all of which are difficult to predict with certainty.

FIXED EXPENSES. Certain expenses of a trust must be met regardless of the profitability of the trust. Such expenses include interest on borrowed funds and compensation to the adviser and trustees.

DILUTION. A trust may be authorized, without approval of the shareholders, to issue additional shares. It may also be authorized to borrow, or in any other manner to raise, money through the issuance of notes, debentures, or other forms of obligations or the trust may be convertible into shares, or may be accompanied by warrants, rights, or options to purchase shares. The exercise of this authority by the trustees may dilute the interest of the shareholders.

OPERATING HISTORY. A trust which has not commenced its operations will, of course, have no operating history. Reliance must be placed upon the real estate experience of the advisers and trustees and the extent to which they will devote their time to the activities of the trust.

LEVERAGE. A trust seeks to increase its yield on investments by the use of leverage, or borrowed funds. Such borrowing may increase the trust's exposure to risk of loss. In order to repay such borrowings, the trust might be required to liquidate investments, which could have an adverse effect on its operations. Further, if the compensation of the adviser is based on the trust's invested assets, the investment of borrowed funds by the trust would increase the compensation payable to the adviser.

USURY. Usury laws may prevent a trust from making loans at rates as high as those which borrowers are willing to pay, thus eliminating profitable investment opportunities. Further, under the usury statutes of many states and the case law interpreting them, legal uncertainties may arise in determining the application of, and compliance with, the usury restrictions in such states in periods in which the current effective rate of interest approaches the usury limits. If any or all of the charges and fees which a trust receives on its loans is held to exceed the legal limit, the trust may be subjected to the penalties imposed by the applicable statutes. Such statutes may require restitution of excess interest or, in some cases, the enforceability of the debt might be impaired.

DISQUALIFICATION. If a trust fails, in any taxable year, to qualify as a real estate investment trust, it will be taxed as a corporation, and distributions to its shareholders may not be deducted by the trust for income tax purposes. The payment of such tax would reduce the funds available for investment or for distribution to shareholders.

DEFAULT. The ability of a trust to realize interest and rental income on its equity and mortgage investments depends on the financial reliability and strength of its borrowers, the attractiveness of the properties in which it invests, the quality of its tenants, the supply of comparable space in the areas in which its properties are located, and general economic conditions. In the event of a default by a borrower or a tenant, the trust may have to bring a foreclosure or eviction proceeding, negotiate revised mortgage loan or lease terms with the borrower or tenant, and expend additional funds to protect its investment. The income received from any new arrangement may be less than the income originally negotiated. Further, the proceeds of the foreclosure of a mortgage loan may be less than the investment of the trust in the property and result in a loss to the trust.

The default of a borrower where the trust's mortgage is subject to prior mortgage liens, or the default of a tenant of a property in which the trust's equity interest is subject to a mortgage lien, would increase the trust's exposure to risk of additional outlay of expense to protect its investment or possible loss through foreclosure.

The trust may lose priority of even a first mortgage lien to mechanic's liens, materialmen's liens, or tax liens, which may be created by acts of the borrower. The trust may find it advisable, in some cases, to make payments in order to maintain prior liens in current status, or to discharge the prior liens entirely, in order to maintain the value of its investment.

SHORT-TERM RISKS. Where the assets of a trust are invested primarily in short-term construction mortgage loans and short-term development mortgage loans, the trust faces the risks normally associated with mortgage lending plus the additional risks of construction and development loans. Additional risks include such factors as inability of the borrower to complete a project as planned, adverse changes in interest rates, and inability to obtain permanent financing.

LONG-TERM RISKS. A trust may invest a substantial portion of its assets in intermediate and long-term first-mortgage loans with equity type participations. The same trust may also invest directly in real estate equities. Such assets tend to be of a more permanent nature than investments in short-term land development and construction loans. The trust is consequently somewhat limited in its ability to change its portfolio quickly in response to changing economic and financial market conditions. Further, the equity investments of a trust are particularly subject to risks associated with general and local economic conditions as well as rent controls, high fixed costs, increasing costs of labor and materials, neighborhood values, quality of maintenance, attractiveness of the property to tenants, and other factors adversely affecting real estate values and reducing yields. Equity investments, particularly in periods of rising costs, involve the risk that rents obtainable on completion of a project under development, or upon the expiration of existing leases, may not be sufficient to cover recurring expenses, such as taxes, maintenance, and debt service.

HIGH LOAN-TO-VALUE RATIOS. A trust may engage in real estate financing techniques which involve loans up to 100 percent of the market value of income-producing properties. A default by a tenant or borrower in such situations increases the risk of loss to the trust on eviction or foreclosure. Net lease financing and land purchase-lease financing are examples of such investments.

COMMITMENTS. A trust may have existing investment commitments which are expected to require cash, in excess of scheduled payments on investments during a given period. It is expected that the trust will continue to increase its investment commitments, thereby increasing its continuing requirements for funds. Trustees believe that funds available to the trust, through short-term borrowings under bank lines of credit, the issuance of commercial paper, and cash generated from the trust's operations, will enable the trust to continue to meet its obligations. The availability of cash flow from the investments of the trust depends, in part, upon the ability of borrowers to repay loans and of tenants to meet their rental obligations. It is conceivable that in the event of defaults by borrowers the trust might not have sufficient funds to fulfill its obligations to pay interest and principal on borrowed funds and to meet its investment commitments. The trust might, in such an event, be required to liquidate certain of its investments under unfavorable conditions.

SHAREHOLDER LIABILITY. The Declaration of Trust usually provides that shareholders shall not be subject to any personal liability for the acts or obligations of the trust and that every written undertaking made by the trust shall contain a provision that such undertaking is not binding upon any of the shareholders personally. It is usually the opinion of the trust's counsel that, except possibly in a few jurisdictions, no personal liability will attach to shareholders for contract claims where trustees give notice of the above provision to all persons with whom they make contracts. There is a possibility that shareholders may be held personally liable for torts, taxes, certain statutory liabilities, and contracts with obligees who are not given the required notice. The Declaration of Trust, however, usually obligates the trust to indemnify and reimburse from its assets any shareholder against whom any such claim is asserted. Therefore, any risk of personal liability is limited to situations in which the assets of the trust would be insufficient to satisfy the claim or to the extent the indemnity is unenforceable as being against public policy. Trustees attempt, of course, to conduct the operation of a trust in such a manner so as to avoid, as far as possible, ultimate liability of the shareholders for liabilities of the trust.

POSSIBLE CONFLICTS OF INTEREST. There is a possibility of conflicts of interest between a trust, its sponsor, and its adviser. For example, ABC Bank sponsors the ABC Mortgage Trust. The trust contracts with ABC Mortgage Advisers, Inc., as adviser to the trust. The adviser is a wholly owned subsidiary of ABC Bank. The principal officer of the trust and chairman of its trustees is also the president of the bank. The same person also serves as the chief executive officer of the adviser. It is possible that substantially all of the officers and directors of the adviser may be affiliated with the bank or one of its subsidiary banks.

The trust and its sponsor or parent company may have the same investment objectives, such as the origination of construction and development loans. Further, the adviser and persons affiliated with the adviser of the trust may render services to the trust, in addition to those required by the advisory agreement, such as servicing of mortgages, sale of insurance, and the making of real estate appraisals. Compensation for such services is agreed upon between such parties and the trust.

EXPANSION

The growth and expansion of an REIT depends upon: (1) its ability to develop sources of money; (2) its ability to use leverage to increase the yield on its investments; and (3) reinvestment of tax depreciation and long-term capital gain benefits, and using proceeds from refinancing existing properties to acquire additional properties.

REIT's have made public offerings in the capital markets of both equity and debt instruments to obtain initial capital. The offerings usually consist of units composed of shares of beneficial interest accompanied by such features as warrants or convertible debentures to make the units more marketable.

Bank lines of credit are a major source of short-term funds. The sale of commercial paper is also an important source of short-term funds. The bank line of credit may be used to cover part of commercial paper issues.

Leverage is the use of borrowed funds to increase the return on capital. The trust seeks to obtain long-term debt at a lower rate than the rate at which the funds can be reinvested. Further, a trust may leverage its equity if it can keep the same return on invested capital and at the same time increase book value per share by selling additional shares at a premium over book value. For example, assume the book value of a share is $30.00 and the trust is earning 10 percent on this equity, or $3.00. The trust sells another share at a premium price of $35.00. The book value is now $32.50 and the 10 percent earnings is increased to $3.25 per share.

Trusts also grow by reinvesting tax savings, such as depreciation and capital gains net proceeds and refinancing proceeds, in additional properties and equity interests in properties of larger market values. Net book value is increased, for example, when the trust sells a property with a book value of $100,000 for $500,000, and then acquires another property for $500,000. Market value of the portfolio, of course, remains the same.

ADVANTAGES TO SPONSER

The organization of an REIT is a detailed, lengthy, and expensive process. Among decisions which must be made are the following: (1) selection of an underwriter that will be able to market the initial offering promptly as well as advise and serve the trust at later dates; (2) determination of the investment policy of the trust; (3) selection of legal counsel; and (4) determination of the size of the offering and the composition of the unit to be offered as to debt, equity, and warrants. The organizers must also select an adviser for the trust and formulate policy as to its services and compensation. Organizers will also be dealing with investment analysts and must learn to communicate with them concerning real estate and mortgage investment techniques and financial reporting methods.

The trust offers a number of benefits to its sponsor or organizer, particularly if the latter is a commercial bank or mortgage banker, and also owns the adviser. Specific benefits to both groups include: (1) substantial fees to the adviser for management of the trust and related activities; (2) offers to customers of more flexible and complete services; (3) better utilization of personnel and acquisition of new skills, such as acquiring equity investments and dealing with the investment banking business; and (4) acquisition of a large pool of money which can be controlled and used by the sponsor largely at its discretion. A trust which is sponsored by a well-known commercial bank, mortgage banker, or life insurance company has the built-in advantage of a known name and is able to have relatively quicker and easier market acceptance than one which does not already have a publicly recognized name.

ADVANTAGES TO INVESTOR

The investor in an REIT share obtains the benefits of investing in real estate: (1) good yield; (2) appreciation of investment; (3) income tax benefits; (4) build up of equity through mortgage amortization; and (5) the opportunity to maximize leverage opportunities. In addition, the REIT offers the benefits of: (1) diversification of investment and spreading of risk; (2) professional management; (3) opportunity to participate in properties which would ordinarily be beyond his financial abilities; and (4) the acquisition of a share which has marketability.

EVALUATION

A trust needs at least two factors to stay in business: (1) production, that is, the ability to originate new investments; and (2) management expertise to handle its assets and liabilities. The trust must be able to raise funds continually in the money and capital markets and to reinvest the funds at a profit. A continual flow of good equity and mortgage investment offerings must be maintained by the trust. A good reputation and a competent professional staff should assist the trust in attracting offerings and in obtaining attractive leverage opportunities.

ROLE OF THE REAL ESTATE BROKER

The real estate broker is a source of business for trusts. The trust needs the broker to bring quality transactions to its attention. The broker must be professional. Presentations to a trust should be good transactions, honestly presented, and accompanied by substantial documentation.[2]

Complete information is essential if the trust is to consider the submission, such as type of property, operating history, financial statement, location features, and information about the developer if the project is proposed rather than existing. A good rapport and working relationship must be developed between the trust and the broker so that each understands how the other performs. Time, patience, and money are necessary to develop the professionalism resulting in a long run relationship profitable to both parties.[3]

REVIEW AND STUDY QUESTIONS

1. Define a real estate investment trust and give a brief history of its development.
2. What is an "adviser" to an REIT and give several reasons as to why an institution forms a REIT and serves as its adviser.
3. What factors have accounted for the growth of REIT's in recent years?

[2] Richard Blagdon, "Where Does the Realtor Fit In?," *Real Estate Today,* July, 1973, p. 51. © National Institute of Real Estate Brokers of the *National Association of Realtors®*.
[3] *Ibid.*

4. What are the basic requirements which an REIT must meet in order to qualify for exemption from the Federal corporate income tax?
5. Define the three types of REIT's, and explain the types of investments made by each.
6. Discuss intermediate-term loans and why REIT's find them attractive.
7. How are REIT's regulated?
8. List the factors of risk which an investor should consider before investing in an REIT.
9. Explain how REIT's grow and expand.
10. What are the advantages of an REIT to: (A) its sponsor, and (B) the investor?

FURTHER READINGS AND REFERENCES

Brewer, Robert E., "REIT's in a Stage of Maturity," *Lawyers Title News.* Richmond, Va.: Lawyers Title Insurance Corporation, July-August, 1973, pp. 8-10.

Korobow, Leon, and Richard J. Gelson, "REIT's: Impact on Mortgage Credit," *The Appraisal Journal,* January, 1972, pp. 42-54.

Lewis, James E., "An Examination of Real Estate Investment Trusts," *The Appraisal Journal,* July, 1973, pp. 350-60.

National Association of Real Estate Investment Funds, *NAREIF Handbook of Member Trusts.* Darien, Conn.: NAREIF.

Schulkin, Peter A., "Real Estate Investment Trusts: A New Financial Intermediary," *New England Economic Review,* Published by Federal Reserve Bank of Boston. November/December, 1970.

Smith, David A., *The Real Estate Investment Trust Industry.* An unpublished research report prepared for a graduate course at Florida International University, Miami, June 15, 1973.

Sonnenblick, Jack E., "The Future of the Mortgage Trust Industry," *Real Estate Review,* Spring, 1971, pp 1-3.

"The Mortgage Banker." Special Real Estate and Mortgage Investment Trust Issue. Washington, D.C.: Mortgage Bankers Association of America, September, 1970.

ELEVEN

Mortgage Brokerage Regulations and Ethics[1]

Mortgage brokerage in most states is regulated under the real estate license law of the state. One state, Florida, regulates the business under a Mortgage Brokerage Act, which is separate from the real estate license law of the state. While the discussion in this chapter is based on the Florida regulations, the discussion provides an example of other states who may be interested in pursuing similar legislation and regulation. The chapter also points out standards of professional ethics for the mortgage brokerage business which, while prepared by Florida mortgage brokers, can be applicable in any state if the mortgage brokerage business in that state wishes to adopt similar standards.

[1] The Florida Mortgage Brokerage Law and Regulations discussed in this chapter are taken from the *Florida Mortgage Brokers Handbook,* 1973 Edition, published by Fred O. Dickinson, Jr., Comptroller of Florida and Mortgage Commissioner, Tallahassee, Florida. The price of the Handbook is $4.00 and is available from the Comptroller's Office.

DEFINITION OF TERMS

MORTGAGE LOAN. "Mortgage loan" means any loan secured by a mortgage on real property.

MORTGAGE BROKER. "Mortgage broker" means any person not exempt under Section 494.03 who for compensation or gain, either directly or indirectly makes, negotiates, acquires or sells, or offers to make, negotiate, acquire or sell a mortgage loan. This section shall not apply to transactions involving the sale or purchase of notes or bonds secured by mortgages which are subject to registration by the Florida Securities Commission.

MORTGAGE SOLICITOR. A mortgage solicitor must be employed by a mortgage broker. In performing the functions of a mortgage broker, his actions must be under the direction, control and management of the broker who employs him. A mortgage solicitor is not bonded.

Exempt Persons

The following persons are exempt from the Mortgage Brokerage Act:

1. Banks, trust companies, savings and loan associations, pension trusts, credit unions, insurance companies, small loan companies or federally licensed small business investment companies and their employees whose mortgage transactions are limited to loans made with their company's funds. Employees of mortgage brokers who have nothing to do with the solicitation of business and who perform strictly routine office duties on a set salary basis.
2. Any person making or acquiring a mortgage loan with his own funds for his own investment without intent to resell said mortgage loan.
3. Any person licensed to practice law in this state, not actively and principally engaged in the business of negotiating loans secured by real property, when such person renders services in the course of his practice as an attorney at law.
4. Securities dealers registered under the provisions of Chapter 517.12, Florida Statutes, servicing corporate clients in the normal course of business.

Non-Exempt Persons

The following persons are not exempt from the Mortgage Brokerage Act:

1. Every person who negotiates a mortgage loan and every person who makes or acquires and sells a mortgage loan must be licensed separately. Individual proprietors, members of a partnership, and officers of a corporation may be licensed as mortgage brokers. Employees, including those occupying supervisory positions, may be licensed as mortgage solicitors only.
2. A person who makes or acquires a mortgage loan for the purpose of selling the mortgage loan.
3. All persons, including real estate brokers, whose services include assistance in securing or arranging for or negotiating a mortgage loan and who receive compensation specifically for the financing service, either directly or indirectly.
4. Employees of exempt organizations who negotiate mortgage loans for other lenders.
5. Loan correspondents who are not employees of exempt organizations, and who receive compensation other than salary for negotiating mortgage loans for the companies they represent.
6. Disabled veterans are not exempt from the payment of the license fee.

APPLICATION FOR REGISTRATION AND LICENSE

Items Which Must Accompany Application for
Registration as a Mortgage Broker

For the principal broker, a license fee of seventy-five ($75.00) dollars and a surety bond; for each of his additional brokers, a license fee of forty ($40.00) dollars. Also, each application requires a $50.00 non-refundable investigation fee. In addition, a copy of the certificate of incorporation and amendments thereto, affirmation as to the residence and U.S. citizenship requirement of the Act, an affirmation of financial solvency, the written recommendation of a currently licensed mortgage broker, fingerprints of the applicants on a card furnished by the Commissioner and taken by a qualified law enforcement officer, must accompany the completed application.

ANNUAL FEE. The annual fee for an officer or member of a corporation, partnership, association or other group, to which a license has been issued to engage in the business of mortgage brokerage, other than the officer or member designated in the application is forty ($40.00) dollars in addition to the fee paid for the first license.

MAXIMUM LIABILITY UNDER MORTGAGE BROKERS SURETY BOND. The maximum liability is $5,000 for the license term.

MINIMUM AGE. The minimum age for a mortgage broker and a mortgage solicitor is 18 years.

CITIZENSHIP AND RESIDENCE. No mortgage broker's or mortgage solicitor's license shall be granted to any person who has not been a bona fide resident of the State of Florida for a period of at least six months immediately preceding the date of application for license, and who is not a citizen of the United States of America. A non-citizen may be licensed if he submits a notarized declaration of intention to become a citizen.

RECOMMENDATIONS. Applications must be accompanied by recommendations from a currently licensed mortgage broker, and of five residents of Florida who are not relatives, former employers, or public officials and their employees.

REGISTRATION, LICENSE, AND BOND PERIOD: RENEWALS

PERIOD FOR WHICH LICENSE IS VALID. All registrations, licenses, and bonds expire the last day of August next following their effective date.

EXAMINATIONS

Examination and Grade

A written examination is required to determine the applicant's knowledge of the mortgage brokerage law and regulations and his competency as to the mortgage business. A minimum grade of 75 percent out of a possible 100 percent is required. If an applicant fails the examination, the earliest date on which he may be re-examined is sixty (60) days after the prior failure.

BRANCH OFFICES

Definition

Even though mortgage negotiations are not customarily conducted at the branch office, any office or location shall be deemed a branch office if the name or advertising of a broker having a principal office located elsewhere shall be displayed in such a manner as to lead the public to believe that business may be conducted there.

Opening a Branch Office

The requirements for opening a branch office to engage in the mortgage brokerage business are an application and payment of a fee of seventy five ($75.00) dollars for each branch office. Each mortgage brokerage office or branch thereof shall be operated under the full charge, control and supervision of a designated mortgage broker employed at such office or branch on a regular and full-time basis to supervise and perform the rendition of mortgage brokerage services. A mortgage broker is permitted to supervise one branch office.

OCCUPATIONAL LICENSES

In addition to the mortgage brokers license or mortgage solicitors license, a licensee must hold such state and county occupational licenses as are required.

SURETY BOND

MAXIMUM LIABILITY. The maximum liability under the mortgage broker's surety bond is $5,000 for the license term.

NAME FOR BOND. The required bond shall be written in the name of the individual, proprietor, or of all members of the partnership, or of the corporation, or of the association as determined by the type of business organization as principal(s) and the bonding company as surety.

RECORDS

Records the Law Requires a Mortgage Broker to Keep

Each mortgage broker must keep the following records:

1. The closing statement signed by each borrower.
2. A complete record of all mortgage transactions, clearly reflecting all payments of commissions, finder's fee, referral fees, or other forms of compensation for services rendered in connection therewith.

HOLDING PERIODS. A mortgage broker must be prepared to make its records available for inspection by the Department of Banking and Finance for a period of at least five (5) years from the date of original entry.

TWO OR MORE OFFICERS. A licensed mortgage broker may operate two or more licensed places of business. General control records for each office do not have to be kept at each office but the records may be kept at any one of the offices upon written request to the Department of Banking and Finance designating therein the office at which such control records are maintained.

EXAMINATION OF RECORDS. The Department of Banking and Finance is authorized to examine the general control records of a licensee once a year. If he has reason to believe the licensee is not complying with the provisions of the Mortgage Brokerage Act, he may conduct examinations more often.

PARTNERSHIP AND CORPORATION

Principal Licensee of Corporation Leaves Corporation

If an officer of a corporation, who has been designated as the principal licensee, ceases to be a member of the corporation, the corporation shall immediately notify the Department of Banking and Finance and designate another officer as its principal broker. If this officer has a current broker's license and is an officer or member of the business organization, no further examination is required and a new license as the principal mortgage broker shall be issued upon payment of $35.00.

License Issued to Corporation

A mortgage broker's license is issued to a corporation. This does not mean that all officers and employees of the corporation are extended the privilege of negotiating mortgage loans. Each officer or employee who negotiates mortgage loans must be licensed separately.

Out of State Corporation

An out of state corporation may be registered. The officer of the corporation who has been designated as its principal licensee must have been a bona fide resident of Florida for a period of at least six months immediately preceding the date of application.

Partnership Principal Licensee and Surety Bond

In a partnership only one person may be designated as the principal licensee; both partners may not be so designated. All members of a partnership, however, must be named in the surety bond as principals.

ADVERTISING

Stipulations

The Act gives certain stipulations regarding advertising by mortgage brokers. All advertisements must contain the broker's name and his office address. No advertisements may be inserted in any publication where only a post office box number, a telephone number or a street number appears. False, misleading or deceptive advertising is strictly prohibited.

Advertising by Mortgage Solicitor

A mortgage solicitor may advertise in his own name those services for which a license is required by the Mortgage Brokerage Act. However, the name and address of the mortgage broker by whom he is employed must be clearly set forth in the advertisement.

MISLEADING PRACTICE

The taking and recording of a mortgage is tantamount to a commitment, and when funds are not available for immediate disbursement to the mortgagor, such procedure will be considered a misleading and deceptive practice, and to warrant suspension or revocation of the license of the registrant who does so, unless, prior to such recording, the licensee informs the mortgagor in writing of a definite date by which payment will be made, and secures the mortgagor's written permission for the delay thus entailed.

DENIAL, SUSPENSION, OR REVOCATION OF LICENSES

The Department of Banking and Finance may, upon its motion, or upon the verified complaint in writing of any person, investigate and suspend a license if the licensee is guilty of certain wrongs. The wrongs and other aspects of violations and penalties are given below:

1. Making any false promises likely to influence, persuade or induce; or pursuing a course of misrepresentation or false promises through agents or solicitors, or advertising, or otherwise.
2. Misrepresentation, circumvention, or concealment by the licensee through whatever subterfuge or device of any of the material particulars of the nature thereof, regarding a transaction to which he is a party, and of injury to another party thereto.
3. Failure to disburse funds in accordance with his agreements.
4. A crime against the laws of this state or of the United States, involving moral turpitude, or fraudulent or dishonest dealing, or if a final judgment has been entered against him in a civil action upon grounds of fraud, misrepresentation or deceit.
5. Failure to account or deliver to any person any personal property such as money, fund, deposit, check, draft, mortgage, or other document or thing of value, which has come into his hands, and which is not his property, or which he is not in law or equity entitled to retain, under the circumstances, and at the time which has been agreed upon, or is required by law,

or, in the absence of a fixed time, upon demand of the person entitled to such accounting and delivery.

6. Failure to place immediately all funds entrusted to him by his principal or others in a trust fund account with some bank or recognized depository and place all such entrusted funds therein upon receipt and have said trust fund account designate him as trustee and all such trust fund accounts provide for withdrawal of the funds without previous notice.

7. Failure to comply with any of the provisions of this act, or with any lawful order, rule or regulation made or issued under the provisions of this act.

8. Conduct which would be the cause for denial of a license.

9. Insolvency.

Penalties

Misdemeanor penalties may be imposed upon a mortgage broker or solicitor who violates any of the provisions of the Mortgage Brokerage Act. The penalty for a misdemeanor of the second degree may be a term of imprisonment in the county jail and/or payment of a fine up to $500.00 or an amount equal to double the pecuniary gain derived from the offense or loss suffered by the victim.

Period of Suspension

The maximum period of suspension under the Act is two (2) years, or until compliance with a lawful order imposed in the final order of suspension.

Hearing

No license shall be suspended or revoked prior to a hearing. The Department of Banking and Finance shall give the licensee at least ten days' written notice, in the form of an order to show cause, of the time and place of such hearing by registered or certified mail addressed to the principal place of business in this state of such licensee. The said notice shall contain the grounds of complaint against the licensee. Any order suspending or revoking such license shall recite the grounds upon which the same is based. The order shall be entered upon the records of the department and shall not be effective until thirty days after a copy of such order of suspension or revocation has been by registered or certified mail furnished to the licensee at such principal place of business.

Review of Suspension or Revocation

Any licensee who has had his license suspended or revoked has a recourse at law. The person aggrieved may, at any time prior to the effective date of the order, apply for a review by petition for certiorari in the circuit court of the county in which he is licensed.

Injunction to Restrain Violations

There are wrong doings which can give rise to investigation of brokers as well as exempt persons by the Mortgage Commissioner. The wrongs are as follows:

1. If the person has employed, employs, or is about to employ any device, scheme or artifice to defraud or to obtain money on property involving a mortgage on real property by means of any false pretense, representation or promise.
2. If the person has made, makes, or attempts to make in this state fictitious or pretended loan commitments or fraudulently accepts a deposit for a mortgage loan commitment.
3. If the person has engaged in, engages in, or is about to engage in any practice or transaction or course of business relating to the purchase or negotiation of a mortgage loan:
    a. Which is in violation of the law; or
    b. Which is fraudulent; or
    c. Which has operated or which would operate as a fraud on the mortgagee.
4. If the person is acting as broker or solicitor within this state without being duly registered as such broker or solicitor as provided in the Act.

The Department of Banking and Finance has recourse against violators of the above provisions. The Department may, in addition to any other remedies, by his own counsel bring action in the name and on behalf of the state against such persons to enjoin them from continuing such fraudulent practices or engaging therein or doing any act in furtherance thereof, in a court of law. The equity courts have jurisdiction of the subject matter in such action.

Effect of Violation on Mortgagee

The validity or enforceability of a mortgage loan is not affected when a mortgage broker fails to comply with provisions of the Mortgage Brokerage Act. That is, there is no effect upon the mortgagee for whom he has negotiated a loan.

COMPENSATION AND FEES

Maximum Fees or Commissions for Mortgage Loans

1. Loan of $1,000 or less; maximum fee, including all closing costs, is $250.
2. Loan which nets borrower in excess of $1,000, but not more than $2,000; maximum fee, including all closing costs, is: $250 for first $1,000, plus $10.00 for each additional $100.00 of the mortgage loan.
3. Loan in excess of $2,000 and not more than $5,000; maximum fee is: $350 for first $2,000 plus $10.00 for each additional $100 of the loan.
4. Loan in excess of $5,000; maximum fee is $250, plus 10 percent of the entire mortgage loan.

Computation Formulas

1. A formula may be used to determine the maximum fees, costs, and commission permitted on the gross proceeds of loans exceeding $1,000 but not exceeding $5,650. Add $1,500 to the gross proceeds of the loan and divide that sum by 11. The result will be the maximum dollar amount that may be charged for negotiating the mortgage loan.
2. A formula may be used to determine the maximum fees, costs, and commission permitted on the gross proceeds of loans exceeding $5,750. Divide the gross proceeds by 11 and to this amount add $227.27. The result will be the maximum dollar amount that may be charged for negotiating the mortgage loan. On loans that are over $5,650 but less than $5,750, the maximum fee is the amount in excess of $5,000.

Items Not Included in Broker's Fee

Certain costs are not considered as part of the closing of a mortgage loan transaction and should not be included as part of the broker's fee. The costs are: hazard insurance premiums, tax escrow deposits, life insurance premiums, recording fees, documentary stamps, intangible taxes, and other similar prepaid items.

Items Included in Maximum Dollar
Amounts That May Be Changed on a Loan

There are certain items that are included in the maximum dollar amounts that may be charged on a mortgage loan. Those items are: the commission, appraisal fees, abstracting charges, title insurance, attorney's fees, and all direct or indirect costs or expenses incidental to the processing and closing of the mortgage loan transaction, excluding recording fees, documentary stamps, and intangible taxes.

Compensation to Unlicensed Broker

An unlicensed person may not charge or receive any commission, bonus, or fee in connection with arranging for, negotiating, selling, or purchasing a mortgage loan. No fee, bonus, gift or gift certificate, or any other gratuity shall be paid or given to any person who submits an application for an FHA appraisal, or conditional loan commitment, or who sells or purchases a mortgage loan, unless the person is licensed as a mortgage broker.

Compensation to Unlicensed Employees of Mortgage Broker

An unlicensed employee of a mortgage broker renders service or assistance to someone in connection with arranging for a mortgage loan. That employee is not entitled to any compensation from either the lender or the borrower. Only persons licensed as mortgage brokers or solicitors may receive such compensation.

Extension of Mortgage and Compensation

A broker procures an extension of the unpaid portion of a mortgage loan previously brokered by him. The maximum charges in total fees and commissions that the broker may charge or receive on both the original transaction and the extension may not exceed in the aggregate the amount of costs and expenses permitted by law.

The Insurance Policy and Compensation

A mortgage broker or solicitor is not entitled to any monetary consideration or inducement in connection with the issuance of a title insurance policy in a transaction.

FHA or VA Commitment and Compensation

No licensee shall gratuitously give or advance, with or without expectation of reimbursement, an FHA or VA conditional or firm commitment to any person. Further, an FHA or VA conditional or firm commitment shall not be discounted or advanced with or without expectation of reimbursement to any person for an amount less than the established charge made by the FHA or VA.

DEPOSITS

If a mortgage broker requires a deposit in connection with an application for a mortgage loan, there must be an agreement in writing, signed by the parties thereto, setting forth the disposition of the deposit, whether the loan is finally consummated or not, and the term for which the agreement is to remain in force before return of the deposit for non-performance can be required.

The mortgage broker or solicitor has a statutory responsibility when he accepts a deposit and/or application for a mortgage loan of less than $25,000. The Mortgage Brokerage Act requires that he deliver to the borrower or prospective borrower a statement in writing setting down the total maximum costs to be charged, "incurred or disbursed" in connection with processing and closing the mortgage loan. Each party must retain a copy of the agreement.

REAL ESTATE BROKER

If a real estate broker offers assistance in securing a loan, or in arranging for the financing of a loan in connection with the sale of property, and the real estate broker receives compensation specifically for that service, either directly or indirectly, he is acting as a mortgage broker and must be licensed as such.

CODE OF ETHICS—FLORIDA ASSOCIATION OF MORTGAGE BROKERS [2]

Preamble

The objectives of this Association are: to promote cooperative business transactions among its members; to increase comprehension of mortgage operations by providing programs; to increasingly protect the industry and the public via legislative actions; and to increase a cooperative liaison with other professional groups.

1. The mortgage broker shall act in accordance with the Mortgage Brokers Act of Florida . . . and in accordance with the by-laws of the FAMB.
2. The mortgage broker shall perform his business in a manner reflecting honor and integrity. He shall avoid and report fraudulent and unethical practices to the Association or Commission charged with regulating the practices of brokers and solicitors in the State of Florida.
3. In accepting employment as an agent, the mortgage broker pledges himself to protect and promote the interests of the client. This obligation of absolute fidelity to the client's interest is primary.
4. The mortgage broker shall abide by generally accepted principles of real estate valuation when reporting to the investor regarding the valuation of the offered collateral for his loan.
5. The mortgage broker shall advise the relevant parties of any equity interest he may have in the collateral offered as security for the mortgage loan.
6. The mortgage broker shall not advise, advertise or intimate terms and conditions not available and not likely to be made available.
7. The mortgage broker should attempt to put all agreements into written form but shall abide by all agreements made by him whether written or oral.
8. The mortgage broker shall maintain special accounts separate

[2] This Code was prepared by the Florida Association of Mortgage Brokers. Specific credits go to FAMB members, Jerry Simon, Harvey Garfield, and Ronald Ames.

from his personal accounts for the deposit of trust or escrow funds.

9. The mortgage broker shall not speak disparagingly of the business practices of his competitor or for a transaction being negotiated by a competitor.

Standards of Professional Practices

1. The mortgage broker shall be remunerated by only one of the two parties (investor and borrower) unless both parties are clearly advised otherwise.
2. The mortgage broker shall secure all information bearing on the collateral or credit so as to permit him to present an objective report to the investor.
3. The mortgage broker shall not advise an investor of the safety or security of the offered collateral unless he has been adequately trained to do so.
4. The mortgage broker shall not indicate or intimate to the borrower or the investor that he is qualified to advise on matters germane to other professions unless he has satisfied the standards set forth for professional acceptability by those other professions.
5. A mortgage broker who has requested and received the requested commitment from an investor shall deliver the mortgage offered to the investor unless prevented by causes beyond his control.
6. The mortgage broker shall keep himself informed on all current thinking and trends in the mortgage industry.
7. The mortgage broker shall keep himself informed of all current trends affecting real estate, which is the collateral for mortgage loans, in such areas as legislation, zoning, city planning and taxation.

REVIEW AND STUDY QUESTIONS

1. Define (A) mortgage broker, and (B) mortgage solicitor.
2. What persons may be exempt from a state mortgage brokerage license act?
3. List the types of wrongs for which a licensee could have his license suspended.
4. What kinds of penalties may be imposed for violation of the mortgage brokerage act?

5. What wrong doings may give rise to investigation of mortgage brokers as well as exempt persons by the regulatory commissioner?
6. Discuss the compensation of a mortgage broker.
7. What must a mortgage broker do with deposits which come into his possession in connection with an application for a mortgage loan?
8. Study the example of the Code of Ethics and Standards of Professional Practices as set forth by the Florida Association of Mortgage Brokers.

FURTHER READINGS AND REFERENCES

Florida Mortgage Brokers Handbook, 1973 Ed. Tallahassee, Fla.: Comptroller of Florida.

Florida Real Estate Handbook. Winter Park, Fla.: Florida Real Estate Commission.

Florida's Mortgage Brokerage Act and Regulations, As Amended July 1, 1971. Tallahassee, Fla.: Comptroller of Florida.

Garrett, Thomas M., "Professions, Associations, and Codes," *The Appraisal Journal,* October, 1965, pp. 555-62.

Kerwood, Lewis O., "Importance of Continuing Education," *The Mortgage Banker,* September, 1971, pp. 4-8.

Mayer, Albert, III, "A Look Into Real Estate's Future," *Real Estate Today,* March, 1973, pp. 10-13.

O'Connell, Stephen C., "Ethics in Business," *The Appraisal Journal,* July, 1966, pp. 359-64.

Ratcliff, Richard U., "The Price and Rewards of Professionalization," *The Real Estate Appraiser,* August, 1967, pp. 3-11.

TWELVE

Creative Financing

Creative financing, also known as sophisticated, imaginative, or intricate financing, is the structuring or packaging of new types and combinations of loans and development of new reasons for using traditional techniques and instruments. There is a wide variety of creative financing techniques. The discussion which follows is a description of some of the more commonly used of these techniques and the reasons for their use.

INVESTMENT FACTORS

Creative financing attempts to give the investor higher yields and protection from inflation. It usually also attempts to maximize leverage benefits for the developer (through reduced or no equity, for example) and to maximize the tax shelter for the developer or owner. One study asked a group of investors to itemize the relative importance of seven financial criteria in their housing investment decisions. The seven investment factors were: annual cash return (cash flow), tax shelter, liquidity or ease of sale, low risk of loss, capital appreciation, financing leverage or minimum equity, and cash fees from packaging or construction. The relative importance was as follows: cash flow, tax shelter, financing leverage, low risk of loss, and capital appreciation. More than one half of the investors believed that tax shelter during construction was very important.[1]

The study also pointed out that the investor could realize cash benefits from appreciation of income property, either by selling the property or by refinancing the mortgage. The study concluded that the investor's holding period for a property was calculated to maximize the tax benefits of the investment. Further, many investors expect to refinance their apartment investments in order to get cash out of the project. Most of the investors planned to refinance between the fourth and twelfth year of the life of a project.[2]

JOINT VENTURE

The joint venture is in effect a partnership between an institutional lender and a developer. The lender usually puts 100 percent of the cash investment into a project and the developer contributes his ability to develop the project. The developer may also contribute land which he owns or on which he has an option. A division of ownership and profits is negotiated between the parties, resulting in a variety of agreements. A common arrangement is for the lender to get back all of his investment with a return on it before any split is made of the net income between the lender and developer. Profits may then be split on a 50-50 basis. Or, the lender may receive a preferred yield, such as 15 percent, then an equal amount is given to the developer, and any excess is divided equally between the parties. The parties may also share in the proceeds of any refinancing or sale of the project, with the lender receiving his investment first, the developer next, and then some form of split between the lender and developer.

The lender may provide mortgage financing as well as equity funds for the project. The mortgage loan is granted on typical mortgage terms, while the equity money is usually provided through a subsidiary real estate holding company of the lender. The permanent mortgage financing may be in the form of a commitment or standby arrangement which will enable the developer to obtain interim financing elsewhere to start de-

---

[1] "What Draws the Pros to Real Estate Investment?" *The Mortgage and Real Estate Executives Report*, September 18, 1973, pp. 5–7. Quoting a report prepared for HUD by the accounting firm of Touche, Ross & Co., entitled "Study on Tax Considerations in Multi-Family Housing Investments."
[2] *Ibid.*

velopment and construction. It is not expected that the commitment will have to be funded since the developer will obtain permanent financing from other sources.

The joint venture benefits both parties. The institutional lender receives a high yield and protection against inflation. The developer receives large sums of cash, which enables him to participate in larger projects. It is likely that the joint venture will remain during periods of tight money as well as easy money. One expert sums up the technique and its future as follows:

> The joint venture in which the investor pays his way and takes the equity risk (described . . . as the joint venture "front money" deal) will seemingly endure. It is not founded on emergent temporary necessities of the developer but in the perennial problems of real estate financing which will become more acute as projects increase in size, cost and complexity. Certainly if the estimates of population increase are at all accurate, and that increased population is to be served with a modicum of required shelter, no other valid financing technique now visible on the horizon can do the job.[3]

WRAPAROUND MORTGAGE

Under a wraparound mortgage the lender, such as a life insurance company, advances funds to the borrower on a property which already has existing first mortgage on it. The existing mortgage is not paid off and remains on the property as a senior lien. The additional loan is possible because of the increased current value of the property. The nature of such a mortgage arrangement is best described as follows:

> The WA (wraparound) mortgage is a second mortgage subordinate in all cases to an existing first mortgage which remains outstanding and unsatisfied. It differs from the conventional second mortgage in that the face amount overstates the actual indebtedness, and also in that it incorporates a special agreement between the parties for payment of the debt service on the first mortgage. The loan is otherwise evidenced and secured by the usual form of promissory note and second mortgage.[4]
> The face amount of the mortgage is the sum of the outstanding balance under the first mortgage plus the amount of additional funds, if any, to be distributed by the WA mortgage, with an annual debt service computed on this face amount. The WA mortgage interest rate is always higher than the interest rate on the first mortgage. This contract rate inevitably is equal to, or slightly less than, the then market rate for conventional first mortgage loans. The WA mortgage is, therefore, generally

---

[3] Mendes Hershman, "The New Look in Real Estate Financing Techniques," *The Appraisal Journal*, April, 1971, p. 221.

[4] Francis P. Gunning, "The Wrap-Around Mortgage . . . Friend or U. F. O.?," *Real Estate Review*. Summer, 1972, p. 36.

effective only in a high-interest period, and is seldom used in a declining interest rate market. The WA loan term and amortization, relative to the maturity of the first mortgage, will vary according to the purpose of the financing.[5]

It is immediately obvious that, if the "contract" rate is computed on the sum of the first mortgage and any new money advanced, a much higher "effective" rate of interest on the new money will result. This provides the leverage incentive for the WA lender.[6]

The developer may use the wraparound mortgage when he wishes to obtain additional cash and the existing first mortgage cannot be prepaid or there is a heavy prepayment penalty, or additional funds are not available under the present mortgage. Conventional second mortgages are too expensive.

BALLON LOAN

The ballon loan provides a type of creative financing. Such a loan occurs when a long term loan extends beyond the term of the lease. An example is as follows:

If a lease with a company has been negotiated for 30 years, and a loan has been committed for 35 years, the 5-year difference is referred to as a "hangout." When the balance of the loan is to be paid at the expiration of the lease, the loan is referred to as a ballon loan.[7]

VARIABLE INTEREST RATE

The variable interest rate on mortgages provides for an adjustment upward or downward in the contract rate on the individual mortgage with changes in interest rates in the economy. The rate is tied to an internal or external index, and as the index changes the rate on outstanding mortgages changes. For example, the index might be the prime lending rate at leading commercial banks. Or it might be the cost of money to the lending institutions, such as the rate paid on savings accounts. The idea behind the concept is to permit lending institutions to increase their income and at the same time permit more rapid increases in the rates paid to savers. It is anticipated that the result would be increased savings flow and the availability of more funds for mortgage

---

[5] *Ibid.*
[6] *Ibid.*
[7] William R. Beaton, *Real Estate Investment* (Englewood Cliffs, N.J.: Prentice-Hall, Inc., 1971), p. 122.

lending. Thrift institutions in particular must "borrow short and lend long," that is, their funds come from fluctuating rate savings and are loaned out in long-term, fixed rate mortgages. The variable interest rate enables these lenders to change the income from their mortgage investments with the fluctuation in market interest rates. Two methods may be used to handle the change in rates: first, the amount of monthly payment may remain the same but the maturity of the mortgage contract is changed; or, second, the maturity of the contract may remain the same, but the amount of the monthly payment is changed.

While the variable rate may tend to offset the problems associated with the instability in interest rates, there are disadvantages or limitations to the concept. Among the possible disadvantages are the following:

1. An increase in monthly payments may work a hardship on borrowers, particularly in periods of inflation, when other prices are also increasing.
2. Maturities could be extended beyond statutory and regulatory limits for some lenders if payments were to remain the same and maturities were extended to accommodate the increase in the interest rate.
3. If payments remain the same, a large increase in the interest rate could result in negative amortization, that is, the interest charges would be larger than the monthly payments. The result would be to reduce the owner's equity in the property each month and increase the risk exposure of the lender.
4. The raising of interest rates on outstanding mortgages as well as on new mortgages raises a public relations problem and possibly one which would not receive widespread public and political support.
5. A stronger demand for funds may come from other sectors of the economy and the variable rate offers no guarantee of adequate funds to thrift institutions if competition for funds results in the payment of higher interest by, say, the U.S. Treasury or private corporations.

SEPARATE FINANCING OF LAND AND BUILDING

There are a variety of techniques which involve the separate financing of land and building. An example will illustrate the concept.[8]

[8] Jack E. Sonnenblick, "The Art of Intricate Financing," *Real Estate Today*, July, 1969, pp. 33–34. © National Institute of Real Estate Brokers of the *National Association of Realtors*®.

Assume a developer acquires land at a cost of $10.0 million on which he will construct an office building at a cost of $21.0 million. A net income, after allowing for vacancy and management, real estate taxes, and operating expenses, of $3.6 million is projected. The appraised value of the land, after the completion of a major office structure, is $12.0 million. A long-term ground rental of $840,000 net per annum is established for the ground, which gives the leasehold position a $2.76 million net annual rental on a free and clear basis. This amount is capitalized at 9 percent, which gives a leasehold appraisal of $30.0 million. A loan on this value is obtained for $22.0 million at 7.75 percent for 30 years.

The fee position, appraised at $12.0, receives $840,000 net income from the building. Long-term financing on the land is obtained in the amount of $9.0 million at 7.5 percent interest with a .5 percent amortization for 25 years.

The result is a total of $31.0 million in long-term financing on a project which has cost the builder an equal amount. Nevertheless, both of the lender's positions are well secured. The land mortgage has a major office building as security, and the mortgagee of the leasehold office building has long-term prime leases to secure the mortgage. The builder will have an annual cash flow of almost $1.0 million from the project.

Income:

600,000 sq. ft. offices	$5,100,000
25,000 sq. ft. stores	600,000
Garage and miscellaneous	100,000
	$5,800,000
Less vacancy & management	300,000
	$5,500,000

Expenses:

Real estate taxes	$1,000,000	
Operating	900,000	
		$1,900,000
Free and clear		$3,600,000
Less ground rental		840,000
Net leasehold profit		$2,750,000

$30.0 million leasehold appraisal
$12.0 million fee appraisal

Leasehold mortgage:	$22.0 million 7.75% 8.6% constant 30 years
Fee mortgage:	$9.0 million 7.75% 8.0% constant 25 years

BASKET MONEY

Basket money is a loan made under state law which permits life insurance companies to make a certain percentage of their loans or investments in properties which would not ordinarily qualify. The incentive for the lender making the unusual or basket money loan is a higher-than-normal yield. Examples of basket money loans include second mortgages and subordinated land projects.

JOINT LOAN CONCEPT

The joint loan concept was introduced by Home Capital Funds in 1967 as an alternative to tight money lending limitations. The concept gave flexibility in the conventional mortgage market. It enabled mortgage bankers to originate joint-mortgage loans for institutional investors and thereby increase the range and volume of mortgage loans they can originate.[9]

A savings bank, for example, may be unable to invest in residential loans which exceed 75 percent of value. The joint loan concept would enable the mortgage banker to originate 90 to 95 percent loans for these permanent investors. The mortgage banker would originate a joint loan which is funded to 75 percent of value by the savings bank, with an added 15 or 20 percent of value funded by Home Capital Funds.[10]

Larger mortgages for higher priced homes may also be funded under the joint loan concept. Permanent lenders are unable to invest in 90 to 95 percent loans over a certain dollar maximum. However, a 90 percent mortgage loan on a $60,000 appraised value property, for example. can be originated. The senior lender would put up $45,000 and the junior lender would fund $9,000, to make a 90 percent loan of $54,000.[11]

The joint loan concept enables the borrower's needs for a 90 or 95 percent loan to be met without the lender increasing his investment risk. Established lending restrictions are adhered to by the lender. The mortgage banker is able to originate more loans in the higher price and higher quality brackets.[12]

[9] "Increased Opportunities, Flexibility Seen in Joint Mortgage Lending," *The Mortgage Banker*, November, 1973, pp. 78–82.
[10] *Ibid.*
[11] *Ibid.*
[12] *Ibid.*

The 75 percent portion of the loan comes from the institutional investor, who has all the rights of the first mortgagee. The 15 to 20 percent portion comes from the junior lender. The loan originator services the combined loan and monthly remits to Home Capital Funds its proportion of borrower payments. Home Capital Funds gains its loan security from the private mortgage insurance that covers the entire mortgage loan. The senior portion of the loan always has priority in the event of a default. In effect, two investors have combined funds to create a single loan.[13]

SALE-LEASEBACK

Under the sale-leaseback arrangement, the developer sells property, such as land, to an investor, such as a life insurance company, at its market value. In the same transaction, the investor leases the property back to the developer at a fixed rent plus maybe a percentage of the income from the property. The developer has received 100 percent financing for his property instead of a smaller loan-to-value ratio if mortgage financing had been secured. Further, the developer retains operational control over the property and is able to deduct the total rent payment, which includes the value of the ground, from his income tax.

INSTALLMENT SALES CONTRACT

The installment sales contract, also known as a sale and repurchase or buyback, is similar to the sale-leaseback. The primary difference is that the owner-developer retains depreciation under the installment sales contract and still obtains the benefits of the sale-leaseback. The owner sells his property to an institution, such as a life insurance company, and the institution simultaneously sells it back to the owner for the same price under a long-term installment sales contract. The institution retains title to the property but the owner has an equitable interest in the property and retains the depreciation tax deduction. The owner is able to obtain 100 percent of his cost and also has the benefit of tax shelter through depreciation and interest deductions. The owner makes payments which include interest and amortization of the contract plus he has the right to pay off the balance of his contract and obtain title to his property after a specified period of years.

[13] *Ibid.*

SECOND MORTGAGE

Second or junior mortgages are subordinate in priority to a first or senior lien on a property. There may be more than one junior mortgage against a property but this discussion is confined to the use of a single second mortgage. Probably the most common use of a second mortgage, particularly in residential property, is to bridge the gap between the price of a property, the amount of the first mortgage, and the amount of downpayment or equity of the purchaser. For example, a property is priced at $50,000 and a first mortgage of $40,000 is available, leaving a needed $10,000 down payment or initial equity investment. If the purchaser only has $5,000, he could consider obtaining the additional $5,000 by a second mortgage to a financial institution, or by means of a purchase-money second mortgage given to the seller.

Second mortgages usually carry a higher interest rate than first mortgages because of the additional risk involved. If the first mortgage is foreclosed and the sale does not bring enough to pay off the second mortgage as well, the second mortgage holder is wiped out. He could, of course, sue on any promissory note which accompanied the second mortgage. Second mortgages also are for a shorter duration than first mortgages, with three to five years being common. They may or may not be amortized. There is no organized market of financial institutions providing second mortgages. Funds are available through a variety of sources, such as individuals, trusts, mortgage bankers, and regulated lenders who are permitted by law to lend on second mortgages. Second mortgage lending is highly speculative and holders of second mortgage paper may dispose of them at substantial discounts.

Second mortgages may also be used in other ways. Four of these ways are as follows:

1. To liquify real estate investments without any tax consequences; in effect, to trade cash flow for instant dollars. For property that has appreciated considerably in value, the appreciation may be pulled out in cash by using a three- or five-year second mortgage. The rate on the second mortgage will be higher than on the existing first mortgage, but the total interest cost will be less than if the entire first mortgage is refinanced at a higher rate. The amortization on the second mortgage will be small during its life, so the investor must be prepared to refinance the loan at its maturity. A higher interest rate may, of course, have to be paid at that time. However, second mort-

gages can often be prepaid at any time without penalty and as a result they may be refinanced if rates decline during their duration.

2. The investor or developer may want to refinance his existing first mortgage to obtain cash but prefer to delay it for a year or two until long-term rates are lower. Second mortgages can provide interim financing. The slightly higher cost during the interim period can be more than offset by interest saved on a refinanced long-term mortgage.

3. One partner in a real estate business may desire to buy out another. The cash may be raised by a second mortgage which provides the cash for an immediate buyout and which can be repaid from anticipated future income that will belong solely to the remaining partner.

4. The second mortgage may be used to increase the leverage return to the investor. Large interest payments on the second mortgage are tax deductible and have a substantially lower net cost to the investor. It must be pointed out, however, that second mortgage financing can increase the risk assumed by the investor substantially. Any significant decline in net operating income could wipe out his cushion and require him to put up additional cash to avoid a default. Periodically, he must refinance the second mortgage, possibly at higher rates. This type of financing, therefore, should be limited to sound, stable properties where income fluctuations should be minimal.[14]

INTERIM LOAN

Interim loans usually run from one to five years and carry interest rates which vary from the permanent loan rate itself to $1\frac{1}{2}$ percent above the prime loan rate. Sources of funds include institutional lenders as well as mortgage companies and real estate investment trusts. The loan may permit prepayment or have a lock-in of up to one-half of the loan term, with a minimum period of six months. Interim loans are also known as "bridge" loans since they bridge the gap between the construction loan and the permanent loan.[15]

Interim or intermediate financing is particularly useful during periods of tight money. Investors are able to use interim financing to avoid being locked in at high interest rates over the life of a permanent loan. If rates on permanent loans drop during the one to five year period of the interim loan, the investor is able to take advantage of the lower rates in negotiating his permanent loan. Interim loans are usually used in newly completed projects. The loan funds are used to take out or repay the construction lender, and the investor is then in a position to

[14] "How to Use Second Mortgages in Today's Real Estate Market," *The Mortgage and Real Estate Executives Report,* April 16, 1973, pp. 1–3. Quoting Jerome J. Hoffman, Managing Partner of Atlantic Continental Co. of New York City.

[15] "Using the Interim Loan to Buy Time," *The Mortgage and Real Estate Executives Report,* September 18, 1973, pp. 1–2.

operate the property for several years before committing himself to permanent financing.[16]

The flexibility created by interim financing can also be used in other ways. With regard to newly completed projects among these ways are:

1. Temporary oversupply. When occupancy in a new building becomes available at a time when vacancy rates are high, the developer may have to sit through a period of several years with large blocks of empty space. Consequently, a permanent loan either may be unavailable or available only at premium rates and at a low loan-to-value ratio.

2. Accelerating demand. A contrasting situation is one in which rents are expected to rise sharply in the next few years; interim financing may enable the developer to obtain a much larger loan by waiting.

3. Temporarily unfavorable conditions. Sometimes, a condition peculiar to the particular project dims the short-term outlook. For example, negotiations with a major tenant may be stalled when the permanent takeout is being sought. Here, an interim loan takeout (often in the form of a standby takeout) gives the developer breathing space.

4. Leases dependent upon completion. Sometimes it is much easier to rent completed or partially completed projects than to obtain leases on blueprints alone. If the permanent financing is dependent upon signed leases, the developer again may be better off with an interim loan takeout to secure the construction lender.

5. Multiphase projects. Shopping centers, industrial parks, and office complexes often are built in phases. As a result, permanent financing for the entire project may be unavailable at the outset; if several lenders are used, complicated legal arrangements must be set up. Interim permanent loans for each phase can provide financing until the entire project is completed.

6. Condominium projects. Here, the condominium developer expects to pay off the construction loan from the proceeds of the sales of individual units. This may put the developer under pressure to meet a deadline. This can be avoided by interim financing.

7. Personal liability. For a number of reasons, including the lack of operating history for the project, a permanent lender may want the developer to assume personal liability. By signing an interim note, the developer limits his exposure to the period before he can refinance a nonrecourse loan.[17]

Interim financing also plays a role in financing and refinancing existing income properties. Examples of such loans include the following:

[16] *Ibid.*
[17] *Ibid.*

1. Superior management. When an existing income property is acquired, the buyer may have to arrange immediate purchase-money financing. If he is convinced that better management will substantially increase the cash flow from the property, an interim loan will enable him to refinance in a few years on substantially better terms.
2. Refinancing prior to loan maturity. An investor, requiring funds, may want to pull cash out of a property by refinancing. But if the existing mortgage is not prepayable, or if its low rate makes prepayment undesirable, an interim second mortgage (often in the form of a wraparound mortgage) can bridge the period until the original mortgage matures.
3. Refinancing when original mortgage matures. In the opposite situation, the existing mortgage may mature at a time when a new permanent mortgage loan cannot be made on advantageous terms because major leases with short terms remaining have not yet been renewed, or for any of the reasons given above. Interim financing can bridge this uncertain period.[18]

OPTION

The option to purchase is both a marketing tool and a financing tool. As a financing device, it may be used as interim financing to hold property pending the organization of a group, such as a syndicate, to acquire it for investment. During this holding period other matters may be taken care of, such as leasing, zoning, and acquisition of any additional parcels needed to create plottage. Further, any increase in the market value of the property during the holding period accrues to the purchaser, assuming, of course, he decides to either sell or exercise the option. If there is no agreement to the contrary, an option may be sold to another party. The person taking an option usually puts down only a small amount of cash and gains the further advantage of not having to pay interest, principal, taxes, insurance, or other carrying charges on the option. If the option is exercised, the downpayment on it applies to the purchase price of the property. If the option is not exercised, the downpayment goes to the seller or property owner.

From an income tax viewpoint, the gain or loss from the sale or exchange of an option, or loss on failure to exercise the option, is determined by the character of the underlying property. The giving or receiving of an option is not a taxable occurrence. Consideration for an option is not deductible when given or taxable when received. When the option is exercised, the consideration given for the option becomes part of the purchase price of the property and is added to the purchaser's basis for the property. The seller treats the proceeds as part of the selling

[18] *Ibid.*

price of the property. If the property is a capital asset, held for longer than six months, the holder of the option realizes long-term capital gain or loss when he sells the option. If the holder of the option fails to exercise it and incurs a loss, the nature of the loss is also determined by the character of the underlying property, namely, if it is a capital asset and the length of its holding period. Gain to the grantor from the holder's failure to exercise the option is ordinary income. For loss purposes, the option is considered to have been sold or exchanged on the date it expired.

TRUST

A method of holding title to property so as not to reveal the identities of the true owners is a trustee agreement. Title is held in the name of a trustee who acts for the owners under a Trust Agreement. The nature of the agreement may be shown by an example of the main provisions of one such trust agreement.[19]

1. Trustee agrees to take title to certain described property and the property is to be held for the use and benefit of the named trustors and subject to the terms and conditions of the trust agreement.
2. The trustors empower the trustee to assume mortgages on the subject property at the time the trustee takes title in a specified amount and terms.
3. It is agreed, for a stated consideration, that the trustee shall hold and administer the subject property, and all other property that may be added to the trust agreement, in trust, for the uses and purposes and upon the terms and conditions as set forth in the trust agreement.
4. Out of the income derived by the trustee from the Trust Estate, the trustee shall first pay all of the necessary costs and expenses of the trust, including outlays necessary for the protection and upkeep for the Trust Estate, interest and premium upon encumbrances, taxes, insurance, and expenses for keeping the property in good condition. The initial trustee shall not receive a fee for acting in such capacity.

[19] Acknowledgement and appreciation is extended to Edgar Schlitt, Realtor, Vero Beach, Florida, who provided the trust agreement from which these provisions are summarized.

5. The purpose of the trust agreement is to acquire the described real property and to hold it for investment purposes. If, within twenty (20) months from closing, the trustee receives a bona fide offer for purchase of the property, he will advise the trustors of the terms and conditions of the offer and shall follow the determination of a majority of the interests of trustors, given in writing, as to the action to be taken with respect to the offer.

6. Cash investment means the amount of cash that has been paid by each trustor into the Trust Estate. It includes both the sums paid for the purchase of the described property and all other sums that are afterwards paid in completing the purchase of the property, together with all expenses incurred in the management of the property, and as may be incurred by the trustee pursuant to the trust agreement.

7. The trustee agrees to an annual audit by a Certified Public Accountant and the audit will be submitted to each trustor. The accountant shall be selected by a majority in interest of the trustors.

8. The trustors will receive, as income during the existence of the trust, or at the termination of the trust, a share of the total of said income in direct proportion to the percentage of contribution of the trustor. In the event of a loss or losses during the existence of the trust, the trustors will be able to use the loss or losses for federal income tax purposes where applicable in proportion to their percentage of contribution.

9. In the event any of the property of the trust is sold, the proceeds of the sale, after payment of all debts and claims against the property sold, will be disbursed to the trustors in direct proportion to the percentage of contribution of each trustor.

10. The trust will terminate upon the sale of all of the property in the trust or twenty (20) years after the death of the last surviving trustor in being at the time of the execution of the trust agreement. The trustee will thereupon transfer, pay over, deliver, and convey the Trust Estate with its accumulation and all undistributed net income to the trustors, their heirs, successors, and their assigns. Or, the trust will terminate by written consent of the trustors holding seventy-five percent (75%) interest of the trust estate.

11. The trustee has the power to transfer, assign, convey, lease, rent, and encumber the Trust Estate upon the written consent

of the trustors owning in excess of fifty percent (50%) interest of the Trust Estate.

12.   In the event that any of the trustors receive an offer to purchase his or their interest in the trust, and the trustor desires to sell his interest, the trustor will notify the trustee and other trustors of the offer and submit to the other trustors a copy of the offer and the price, terms, and conditions of the sale. The other trustors are given the privilege of purchasing the interest of the trustor at a price and upon terms not less than those received by the trustor from the third party. If the other trustors do not exercise the privilege within forty-five (45) days after receiving notice of the offer, the trustor desiring to sell his interest will have the right to do so.

13.   The percentage of contribution of the trustors is set forth in this provision.

14.   The articles of the trust may be amended with the consent of the trustors holding a seventy-five percent (75%) interest in the trust. The amendments do not take effect until they are recorded in the public records.

15.   The originating capital for the purchase of the described property is a specified amount. A certain amount is paid to the trustee at the execution of the trust agreement and the balance is paid in specified annual installments.

16.   There is no personal liability on the party of an trustor for any payment in connection with the trust agreement, except for his liability to make his contribution to the trust as agreed upon. Any and all other payments required to be made by a trustor will, if not made, result in a readjustment of interests but not in any personal liability. No trustor will have any liability of any type to any third party.

17.   Expenses of the Trust Estate are to be shared by the trustors in an amount equal to their percentage of contribution. They must promptly contribute their share to the trust upon written demand by the trustee, itemizing the expenses and their proportionate share. The trustee will give each of the trustors written notice of the amount of the trustors' shares of the common expenses and the expense is immediately due and payable to the trustee. In the event that one or more of the trustors is unable, for any reason, to pay his share of the common expenses, after having received thirty (30) days' notice, the remaining trustors will immediately have the option to

purchase the delinquent trustor's percentage of contribution in the trust for the amount of cash the delinquent trustor has invested in the trust. The remaining trustors will immediately contribute proportionately to the trustee the additional amount needed to pay the common expenses of the delinquent trustor.

If the remaining trustors elect to purchase the interest of the delinquent trustor, the delinquent trustor's percentage of contribution in the trust will be paid to him within fifteen (15) days after notice of the election to purchase has been given to the trustee. In the event that the trustors do not elect to purchase the percentage of contribution of the delinquent trustor, the remaining trustors will pay the delinquent trustor's share of the common expenses. The payments made by the remaining trustors, in excess of their required percentage of contribution, will bear interest at the rate of 10 percent (10%) per annum, payable semiannually. In the event that one or more of the trustors remains delinquent in his share of the common expenses for a period in excess of six (6) months, the remaining trustors, at their election, by notice to the trustee, may treat the payment that they made, by reason of failure of the trustor to pay his share of the common expenses, to be an additional contribution to the trust, and their percentage of contribution is increased proportionately, and the delinquent trustor's percentage of contribution is likewise reduced proportionately.

18. If one or more of the trustors dies during the existence of the trust agreement, the remaining trustors have the option to buy the deceased trustor's percentage of contribution from his personal representative for a sun that would equal the total amount of capital invested in the trust by the deceased trustor, plus ten percent (10%) interest per annum on the invested capital.

19. In the event of the death of the named trustee, or in the event of his disability or removal or resignation, another specified trustee is named as successor. The successor trustee accepts the office by written instrument, and assumes the duties of the office immediately upon delivery of the instrument to the other trustee then serving. If no other trustee is then serving, delivery is made to the trustors, without the necessity of any other act, conveyance, or transfer.

20. The trustee will distribute all net income received by him during each year of the existence of the trust. The distribution will be on at least a quarterly basis.
21. The trustee also secures title insurance, insuring the title to be fee simple. Certain exceptions are specified, such as taxes for the current year, boundary lines, and the like.

KICKERS

Kickers or sweeteners provide the lender with an income beyond what he would receive under a straight interest loan. Kicker arrangements, or equity participations, usually are popular with some lenders during periods of tight money. Lenders seek some degree of protection from inflation by arranging to share in the growth and profit of an investment. The kicker may, in fact, be the incentive that makes the unusual loan acceptable to the lender.

There are many forms of kickers which have been used by lenders. The more common forms include the following:

1. Rental participation, whereby the lender receives a percentage of the gross rentals from the property.
2. Profit participation, in which the lender participates in the profits of the venture.
3. Participation in the gain from sale of the property.
4. Share in the proceeds of any refinancing on the property.
5. Share in the equity ownership of the property.
6. Charging of nonrefundable fees and discounts by the lender.
7. Participation in the form of stock ownership or stock options.

Kickers, of course, give the lender a larger return on his investment and make possible loans which otherwise might not be given. Developers or borrowers need larger loans for larger and more sophisticated projects and are willing to pay the kickers in order to obtain the loans as long as the project will profitably absorb the participation.

Kickers, however, are not readily accepted by all lenders and developers, and during periods of easy money there may be little interest in them. Loans with participations may be more difficult to administer than straight interest loans and the additional return may be less than anticipated. It is also felt by some developers that lenders' demands have not always been in proportion to the risk in the loan. There is also the question of whether usury statutes might be violated with some participation arrangements. Finally, participations may affect the resale of properties if the participation tends to influence the market value of the property adversely.

Certain guidelines for kicker loans have been set forth by several experts on the subject. It is generally agreed that when kickers are used, the following guides should be observed:

1. Favor high turnover properties. Kickers work best when the gross income for the property involved is not held down by long-term leases. Thus, apartment projects and motels are suitable because short-term leases in the one and the absence of fixed rates in the other enable gross income to keep pace with inflation. On the other hand, a property subject to a long-term lease with no step-up in rentals will throw off no additional return to the participating lender.

2. Require estimated payments in advance. The lender should not wait until annual financial statements are prepared to receive its participating share. Hartford (Life Insurance Company), for example, seeks monthly estimated payments which are then adjusted up or down at the end of the year. This makes the pill less bitter for the developer and reduces the risk that figures will be misrepresented. It may also be a good idea to require quarterly profit and loss statements.

3. Provide continuous supervision. A company with a large number of participation agreements should have a full-time person following developments in the properties covered.[20]

SUBCHAPTER S CORPORATION [21]

While it would appear on the surface that a sub-S corporation is the best of all possible worlds for real estate investment, providing limited liability coupled with deductibility of losses, a review of the requirements for qualification shows that there are pit-falls for the unwary and restrictions as to the use of this vehicle. In order to qualify, a corporation must meet all of the following requirements:

[20] "Do Kickers Have a Future?," *The Mortgage and Real Estate Executives Report,* November 15, 1973, pp. 1–2.
[21] This section was prepared by Mr. Lynn Stokes of Haskins & Sells.

1. It must be a domestic corporation with 10 or fewer shareholders all of whom are individuals or estates and none of whom is a non-resident alien.
2. It may not be used as a holding company because it may not be a member of an affiliated group under section 1504 of the Internal Revenue Code.
3. It may not have more than one class of stock.
4. It must not have more than 20 percent of its gross receipts in the form of "passive income" and not more than 80 percent of its gross receipts may be from outside the United States.

Failure to meet any of the above results in a termination of the corporation's election and a ban on re-electing for five years. The greatest danger of losing its election, however, is that the election may be lost through inadvertance and its loss may not be discovered until it is too late, that is, until several years have already passed. Such a discovery would not only undo all the taxplanning done in the interim but might significantly change the taxability and, therefore, the economics of many of the intervening transactions. For example, a sale of real property would now be taxed at two levels rather than one (once to the corporation as gain on the sale of the property with the subsequent distribution to the shareholder taxed as a dividend at the ordinary income rates) thereby giving the shareholder a smaller return than he had planned on when negotiating the sales price.

Assuming that the participants are willing to accept the risks of accidental disqualification inherent in this vehicle, some of the restrictions are as follows:

1. If the lender is a corporation it cannot be given a piece of a sub-S developer as an equity kicker because this would break the sub-S election. (All shareholders must be individuals or estates.)
2. If the investment objective is speculation the size of the group must be limited (no more than 10 shareholders) and its composition must be monitored (no shareholders other than an individual or an estate and no non-resident aliens) for initial as well as subsequent shareholders.
3. If the property is to be located in the U.S. it should not be difficult to prevent more than 80 percent of the corporation's gross receipts from being from outside the U.S. However, com-

plying with the limitation on passive income, 20 percent or less of gross receipts, will be difficult for any real estate venture. This is true for several reasons:

a. Rents are deemed to be passive income for this purpose, unless significant services (such as in a hotel) are provided, and

b. the definition of gross receipts is very broad. As an example, if a speculative syndicate is holding farm land and allows a farmer to use it in return for his paying the real estate taxes or other expenses, this would constitute gross receipts from passive rents and would break the sub-S election unless the corporation had sufficient active income to offset it.

In addition to the problems discussed above, it should be remembered that the losses of a sub-S corporation may only be deducted by the shareholder to the extent of his basis in his stock and his loans to the corporation (guarantees of third party liabilities do not count), and if not utilized in the year incurred are lost forever. This is contrasted with the situation of the partner or limited partner who may be allowed to add his share of third party liabilities to his basis even if he is not personally liable and whose losses may be deducted in a later year, when he makes additional contributions, even if not deductible in the year when the loss is incurred.

Based on the foregoing it would appear that a sub-S corporation will be valuable to the real estate entrepreneur in two instances:

1. If a syndicate of individuals investing in raw land on a leveraged basis seek limited liability and will fund the current operating loss of the venture by annual contributions to pay interest, taxes, etc. An example of this format is William B. Howell, 57 TC No. 58, where the Internal Revenue Service argued alternatively that (1) either the corporation was passive and could not elect sub-S or (2) that it was active and the gain on the sale of its real property could not be capital. The court held for the taxpayer on both points.

2. In a situation where a group is constructing or rehabilitating property for rental use and wishes to deduct the losses during the construction phase. In this situation an exhaustion of the shareholders basis and, therefore, a loss of tax benefit may be avoided by electing to capitalize a portion of the construction period carrying charges under section 266 IRC.

If the entrepreneur uses this vehicle he should remember that there are many administrative complexities. He should engage competent tax advisors to help him achieve his objectives.

REVIEW AND STUDY QUESTIONS

1. What is meant by creative financing and what factors have prompted investors, developers, and lenders to enter into creative financing arrangements?
2. Explain the joint venture and give an example.
3. What is a wraparound mortgage and why is it used?
4. Discuss the variable interest rate and its advantages and disadvantages to the lender.
5. Discuss separate financing of the land and building.
6. What is basket money?
7. Discuss the joint loan concept.
8. Discuss: (A) the sale-leaseback, and (B) the installment sales contract.
9. Discuss the ways in which second mortgages may be used in financing real estate.
10. Define interim financing and give several ways it is used.
11. Discuss the use of options in financing real estate.
12. What are the main provisions of a trust agreement when title to property is held by a trustee.
13. Define "kickers," give several examples, and explain certain guidelines for their use.

FURTHER READINGS AND REFERENCES

Beaton, William R., *Real Estate Investment,* Chapter 7, "Creative Financing." Englewood Cliffs, N.J.: Prentice-Hall, Inc., 1971.

"Do Kickers Have a Future?," *The Mortgage and Real Estate Executives Report,* November 15, 1973, pp. 1-2.

Gunning, Francis P., "The Wrap-Around Mortgage . . . Friend or U. F. O.?" *Real Estate Review,* Summer, 1972, pp. 35-48.

"How to Use Second Mortgages in Today's Real Estate Market," *The Mortgage and Real Estate Executives Report,* September 18, 1973, pp. 1-2.

"Increased Opportunities, Flexibility Seen in Joint Mortgage Lending," *The Mortgage Banker,* November, 1973, pp. 78-82.

Miller, R. A. Stuart, and James C. Kafes, "Mortgage Participation: Effects on Real Estate Investments," *The Appraisal Journal,* pp. 178-193.

Sonnenblick, Jack E., "The Art of Intricate Financing," *Real Estate Today,*
    July, 1969, pp. 26-35.

"Using the Interim Loan to Buy Time," *The Mortgage and Real Estate
    Executives Report,* September 18, 1973, pp. 1-2.

THIRTEEN

Syndication, Tax Shelter, and the Limited Partnership

A real estate syndicate is a method of raising equity capital. The "syndicate" is a group of persons who organize in some form of legal entity, such as a corporation or limited partnership, and pool their funds for investment in real estate. The group is dissolved when the objective of the syndicate is accomplished.

REASONS FOR SYNDICATION

Syndication has always been an attractive way to finance real estate though the degree of popularity of the method has gone through cycles. A number of factors in the economy in recent years have accounted for increased interest in syndication. Further, real estate brokers, who often promote syndicates and participate in them, find that syndication offers benefits to their business.

Factors of Growth

1. People today are more knowledgeable about real estate and its investment advantages. They see new developments; news and magazine articles on real estate appear frequently; and educational programs and courses in real estate have attracted enrollment of the public. Knowledge and awareness have resulted in increased demand for participation in real estate investments and the syndicate is one way to meet the demand.

2. The increased demand is supported by the financial ability to satisfy that demand. People have higher incomes and increased public and private retirement benefits.

3. There have been more syndicates organized in recent years and and wider promotional efforts in selling them. People have more opportunities to invest in this medium and are more likely to be offered a participation.

4. The population make-up or "mix" is favorable to syndication. Syndicate investors are typically in the 30 to 55 years of age range and this group constitutes a substantial segment of the population. They also have a strong earning power and can handle the typical syndicate investment of $2,500 to $10,000 easily. Further, there is considerable activity in syndicate organization and promotion by persons in the 24 to 29 years of age bracket.

5. There are more and better properties suitable for syndicate investment available today. Typical of the types of attractive properties are apartment complexes, shopping centers, office buildings, industrial buildings, warehouses, and raw acreage.

6. While the income tax benefits of real estate investment have been modified in recent years, real estate continues to offer advantages taxwise. Syndication provides a good vehicle for maximizing these benefits to the individual investor.

7. Prices of sound investment real estate are generally high and have been steadily increasing over the long-run. Inflation has been a contributing factor. Large sums of money are needed for the acquisition of properties. Syndication has proven to be an excellent method of raising the needed sums.

8. Investment real estate has acquired a broad-based national market. Investors are willing to participate in properties outside of their local areas. Syndicates have provided an opportunity for national investment outlets.

Benefits to the Broker

The real estate broker renders a service to the public. A profit should come from an efficient and knowledgeable service. Syndication can increase profits of the broker in two ways:

1. Knowledge of syndication will enable the broker to offer a wider real estate service. Persons interested in syndicate organizations or investment will seek out his services.
2. Syndication requires a working knowledge of many subjects, such as income taxation, business organization types, creative financing, and economics. The broker who engages in syndication will broaden his educational horizons and keep current with advances in knowledge. Syndication prompts continuing education.

INVESTOR'S PROFITS

Both the investor and the syndicator are attracted to syndication because of the profit maximizing potential of the arrangement. The investor (that is, the person who buys a share of the syndicate) has five possible sources of profit or income from a properly structured syndicate: (1) net cash flow; (2) tax shelter or tax write-offs; (3) equity build-up; (4) capital appreciation; and (5) leverage.

Net Cash Flow

Net cash flow is a primary objective in a real estate investment. It is computed as follows: gross income from the property; less vacancy allowance, operating expenses, and reserves; and less the mortgage payments or debt service.

Tax Shelter

The investor would like to reduce his taxable income as much as legally possible so as to increase his "take-home" or "money in-pocket" income from the property. Tax shelter means that he seeks to offset or shelter income with tax deductions. Typical of such deductions are mortgage interest and depreciation. Taxable income is computed as follows: Gross income from the property, less vacancy allowance and operating expenses, including property taxes. The result is net operating income, from which is deducted mortgage interest and depreciation to arrive at taxable income. Note that net cash flow and taxable income are different concepts. Capital gain is also a tax benefit to the investor in that it permits gain on the sale of property to be taxed at more favorable rates than if the gain were all from ordinary income.

Equity Buildup

Each payment on a mortgage, assuming the payment includes an amount to be applied toward both principal and interest, reduces the principal sum of the debt and increases the owner's equity, or ownership interest, in the property. The periodic amortization of principal and reduction of dollar liability on the debt may be considered as a source of profit, gain, or income to the investor. The equity buildup is converted to cash upon disposition of the property or by its refinancing.

Equity buildup is quoted as a percentage of the investor's equity in the property or on the total value of the property. It should be remembered that as the investor's equity increases, the percentage rate of return on equity will decrease.

Capital Appreciaiton

Investors anticipate that the capital value of their investment will increase or appreciate during the term of the investment. Appreciation is considered to be a source of profit or income and the increase each year is quoted as a percentage return on equity, or on the total value of the property. Capital appreciation is realized upon disposition of the property or by its refinancing.

Leverage

Most real estate is financed through borrowed funds, usually with a mortgage loan in some form. Borrowed funds, when properly used and with a sound financing arrangement, will increase the rate of return on equity if the earnings on the investment exceed the cost of the borrowed funds.

SYNDICATOR'S PROFITS

The person who organizes a syndicate is known as the syndicator; the syndicator may also be an investor. The incentive is profit, which may come from several sources: (1) income participation with the investors in the net cash flow, income tax benefits, equity buildup, capital appreciation, and leverage benefits of the syndicate; (2) property management fees; (3) real estate commissions on acquisition and disposition of syndicate property; (4) development and construction profits; and (5) leases and rents.

Income Participation

The syndicator may receive a share of the income from the property, including tax savings, mortgage reduction, leverage, and gain upon disposition of the property. One arrangement might be for the investors to receive their designated share first, with the syndicator then receiving an equal amount. Income remaining is distributed according to a formula agreed upon at the inception of the syndicate.

Property Management Fees

The syndicator may receive a fee for the management of the real estate of the syndicate. The management function includes receipt of the income from the property and responsibility for the payment of operating expenses and distribution of income to the investors. Management also includes physical maintenance of the real estate so as to maintain and enhance its capital value.

Real Estate Commissions

Syndicates are frequently organized by licensed real estate brokers. The brokers may, in addition to providing management and promotional expertise, actively acquire and dispose of investment property for the group. The broker may charge the syndicate a commission for these services.

Development and Construction Profits

The funds of a syndicate may be used for the development and construction of a project. The syndicator may be the developer and builder of the project and receive construction profit from the syndicate for these services.

Leases and Rents

The syndicator may receive income in the form of rents over a certain level. A property may, for example, be sold to the syndicate at a given schedule of rents. The syndicator may arrange to receive a portion of or all increases in the rental schedule.

SELECTION OF A LEGAL ENTITY

The syndicate is not a separate legal entity or form but a group of people brought together for a common objective, namely, to pool their funds for investment in real estate. The syndicate must select a form of legal ownership in which to hold and manage its property.

Consult Professional Counsel

Syndication is heavily and strictly regulated by all levels of government. Selection of an ownership form involves legal and income tax considerations which are subject to change. There is considerable work and risk in the organization and promotion of the syndicate and detailed processes must be followed to meet legal and income tax regulations. Professional counsel should be retained in any syndication for legal and tax matters.

Objective

The selection of an ownership form will be determined in part by the objective of the investors and the type of property to be acquired. If the objective is to receive cash flow, income producing property will be acquired and held in a form, such as limited partnership, which will permit maximum income to be passed through the entity to the investors. If the objective is to acquire raw land and hold it for capital appreciation, the ownership form may be a joint venture arrangement which permits the group to be called upon for additional cash if needed. Land may also be held in a limited partnership and many syndicators use this form of ownership for land.

TYPES OF SYNDICATES

Syndicates may be divided into four categories: (1) blind pool offering; (2) specific property offering; (3) interstate offering; and (4) intrastate offering. In a blind pool offering the syndicator raises the money first, and has no specific property in mind for an investment. He seeks out properties to buy after acquiring a pool of capital. The syndicator has the advantage of being able to negotiate and close a transaction quickly since the cash is in hand. A disadvantage is the possibility of the syndicator making investment without adequate investigation because of pressure to spend the capital pool.

In the specific property offering, the syndicator raises money to acquire or contract for a particular property. The syndicator enters into a contract with the developer or owner to acquire the property and raises the money to close the transaction at a specified time.

The interstate offering involves promotion and sale of syndicate shares or units in more than one state. It is usually a large public offering and shares are sold to hundreds of investors. Such an offering requires registration with the Federal Securities and Exchange Commission (SEC). The registration and approval process may take several months, and the syndicator should allow for this time factor in planning the acquisition of properties for the proposed syndicate.

Intrastate offerings are confined to a particular state and are governed by state law. The property, the business, and the investors are all in one state. The state law may provide, for example, that: (1) solicitation is limited to not more than 25 persons; (2) they must all be known to you previously; (3) the offering may not be advertised; and (4) subscribers are limited to not more than 15 persons. A larger offering must be registered with the state securities commission.

LIMITED PARTNERSHIP

The limited partnership legal entity is commonly used in real estate syndication. The form has both benefits and limitations.

Benefits

There are a number of benefits to the investor, among which are the following:

1. Cash flow and tax shelter are passed through the limited partnership directly to the investor.
2. Professional management is given by the syndicator, who is usually the general partner.
3. There is limited liability of the limited partners.
4. A share in a soundly conceived limited partnership has good liquidity.
5. There is a definite life of the syndicate.
6. There is leverage; good buying power and good financing power of a soundly conceived limited partnership group.

Risks and Limitations

The purchase of units or shares in a limited partnership involves elements of risks and limitations. While details will vary with a given entity, the below factors should be considered in any purchase:

1. A limited partnership may be declared an association and taxed as a corporation.
2. Income tax laws and regulations change and may result in the limited partnership losing some or all of its present tax benefits.
3. Management has complete discretion in property acquisitions.
4. There is no assurance that a syndicate will be profitable or that the objectives of the group will be realized at any time.
5. A syndicate unit or share may not have a public market and thereby have limited liquidity. Limited partnership units usually may not be assigned without written consent of the general partner and thereby have limited transferability.
6. Management may have little, if any, experience in investing in certain types of properties. Also, it may not be familiar with many geographic areas in which it is permitted to invest the funds of the group.
7. A syndicate, like any business enterprise, is subject to the competition and risks of the highly competitive field of real estate investment. A new syndicate faces competition from established groups as well as from groups with greater experience and financial resources.
8. A limited partner has no control over the general partner and may not exercise any voice in management.
9. Any property acquisition by the syndicate involves the usual risks of investing in real estate. Market changes in demand and supply, rents, and operating expenses can materially affect the value of the property. There are the usual risks of construction when the syndicate uses its funds to develop and construct property.
10. Syndicates depend heavily on the use of borrowed funds, that is, leverage, which involves the possibility of loss as well as gain. Further, a syndicate has no assurance that it will always be able to obtain financing, or that desired terms will be available, or what limitations lenders may impose on the syndicate.

11. A syndicate is always subject to the risks of changes in the money market, general economic conditions, and governmental controls in the economy. Further, it is difficult to predict the effect of changes in federal and state regulations on syndicate operations. Examples of such regulations are environmental and ecological standards, wage and price controls, and rent controls.

TAX ASPECTS OF LIMITED PARTNERSHIP

Tax counsel to a limited partnership usually requests a ruling from the Internal Revenue Service to the effect that the limited partnership will be treated as a partnership and not as an association taxable as a corporation. A favorable ruling includes at least two conditions:

1. The net worth of the general partner at all times must be at least 10 percent of the total capitalization of all partnerships of which it is the general partner. In computing the net worth of the general partner for this purpose, its interest in the limited partnership, plus any interest it has in other limited partnerships, and all notes or accounts receivable from or payable to any limited partnership in which it has an interest, must be excluded; and,
2. Limited partners may not at any time, directly or indirectly, either individually or collectively, own more than 20 percent of the capital stock of the general partner or any of its affiliates.

Three conditions might result in the limited partnership losing its favorable tax ruling and being declared as an association taxable as a corporation: (1) a change in the Internal Revenue Code or regulations; (2) a change in the Limited Partnership Agreement; and (3) failure of the general partner to meet the net worth or other requirements of the Internal Revenue Code or regulations. If a limited partnership is treated for Federal income tax purposes as a corporation in any taxable year, the limited partnership would be required to pay taxes on its income, deductions would be made only on its tax return, and distributions to the limited partners may be taxable to them as dividend income.

A summary is presented below of some of the Federal income tax consequences to limited partners in a limited partnership. Two factors must be remembered: (1) income tax laws and regulations change; and

(2) the discussion below is brief and is no substitute for advice from competent tax counsel when considering a specific situation.

1. A limited partnership is not subject to the payment of federal income tax. Each limited partner is required to report, on his personal tax return, his prorata share of the taxable income of the limited partnership, whether or not distributed to him. It is possible that the tax liability of a limited partner may exceed the cash distributed to him in a given year, that is, he may be required to recognize taxable income attributable to his interest in the limited partnership without receiving cash distributions with which to pay the taxes. Such a situation could arise, for example, in the sale of property on the installment plan where a large part of the cash received on sale is paid out for real estate commissions. The commissions are not deductible in full in the year of payment unless the taxpayer is classified as a "dealer".

2. A limited partnership may prepay interest on certain indebtedness for periods up to twelve months of the taxable year in which the prepayment is made. Such deductions are considered by the Internal Revenue Service on an individual case basis to determine whether a material distortion of income has resulted. Where a material distortion of income has been found to result from the deduction of prepaid interest, the Internal Revenue Service requires a cash basis taxpayer to change his method of accounting with respect to such prepaid interest in order to allocate it to the years to which such interest relates.

3. The tax basis of a limited partnership interest is generally equal to its cost, reduced by the limited partner's share of partnership income. Further, the tax basis of the limited partner's interest is increased by his proportionate share of liabilities to which partnership assets are subject, but for which no partner or the partnership is liable, such as real estate acquired subject to a mortgage which is not assumed by the partnership or any of its partners. The proportionate share for this purpose is the proportion in which the partners share profits of the partnership. A decrease of a limited partner's share of the above type of liability is treated for tax purposes as though it were a cash distribution, which may or may not be taxable. Examples of actions resulting in such a decrease in liability would be: (1) sale of a property subject to the mortgage; (2) payment of the mortgage in part or in whole; (3) foreclosure of the mortgage; and (4) sale of the limited partner's interest.

4. If the cash distributions to a limited partner in any year, including his share in any reduction of liabilities, exceed his share of the limited partnership's taxable income for that year, the excess constitutes a return of capital to the limited partner. A return of capital is not reportable as taxable income by a recipient, but it will reduce the tax basis of his partnership interest. If the tax basis of a limited partner's interest is reduced to zero, his share of cash distributions for any year, including his share in reduction in liabilities as described above in excess of his share of partnership taxable income, is taxable to him as though it were a gain on the sale or exchange of his partnership interest. A limited partner's share of a partnership loss is not deductible if the tax basis of his interest is reduced to zero.

5. The income tax cost to each limited partner upon the sale of partnership properties depends upon a number of factors. A gain or loss at the time of sale is taxed as a capital gain or loss if the properties are held for investment and not primarily for sale to customers in the ordinary course of the business or trade of the partnership. Any of the gain which represents excess depreciation and is subject to recapture must first be reported as ordinary income, and the remaining gain will be taxed at capital gain rates. If the partnership is determined to be a "dealer" and its investment in a given property is ruled not to be a capital asset, any gain or loss on the sale or other disposition of the property is treated as ordinary income or loss. A limited partnership for investing in real estate usually has the intention of conducting its business in such a manner as to not be declared a "dealer" in real estate, thereby permitting limited partners to report their respective share of gains as capital gains.

6. Gain or loss realized on the sale of a limited partnership interest by a limited partner who is not a "dealer" in securities and who has held the interest for more than six months is a long-term capital gain or loss. The portion of the sale proceeds attributable to the limited partner's share of substantially appreciated inventory items and unrealized receivables, as well as any applicable depreciation recapture, is taxed at ordinary income rates. It is possible that the Federal income tax payable upon sale of a limited partner's share could exceed the actual cash proceeds of the sale because a limited partner, upon sale or other disposition of his interest, is deemed to receive a cash distribution to the extent of his proportionate share of liabilities against the assets of the partnership.

7. The limited partnership in real estate usually files, under Sec-

tion 754 of the Internal Revenue Code, an election to adjust the basis of partnership property in the case of a transfer of a limited partnership interest. The effect of this election is that, with respect to the transferee partner only, the basis of the partnership's property will either be increased or decreased by the the difference between the transferee's basis for his partnership interest and his proportionate share of the partnership's adjusted basis for all partnership property. Any increase or decrease resulting from such adjustment is allocatable among the partnership's assets in accordance with rules and regulations in the Internal Revenue Code. After such adjustment is made, the transferee partner's share of the adjusted basis of the partnership's property is equal to the adjusted basis of his partnership interest. If this election is not made, the amount of a transferee partner's taxable income from the partnership would be determined with reference to a basis reflecting his predecessor's cost, unadjusted to reflect the amount paid by the transferee partner for his interest in the limited partnership.

TAX REFORM ACT OF 1969

The Tax Reform Act of 1969, which amended the Internal Revenue Code of 1954, made several changes affecting the tax benefits traditionally associated with the ownership of real estate. The following items are among the provisions of that Act affecting limited partners.

1. The 25 percent alternative tax rate applicable to the excess of long-term capital gains over short-term capital losses is eliminated except as to aggregate net long-term capital gains which do not exceed $50,000. The maximum rate for individuals on the excess over $50,000 is 35 percent. Only one half of long-term capital losses may be used for the $1,000 annual deduction from ordinary income available to individuals.
2. A new 10 percent additional tax is imposed on certain tax "preferences". The preferences include the excess of accelerated over straight line depreciation on real property, and the amount allowable to an individual taxpayer under the 50 percent capital gains deduction. The amount subject to the 10 percent tax is the aggregate of tax preference items reduced by: (1) a specific exemption of $30,000; (2) the taxpayer's regular income tax, less certain tax credits, for such taxable year; and (3) any

amount of the taxpayer's "tax carry-overs" for the seven preceding years, excluding any year before 1970. The extent to which the tax preferences of a limited partner are subject to the 10 percent tax depends on his overall tax situation.

3. A limitation is placed, for any taxable year, upon the deductibility of interest on funds borrowed to acquire or to carry investment assets. In general, interest is deductible in such cases by non-corporate taxpayers only to the extent that it does not exceed the sum of the following items: (1) $25,000, but only $12,500 for a married taxpayer filing a separate return and zero for a trust; (2) net investment income, that is, the excess of non-trade or business income from interest, dividends, rents, royalties, and net short-term capital gain from investment property over expenses, including straight-line depreciation, incurred in earning such income; (3) net longer-term capital gain in excess of net short-term capital loss from the disposition of investment property; and (4) one-half of the excess of investment interest over the total of the three items given above. That is, only one-half of the excess investment interest is disallowed as a deduction, but it may be carried over to subsequent years within certain limits. Interest incurred in real estate ventures, if the property involved is rented under a net lease (and this may be the case with certain investments by a limited partnership), is regarded as "investment interest," subject to disallowance, as distinguished from business interest, which remains fully deductible. The effect of this change is that under certain circumstances the full amount of mortgage interest passed through from the partnership to the limited partners might not be allowable as a deduction to some or all of the limited partners where property is rented by the partnership under a net lease. Also, long-term capital gains used to offset investment interest are treated as ordinary income for tax purposes.

4. A limited partnership may elect to use accelerated methods of depreciation, that is, methods which give a faster write-off than the straight line method. Double declining balance and the sum-of-the-years digits methods may be used for new residential rental real property where at least 80 percent of the gross rental income for the year is from dwelling units, such as apartment houses. Other new buildings are limited to the 150 percent declining balance method. Used buildings are limited to straight-line depreciation, except for residential rental property with a useful life of twenty years or more at acquisition, which is allowed 125 percent declining balance depreciation.

5. Excess depreciation, which is the excess of accelerated depreciation over straight-line depreciation, on depreciable real property, other than residential rental property, is subject to being fully recaptured as ordinary income when the property is sold, regardless of how long it is held before such sale. Excess depreciation on residential rental property is subject to being fully recaptured only if it is held for less than 100 months. The recapture of excess depreciation on residential property is decreased by one percent for each month such property is held beyond 100 months so that there is no recapture if the property is held for 16 years and 8 months. All recapture of excess depreciation is recognized by a limited partner at the time he disposes of his limited partnership interest. Such recapture could cause part or all of the consideration received by the limited partner to be taxed as ordinary income. Depreciation taken on personal property also continues to be subject to recapture to the extent of gain realized on sale of the property.

STATE AND LOCAL TAXES

In addition to Federal income tax considerations, a limited partnership may be subject to state and local taxes in jurisdictions in which the partnership is deemed to be doing business or in which it owns property or other interests. Prospective investors need to consider potential state and local tax consequences on an investment in a limited partnership.

THE LIMITED PARTNERSHIP AGREEMENT

A limited partnership is created under the laws of a particular state. The rights and liabilities of the parties are provided in the partnership laws of the respective state and, along with the provisions of the agreement between the parties, govern the operations of the group.

The provisions of a Limited Partnership Agreement vary with the nature of the particular group, its objectives, and desired operating policies. The provisions discussed below give an example of one agreement.

FORMATION. Parties form the limited partnership under the Uniform Limited Partnership Act of a specified state.

NAME. This is the name under which the business of the limited partnership will be conducted.

PRINCIPAL PLACE OF BUSINESS. This is the address of the principal place of business of the limited partnership, and the addresses of the limited partners.

PURPOSES. The aims are acquiring, owning, leasing, operating, improving, selling, exchanging, and otherwise using interests in real estate for profit; doing and engaging in any and all activities related to or incidental thereto; real estate interests include fee, leasehold, equitable, and land contracts, as well as legal interests.

DEFINITIONS. These are the meanings of terms used in the limited partnership agreement, such as general partner, limited partners, net profits, net losses, unit of limited partnership interest, cash available for distribution, and limited partnership asset.

CAPITAL CONTRIBUTIONS. The general partner is not required to make cash contributions to the limited partnership; the general partner may purchase shares or units and be a limited partner with respect to these shares. Public offering of a specified number of shares or units, procedure for handling subscriptions and monies, and termination of offering.

ALLOCATIONS. Net profits and losses are allocated entirely to limited partners; quarterly distributions of available cash are made entirely to limited partners in proportion to their respective ownership of shares or units. Compensation of a general partner consists of: (1) its share of profits and losses and distributions of cash as owner of shares or units; (2) a fee upon the sale of partnership assets; for example, 15 percent of the net gains realized on the sale; (3) an organizational fee; for example, 7 percent of each share or unit sold by the limited partnership; (4) a management fee; for example, a fee equal to 10 percent of the gross revenues of the limited partnership from operations, but not from the sale of partnership assets, before deduction of partnership expenses; (5) reimbursement of expenses in administering the partnership, except salaries paid by the general partner to its officers and employees.

RIGHTS AND DUTIES. The general partner has complete and exclusive control over the management, conduct, and operation of the limited partnership and makes all decisions affecting its business. The power and authority is granted to do, but not limited to, the following: (1) acquire interests in real estate; (2) sell and convey all or any part of the property owned by the limited partnership; (3) execute or modify leases on real estate owned by the limited partnership; (4) borrow money and encumber partnership property as security; (5) prepay, refinance, recast, increase, modify, or consolidate mortgages or other encumbrances on the limited partnership property; (6) formulate a program for the investment of the assets of the limited partnership and select and evaluate potential projects for investment; (7) employ persons whose services are necessary for the operation of the limited partnership; (8) manage, improve, alter, and further develop the assets of the limited partnership; (9) enter into and execute agreements and documents customarily used in the real estate industry in connection with the acquisition, sale, development, and operation of real properties; (10) maintain adequate records and accounts of all operations and expenditures and furnish limited partners with annual statements of accounts together with tax reporting information; (11) purchase insurance to protect the limited partnership's properties and business; (12) make elections under tax laws as to treatment of items of limited partnership income, expense, gain, loss, credit, and other relevant matters; and (13) perform any and all other acts or activities customary or incident to the acquisition, ownership. management, improvement, leasing, and disposition of real estate, and to the investment in mortgages and the conduct of other real estate financing activities.

A general partner may sometimes engage "affiliates" to perform services for the limited partnership. Affiliate means a company or other entity controlled by officers and directors of the general partner or in which they have a material interest, and it may include the general partner and its subsidiaries. Affiliates may be used for such services as: real estate brokerage, real estate management, insurance, financing, title abstracting, title insurance, accounting, legal, and administrative activities.

LIMITED PARTNERS. The shares or units of the limited partners are fully paid and non-assessable; a limited partner shall not become personally liable for debts of the limited partnership in an amount exceeding the capital contributed by him plus his share of undistributed profits and cash available for distribution. Limited partners do not take part in the management of the limited partnership business or transact any business for the limited partnership, and do not have the power to sign for or bind the limited partnership to any agreement or document.

TRANSFERS. A limited partner may assign his shares or units and have the assignee become a substituted limited partner provided certain conditions are met: execution and filing by the assignor of an assignment instrument; payment of a transfer fee ($50.00, for example); execution by the assignee of a power attorney; and acceptance of the assignment and admission of the assignee as a substituted limited partner by the general partner. Death, legal disability, bankruptcy, or dissolution of a limited partner does not dissolve the limited partnership, but his interest passes to his legal representative who has the rights of a limited partner for the purpose of settling the estate or business of such limited partner, including the right to transfer such interest or to be substituted as a limited partner.

DURATION. A limited partnership may be terminated in several ways. Examples of events which will dissolve the entity include one or more of the following: (1) written consent or affirmative vote of limited partners owning more than 50 percent of the capital of the limited partnership; (2) disposition of all interests in real estate and other assets of the limited partnership; and (3) expiration of a specified number of years (15 or 30 years, for example) from the date of formation of the limited partnership.

REVIEW AND STUDY QUESTIONS

1. Define a syndicate and list the reasons accounting for their recent growth.
2. How can engaging in syndication activity increase the profits of real estate brokers?
3. What are the five possible sources of profit to the investor in a real estate syndicate?
4. What are the five possible sources of profit to the syndicator, that is, the person who organizes a syndicate?
5. How does a syndicate go about selecting a legal entity or form of legal ownership in which to hold or manage syndicate property?
6. Define the four categories of syndicates.
7. What are the benefits and limitations of the limited partnership as a legal entity?
8. Discuss the income tax aspects of the limited partnership.
9. List some of the provisions which may be found in the limited partnership agreement.

FURTHER READINGS AND REFERENCES

Augustine, Don, and Ronald R. Hrusoff, "The Growing Pains of Public Real Estate Syndicates," *Real Estate Review*, Fall, 1971, pp. 22-27.

Beaton, William R., *Real Estate Investment*, Chapter 5, "Ownership Forms." Englewood Cliffs, N.J.: Prentice-Hall, Inc., 1971.

Berman, Daniel S., *How to Reap Profits in Local Real Estate Syndicates*. Englewood Cliffs, N.J.: Prentice-Hall, Inc., 1964.

Casey, William J., *Real Estate Investment Planning.* New York: Institute for Business Planning, 1965.

Dinehart, Mason A., "Selling Syndication Shares Successfully: A Professional's Approach," *Real Estate Review,* Fall, 1972, pp. 38-43.

Hussander, Martin, *Real Estate Syndicator's Manual and Guide.* Englewood Cliffs, N.J.: Prentice-Hall, Inc., 1969.

Malkan, Willard, "Who Gets What in a Tax-Shelter Syndicate," *Real Estate Review,* Fall, 1972, pp. 26-31.

Roulac, Stephen E., *Real Estate Syndication Digest: Principles and Applications.* San Francisco: Real Estate Syndication Digest, Inc., 1972.

Glossary

ABSTRACT COMPANY. Also known as a title company. A business which prepares abstracts of title for a fee.

ABSTRACT CONTINUATION. Extension or continuation of an abstract of title commencing with the date of the previous abstract.

ABSTRACT OF TITLE. A condensed history or summary of the title to a parcel of real estate.

ACCELERATION CLAUSE. A clause in a note, bond, mortgage, or deed of trust which provides that in the event of default by the borrower, the entire balance of the obligation shall become due and payable at once.

ACKNOWLEDGEMENT. A formal declaration before a duly authorized person, such as a notary public, to the effect that the person executing the instrument is performing his free act and deed and that the signature is genuine.

ADD-ON INTEREST. Interest for the term of the loan is added to the principal of the loan. Borrower, however, receives only the principal but signs a note for both principal and interest.

ADMINISTRATOR. A person appointed by a court to administer the estate of a deceased person who left no will (died intestate).

AD VALOREM. A tax according to value; used in real estate taxation.

AFFIDAVIT. A written statement or declaration sworn or affirmed to before an authorized officer.

AIR RIGHTS. Ownership or interest in the air space over a given property.

AMENITY. The tangible or intangible quality aspects or benefits of a property which give satisfaction to its owner rather than money income.

AMORTIZATION. The repayment of the principal of a loan in periodic installments; payments usually include principal and interest and often an amount to an escrow account to pay property taxes and hazard insurance premiums when due.

APPRAISAL. An opinion and estimate of value.

ASSESSED VALUE. The valuation placed upon property by a public body for purposes of taxation.

ASSESSMENT. The valuation of property for tax purposes; also refers to a tax levied against property for a special purpose.

ASSIGNMENT. A transfer of an interest in property from one person to another. The party who transfers the right or interest is known as the assignor and the party to whom the interest is transferred is known as the assignee.

ASSUMPTION OF A MORTGAGE. The agreement between buyer and seller whereby the buyer takes over personal liability for an existing mortgage debt on a property.

ATTACHMENT. A legal process whereby a defendant's property is seized by court order to have it available if needed to satisfy a judgment in a pending court action.

ATTEST. To witness or affirm that a document is genuine or true.

ATTORNEY IN FACT. A person legally appointed by another to transact business for him.

BALLOON PAYMENT. The final payment on an obligation, with the payment being greater than any of the preceding ones.

BLANKET MORTGAGE. One mortgage which covers more than one parcel of real estate.

CAPITALIZATION. The process of converting an income stream into a capital value figure.

CASH THROWOFF. Net operating income less debt service on the mortgage.

CAVEAT EMPTOR. Let the buyer beware.

CHATTEL MORTGAGE. A mortgage on personal property.

CLOSING. The final settlement between a buyer and seller of real estate in which title is transferred and an accounting of funds is made by all parties to the transaction.

CLOSING STATEMENT. A written itemized accounting of income and expense funds between buyer and seller when a real estate transaction is closed or completed.

CLOUD ON TITLE. A claim on the property which, if valid, could be a defect impairing the title.

COLOR OF TITLE. A title which appears to be good but which in reality is not a good title.

COMMITMENT. A promise or pledge by a lender to make a loan on specified terms at a given time in the future.

COMPOUND INTEREST. Interest paid on the original principal and all other interest accrued or earned; interest paid on interest.

CONDOMINIUM. Ownership of a single unit in a multiple unit building, with joint ownership in the common elements of the property, such as the land and recreational facilities.

CONSTANT. A level payment on a mortgage which includes both principal and interest.

CONSTRUCTION LOAN. An interim or temporary loan to finance the construction of a building and other improvements on a site; loan disbursements are made in stages as the construction progresses.

CONVENTIONAL LOAN. A mortgage which is not insured or guaranteed by a government agency.

CONVEYANCE. Transfer of title from one person to another. Also, the instrument by which the transfer is made, such as the deed.

COOPERATIVE. Ownership of a unit in a multiple unit building; the individual owns stock in the corporation which grants him a proprietary lease to his unit.

CORRESPONDENT. A mortgage banker who originates and services loans for an investor, such as a life insurance company.

COVENANT. A written promise or agreement between two or more persons in a legal instrument, such as a contract, deed, or mortgage in which one of the parties promises the performance or nonperformance of certain acts, or that a given state of facts does or does not exist.

CURTESY. The interest of a husband in the real estate owned by his wife.

DEBENTURE. A form of note or bond backed by the general credit of the issuer. Also, a form of payment made by FHA to mortgage lenders when a mortgage is foreclosed and title is transferred to FHA.

DEBT. An amount of money due by certain and express agreement.

DEBT SERVICE. The annual payment made on a mortgage loan, including principal and interest.

DEED. The written instrument which transfers title to real estate.

DEED OF TRUST. Conveyance of title to a trustee as security for a debt; in the event of default the trustee has the power to sell the property. When the debt is paid the trustee reconveys the title to the debtor.

DEED RESTRICTION. Provisions in a deed limiting or restricting the use of the property.

DEFAULT. Failure to meet a legal obligation in a contract, note, or mortgage, such as failure to make the monthly payments on a mortgage.

DEFICIENCY JUDGMENT. When a foreclosure sale of property does not bring sufficient funds to pay the debt, the court may issue a judgment against the debtor for the deficiency.

DELINQUENCY. Failure of the debtor to pay an obligation when due.

DEMAND MORTGAGE. A mortgage payable on demand of its holder.

DENSITY. Number of lots per acre of land.

DEPRECIATION. Loss of value in real estate from any cause; usually due to physical deterioration, functional obsolescence, and economic obsolescence.

DEVELOPMENT LOAN. A loan for the purpose of developing raw land so that construction of buildings may start, such as grading for roads and the installation of utilities.

DISCOUNT. The fee or interest deducted from a loan at the time it is made or sold; the difference between the principal amount of the loan and the actual amount loaned, expressed as a percentage of par value. Discounts are commonly used with FHA and VA mortgages to adjust their fixed interest rates to the current market rate.

DISCOUNTING. The process of converting an income stream into present value by means of a rate.

DISINTERMEDIATION. The withdrawal of money from savings institutions (intermediaries) and investment of it in direct market instruments, such as U.S. Treasury bills.

DOWER. The interest of a wife in her husband's estate at his death.

EMINENT DOMAIN. The right of government to acquire private property for public use upon payment of just compensation.

ENCROACHMENT. An improvement which extends beyond the property line and intrudes upon the property of another person.

ENCUMBRANCE. A lien or claim upon title to real estate, such as a mortgage or easement.

ENTITLEMENT. The insurance or guaranty benefit available to a qualified veteran.

EQUITABLE MORTGAGE. A financial arrangement which on its face is not a mortgage but whose intent is to create a mortgage in fact.

EQUITABLE RIGHT OF REDEMPTION. The right of the borrower to redeem his property during a stated period of time after the foreclosure sale.

EQUITY. The difference between the market value of the property and the mortgage amount and other liens against it.

EQUITY OF REDEMPTION. The right of the borrower to redeem his property before the foreclosure sale by payment of the debt, costs, and interest.

ESCHEAT. Reversion of property to the government when the owner dies and leaves no will or heirs.

ESCROW. Monies and instruments delivered to a third person to be held in trust for a specified use and under stipulated conditions.

ESCROW ACCOUNT. An account set up by the lender into which the borrower makes periodic payments, usually monthly, for taxes, hazard insurance, assessments, and FHA mortgage insurance premiums. The funds are held in trust by the lender who disburses the sums as they become due.

ESTATE. The degree, quantity, nature, and extent of interest which a person has in property.

ESTOPPEL. A statement of facts, about a mortgage, for example, which prevents the person making it from denying the facts at a later date.

EXCULPATORY CLAUSE. The clause in a mortgage which releases the debtor of any personal liability for the debt; the lender can look only to the mortgaged property as security for the debt.

EXECUTOR. A person designated in a will to carry out its provisions.

FANNIE MAE (FNMA). A secondary mortgage market.

FEDERAL HOME LOAN BANK SYSTEM. A credit reserve system for savings and loan associations, mutual savings banks, and life insurance companies; a system of regional banks designed to supply credit to its member institutions; used primarily by federal savings and loan associations.

FEDERAL HOME LOAN MORTGAGE CORPORATION. A secondary mortgage market under the Federal Home Loan Bank System; buys and sells conventional, FHA, and VA mortgages.

FEDERAL HOUSING ADMINISTRATION. An agency within the Department of Housing and Urban Development which insures loans on real estate.

FEDERAL SAVINGS AND LOAN INSURANCE CORPORATION. An agency of the Federal government, operating under the Federal Home Loan Bank Board, which insures savings accounts in member institutions.

FHA MORTGAGE. A loan that is insured by the Federal Housing Administration.

FEE SIMPLE. The largest estate or interest in real estate; owner has all rights in the property and there are no limitations on heirs. Also, known as fee and fee simple absolute estate.

FIDUCIARY. One who acts in a position of trust or confidence for the benefit of another party, particularly with respect to property and money.

FINANCIAL INTERMEDIARY. A financial institution, such as a savings and loan association, which acts as an intermediary between savers and borrowers; uses the funds of savers to lend to borrowers, such as on mortgage loans.

FINDER'S FEE. The fee or commission paid to a mortgage broker for bringing the lender and borrower together or for referring a loan to a broker.

FIRM COMMITMENT. A promise by an investor to purchase a specified mortgage loan; also, a commitment by FHA or VA to insure or guarantee a loan on a specific property and borrower.

FOREBEARANCE. A lender refraining from enforcing the terms of a mortgage or note for a given period of time.

FORECLOSURE. A legal process whereby property pledged as security for a debt is sold, in the event of default, to pay the debt; the property is usually sold at public auction by an officer of the court, such as the sheriff.

FUNCTIONAL OBSOLESCENCE. Decline in the value of property due to changes in style, design, technology, floor plan, and the like; the building is no longer adequately able to perform its intended function.

GARDEN APARTMENT. A multi-family dwelling, usually two or three stories, surrounded by grass and open space.

G.I. LOAN. A mortgage loan guaranteed to the lender by the Veterans Administration.

GRACE PERIOD. A period of time after which a loan payment is due in which the lender makes no charge or penalty.

GRANTEE. The person to whom real estate is conveyed.

GRANTOR. The person who conveys title to real estate.

GROSS INCOME. Total income from a property before deduction for expenses and debt service.

GROSS INCOME MULTIPLIER. A figure by which the gross income of a property is multiplied to arrive at its capital value.

GROUND RENT. Rent paid for the right to use a parcel of land for a given period of time.

HAZARD INSURANCE. A form of insurance whereby the insurance company protects the insured from specified losses, such as fire, windstorm, and the like.

HIGHEST AND BEST USE. That use of property which will produce the most profitable use of the site under existing legal and zoning restrictions.

HOMESTEAD. Real estate occupied by the owner as a home and used as his primary residence.

INCOME APPROACH. A method of appraising real estate in which the value is the present worth of future income from the property.

INCOME PROPERTY. Property which produces money income to its owner.

INFLATION HEDGE. An investment which appreciates in value during periods of inflation.

INSTRUMENT. A written document that gives formal expression to a legal agreement.

INTEREST. Rent or charge paid for the use of money.

INTERIM LOAN. A short-term mortgage loan, usually in the form of a construction loan, to finance improvements on land.

JOINT TENANCY. Ownership by two or more persons; upon the death of one person the surviving persons receive his portion of the estate.

JUDGMENT. Decision of a court as to the claims of persons involved in a legal action.

JUNIOR MORTGAGE. A lien subordinate to a prior mortgage.

KICKER. A payment on a loan in addition to principal and interest; also called a sweetener.

LAND ACQUISITION LOAN. A loan for the purpose of acquiring raw land for development.

LAND CONTRACT. A contract used to purchase property, particularly land, on the installment basis; title remains with seller until most or all of the purchase price is paid.

LATE CHARGE. An additional charge or penalty the lender imposes on a borrower who fails to make a payment when due.

LEASE. A contract by which the possession and use of land and buildings is given to another party for a period of time and at a specified rent.

LEASEHOLD. The interest or estate of the lessee under a lease.

LESSEE. The tenant under a lease.

LESSOR. The landlord or owner under a lease.

LIEN. A claim or charge which one person has upon the property of another, such as a tax lien or mortgage lien.

LIMITED PARTNERSHIP. A form of ownership in which the general partner actively manages the operations of the group, while limited partners are passive investors.

LIQUIDITY. The ability of a person or institution to convert assets into cash quickly, usually with a minimum of loss.

LOAN FEE. The charge or fee made by a lender when a loan is closed; it is in addition to the interest on the loan.

LOAN SERVICING. The steps necessary to keep a good loan in good standing from its inception to its final payment.

LOAN-TO-VALUE RATIO. The relationship between the amount of the mortgage loan and the appraised value of the property, and usually expressed as a percentage.

LOCK-IN. The period of time during which the lender will not permit the borrower to prepay the loan.

MARKETABLE TITLE. A title which a court would consider to be acceptable by a purchaser in the market; free of reasonable defects. Also, known as a merchantable title.

MARKET APPROACH. A method of appraising real estate in which the property being appraised is compared with comparable properties which have recently sold.

MARKET VALUE. The highest price estimated in terms of money which a property will bring if exposed for sale in the open market, allowing a reasonable time to find a knowledgeable purchase.

MATURITY. The term of a loan; the due date of a mortgage or other instrument.

MECHANIC'S LIEN. A lien created by statute in favor of persons who have performed work or furnished materials for the erection or repair of a building.

MILL. The measure used to specify property tax rates; a mill is one-tenth of one cent, or one dollar per $1,000 of assessed valuation.

MODIFICATION. Changing the terms of a note or mortgage.

MORATORIUM. A temporary suspension by the lender of the enforcement of a borrower's debt.

MORTGAGE. A pledge of specific property as security for a debt.

MORTGAGE BANK. A financial intermediary which serves as a middleman between borrowers and lending institutions; originates and services mortgages for institutional investors.

MORTGAGE BROKER. Brings together borrowers and lenders of mortgage funds; usually does not service the mortgages it finds or originates.

MORTGAGEE: The lender under a mortgage.

MORTGAGE INSURANCE PREMIUM. The fee or premium paid by the borrower for FHA insurance of a mortgage loan.

MORTGAGE PORTFOLIO. The total amount of mortgage loans held by the lender, such as a commercial bank or savings and loan association.

MORTGAGOR. The borrower under a mortgage.

MUTUAL MORTGAGE INSURANCE FUND. A fund into which FHA mortgage insurance premimus are paid and from which losses are met.

NOTE. A written promise to pay a debt.

OBSOLESCENCE. Loss of value due to changes in demand for a property when its usefulness and desirability are impaired when contrasted with modern properties.

OPEN-END MORTGAGE. A mortgage which provides for additional advances under the same mortgage.

OPTION. The right given to purchase or lease a property for a specified period of time on specified terms for which a consideration is paid.

ORIGINATION FEE. The initial fee charged by a mortgage lender for originating and processing a loan.

PACKAGE MORTGAGE. A mortgage which covers both realty and personalty, such as household appliances.

PARTICIPATION LOAN. A loan in which more than one lender has an interest.

PERCENTAGE LEASE. A lease of property in which the amount of rental is based upon the volume of business done by the tenant, such as a percentage of gross sales.

PERMANENT FINANCING. A long-term mortgage loan.

PERSONALTY. Property which is not real estate; also, known as chattels.

PHYSICAL DETERIORATION. Depreciation of property due to wear and tear and the action of the elements.

PLANNED UNIT DEVELOPMENT. A planned combination of various land uses in one location, such as residential, non-residential, and open space.

PLAT. A map or plan of a given area of land, such as a subdivision.

PLAT BOOK. Books in the court house which are a public record of the recorded plats for a given county or area.

POINTS. The amount of discount on a mortgage, usually expressed as a percentage.

POWER OF ATTORNEY. An instrument authorizing one person to act for another. The person authorized to act is known as an attorney in fact.

PREPAYMENT. A privilege in a note, bond, or mortgage permitting the borrower to make payments in advance of their due date.

PREPAYMENT PENALTY. A penalty sometimes charged by the lender for payment of a debt before it becomes due.

PRESENT VALUE. The present worth of an income stream to be received in the future.

PRIMARY MARKET. The market in which mortgage loans are originated.

PRINCIPAL. The amount of the mortgage debt, exclusive of interest.

PRIVATE MORTGAGE INSURANCE. Insurance issued, by a private company, to a lender to protect the lender against loss on high loan-to-value mortgages, such as 90-95 percent loans.

PURCHASE MONEY MORTGAGE. A mortgage given by the buyer to the seller as a part of the purchase price of a property.

QUIT CLAIM DEED. A deed to release any interest a person may have in a property; contains no warranties.

REAL PROPERTY. Land and all the improvements permanently affixed to the land.

RECEIVER. A person appointed by the court to manage a property being foreclosed.

RECORD. To place an instrument on the public records.

RECOURSE. The right to claim or require performance of an obligation against a prior owner or holder of an instrument.

REFINANCING. The payment of a debt with monies obtained through a new obligation.

REFUNDING. Refinancing or replacement of an outstanding debt; usual purpose is to reduce the interest or extend the maturity date.

RELEASE CLAUSE. The lender releases his lien on a given portion of the land under a blanket mortgage.

REPLACEMENT COST. The cost of replacing improvements, such as a building, with improvements of equal utility though not identical.

REPRODUCTION COST. The cost of reproducing identical improvements on a site, less depreciation.

RIGHT OF REDEMPTION. A statutory right, in some states, giving an owner the right to reclaim title to his property within a specified period of time after a foreclosure sale.

RIGHT OF RESCISSION. The statutory right of a borrower, under the truth-in-lending law, to rescind a transaction within a period of three days after its completion.

RISK RATING. A process of analyzing the risks in a mortgage loan and determining its soundness.

SATISFACTION OF MORTGAGE. Settlement in full of a mortgage debt; lender gives satisfaction piece instrument which is recorded.

SAVINGS AND LOAN ASSOCIATION. A financial intermediary which receives savings deposits and invests these deposits primarily in real estate mortgages.

SAVINGS BANK. A financial intermediary, usually a mutual institution, which receives savings deposits and invests them in mortgages and other securities.

SEASONED LOAN. A loan which has been in existence long enough to indicate that it is a sound loan.

SECOND FINANCING. A loan whose security is a second mortgage or deed of trust on real estate.

SECONDARY MORTGAGE MARKET. The market in which existing mortgages are bought and sold.

SECOND MORTGAGE. A mortgage whose claim is subordinate to a prior claim.

SECURITY. Property given or pledged to secure a debt, such as real estate used as collateral for a mortgage debt.

SEED MONEY. Monies needed to cover the cost of planning and initiating a project.

SERVICING. All the steps and operations a lender performs to keep a loan in good standing, such as collection of payments, payment of taxes and insurance, property inspection, and the like.

SINGLE-FAMILY PROPERTY. A property intended for ownership and occupancy by one family.

SPECIAL ASSESSMENT. A charge levied against a property by government to finance improvements which benefit the property, such as street paving or a sewer line.

STATUTE OF FRAUDS. A legislative act requiring that certain contracts relating to real estate must be in writing in order to be enforceable.

STATUTE OF LIMITATIONS. A legislative act which states that a legal action may not be taken after the passage of a specified period of time.

STRAIGHT REDUCTION PLAN. Mortgage amortization with a fixed amount applied regularly to principal reduction, and interest payable on the balance.

STRAIGHT TERM MORTGAGE. A mortgage for a given term of years with the total amount due at the expiration of the term.

STRICT FORECLOSURE. A legal foreclosure proceeding in which title goes to the lender without a public foreclosure sale.

SUBJECT TO. A purchaser acquiring a property "subject to" an existing mortgage is not held personally liable for the debt in the event of foreclosure; he is not liable for a deficiency judgment.

SUBORDINATION. A lender permitting a debt due to him to be subordinate or inferior to the debt of another lender on the same property.

SUBROGATION. Substitution of one person in the place of another with reference to a lawful right or claim.

SUPERVISED LENDER. Lenders subject to supervision and examination by a governmental agency.

TAKEOUT. The commitment issued by a permanent lender to acquire a mortgage loan from the originating lender. The permanent lender or investor agrees to make a long-term, permanent loan, the proceeds of which are used to pay off a short-term loan, such as a construction loan.

TAX DEED. A deed conveying property sold at public auction as a result of the owner's nonpayment of taxes.

TAX LIEN. A claim against property for nonpayment of property taxes.

TENANCY IN COMMON. Ownership by two or more persons; interest of a deceased owner passes to his heirs.

TERM. The period of time between the original date of a mortgage and its termination date.

TERM MORTGAGE. A mortgage in which only interest is paid during its term, with the total principal coming due at the end of its term.

TITLE. Evidence of ownership in real estate.

TITLE INSURANCE. Insurance which protects the owner of real estate against loss due to defects in title.

TITLE REPORT. The report from a title company as to the condition of a given title on a specified date.

TITLE SEARCH. An analysis of all of the instruments affecting a given parcel of real estate.

TRUST DEED. Transfers title to a third party to be held in trust for the repayment of a debt.

TRUSTEE. A party who holds property in trust for another for a given purpose, such as the performance of an obligation or duty.

TRUTH-IN-LENDING. The Consumer Credit Protection Act of 1968 which requires lenders to disclose the costs of a loan to a borrower.

UNDERWRITING. Determining the risks in a given loan and setting loan terms.

USURY. Charging more than the legal rate for the use of money.

VA LOAN. A mortgage loan guaranteed by the Veterans Administration; also called a G. I. Loan.

VALUATION. An estimate or opinion of the value of a given property; also, the act of estimating the value of property.

VALUE. Present worth of future benefits.

VARIABLE RATE MORTGAGE. A mortgage whose interest rate increases or decreases according to some index.

VENDEE. The buyer of real estate.

VENDOR. The seller of real estate.

VETERANS ADMINISTRATION. A Federal government agency which, among other programs, administers the VA loan guaranty programs for veterans.

VOLUNTARY CONVEYANCE. The voluntary conveyance of property by the borrower to the lender in lieu of foreclosure.

WAIVER. Voluntary relinquishment of a right.

WAREHOUSING. Usually a mortgage banker obtaining short-term funds from a commercial bank between time of origination of a mortgage loan and its ultimate sale and transfer to a permanent investor.

WARRANTY. A promise or guarantee.

WARRANTY DEED. Grantor warrants good title and guarantees to defend it against all claimants.

WASTE. Willful damage to property, such as by neglect.

YIELD. The annual earnings by an investor on a property.

ZONING. Restrictions placed upon the use of real estate by a governmental body.

Index